Social Impact Analysis and Development Planning in the Third World

Social Impact Assessment Series
C. P. Wolf, General Editor

†Available in paperback only.

About the Book and Editors

Although national governments and international agencies have committed vast sums of money to development, many projects have not only failed to improve the lives of the poor but in some cases have created additional social and economic problems. Such failures can often be traced to an inadequate understanding of the socio-cultural reality of the people most directly affected and to a lack of their participation in project planning, implementation, and evaluation.

In this collection of essays, scholars and practitioners from diverse disciplines examine many of the perplexing social issues of development planning from the perspective of social impact analysis. Drawing on national, regional, and local case studies, the authors demonstrate why socio-cultural factors are seldom adequately understood and discuss how they can be effectively incorporated into the planning process.

William Derman is professor of anthropology and African studies at Michigan State University. He has most recently been studying potential dam impacts and irrigation projects in the Gambia River Basin. His more general interests include rural transformation, peasantries, river basin development, and West Africa. **Scott Whiteford** is associate professor of anthropology at Michigan State University. He has done extensive research on political economy, agrarian change, and labor migration in Latin America. His most recent research has focused on the salinization of the Colorado River and the social, political, and ecological impact of that process on northern Mexico.

Social Impact Analysis and Development Planning in the Third World

edited by William Derman and
Scott Whiteford

Westview Press / Boulder and London

The paper used in this publication meets the minimum requirements of the American National Standard for Permanence of Paper for Printed Library Materials Z39.48-1984.

Social Impact Assessment Series

Chapter 9 ("Nutrition, Social Impact, and Development: A Mexican Case," by Kathryn G. Dewey) includes material that originally appeared in an article in *Medical Anthropology* 4, no. 1 (Winter 1980), © Redgrave Publishing Co., Bedford Hills, NY 10507. Reprinted with permission.

Published in 1985 in the United States of America by Westview Press, Inc.; Frederick A. Praeger, Publisher; 5500 Central Avenue, Boulder, Colorado 80301

Library of Congress Cataloging in Publication Data
Main entry under title:
Social impact analysis and development planning in
  the Third World.
  (Social impact assessment series; v. 12)
  Includes index.
  1. Rural development—Social aspects—Case studies.
2. Social indicators—Developing countries—Case
studies. 3. Developing countries—Social conditions—
Case studies. I. Derman, William. II. Whiteford,
Scott, 1942-   . III. Title. IV. Series.
HN980.Z9C67 1985   307'.14   84-27142
ISBN 0-86531-786-0

Printed and bound in the United States of America

10   9   8   7   6   5   4   3   2

Contents

Illustrations

Preface

This volume is the product of a conference on social impact and development, a series of invited lectures on the topic, and two graduate seminars on social impact assessment. As editors, we are grateful to the Midwest Universities Consortium for International Assistance, the Michigan State University Center for Advanced Study of International Development, and a University Title XII Strengthening Grant for making this volume possible. Strong institutional support for the conference and publication came from Dr. Ralph H. Smuckler, dean of International Studies and Programs; Dr. David Wiley, director of the African Studies Center; and Dr. Bernard Gallin, chairperson of the Department of Anthropology, Michigan State University. The volume would not have been completed without the opportunity for support writing and editing provided by the School of American Research and the Center for U.S.-Mexican Studies at the University of California, San Diego, funded by the National Endowment for the Humanities and the Mellon Foundation.

Editing the book was a joint effort that survived long-distance communication between the editors who were in Senegal and Mexico during critical phases of manuscript preparation. The editors are listed alphabetically. From its inception, the book was a product of both editors' concern for the plight of the disadvantaged, frustration with traditional development programs, and hope for the future. The volume reflects the conviction that knowledge generated and shared by people involved in projects can make a difference in the outcome, but not as much as one might like.

William Derman
Scott Whiteford

Introduction: Issues in Social Impact Analysis and Development

William Derman
Scott Whiteford

Economic development has been a dominant goal espoused by world leaders. Pursuing a variety of strategies, governments have created development programs and projects ostensibly to achieve higher standards of living for their citizens. In many cases loans, modern technology, and ideology have been borrowed from the more highly industrialized nations in an effort to increase production and create development. The history of these efforts is etched in the growing poverty, hunger, and declining standards of living of large segments of the world's population as, simultaneously, national military establishments are expanding with new weapons systems, export agriculture is increasing, and high technology industrial parks are being built. Despite many of the growing problems, people throughout the world continue to see "the government" as the mechanism for bringing about development.

The vast array of projects and programs designed to modernize nations is reflected in the burgeoning literature examining the development-underdevelopment process, a body of literature that is constantly under revision. Much of the analysis has focused on the national and international levels, while much of the planning at those levels has excluded from the decision-making process the people encompassed in the programs. Often, the consequences of the process and the projects have created more problems for the people involved than they have solved. This problem has led to the emergence of social impact assessment (SIA) in the United States and Canada. SIA represents an effort to increase knowledge before, during, and after development projects and to incorporate the "target" population into the planning and active stages of the project.

Although SIA was developed in industrialized nations, there have been recent efforts to transfer the methodology to development agencies working in Latin America, Africa, and Asia. As a result, the Inter-American Foundation, the Agency for International Development, and

1

the World Bank, among other organizations as well as some Third World governments, have incorporated dimensions of the process into their projects. The increased recognition of the importance of sociocultural variables in project planning and implementation is critical, but merely incorporating some type of social analysis may only serve to legitimize the project without changing the outcome or increasing local control over the process. The structural relationship linking center and periphery nations coupled with the complex mosaic of class, regional, and often ethnic differences raises another layer of methodological, ethical, and political issues for social scientists working in applied programs.

This volume is exploratory, presenting diverse approaches to an emerging field that has very diffuse boundaries. It is designed to bridge the gap between the growing literature on social impact studies in the United States and Canada and the rich, but diverse, body of reseach and theory on development. We recognize the difficulty of linking the development literature with that of social impact studies. The chapters, which are a first step in this exploration, share a common subject, social impact analysis, a general term we use to refer to the study of the social consequences of planned development projects, programs, and policies designed to produce changes in society. Within this framework, the potential and liabilities of social impact assessment in the international context emerge as a central subject. Although there are different perspectives of what constitutes social impact assessment and its uses, these are less profound than the differing (or more accurately, competing) theoretical paradigms explaining development and underdevelopment.

Let us discuss development first, and then return to SIA in the international arena. Developed, developing, underdeveloped, less developed, and least developed are descriptive categories, often based solely on economic indicators such as per capita income. More sophisticated criteria are now being developed such as quality-of-life indices, but how development is defined is highly ideological, and it will remain so for the foreseeable future. Issues of equity, freedom, and participation are important criteria used by many people in measuring development. Which nations are indeed "developed" is not an easy issue, especially if one adds the criterion of the quality of the natural environment. If ecosystems are in jeopardy because of developed technological systems, can the nations indeed be labeled as "developed" in any meaningful way?

The nature of the structures and processes that link populations that are described as developed, or developing, is a critical topic of theoretical debate. Among the central issues of the debate is the nature of socio-economic change. Understanding this process is important to individuals in a range of organizations including national governments, nongovernment organizations, and international donor agencies, all of which are trying to exercise some control over the changes taking place. Whether these changes are good or bad, for whom they are good or bad, what the outcomes of these changes are for the populations in less developed countries, and what type of relationships these nations have with Western nations are issues that will be debated for years to come and will serve as a framework for action. For example, for the proponents of capitalism, market incorporation is a "good thing"; for those opposed to capitalism because of its destructive consequences, incorporation is either undesirable or is a necessary and temporary evil that may lead to a. better system. Although there are those individuals who wish to strip the "development process" away from ideology, it is important to point out that efforts to influence socioeconomic change are seldom neutral. Equally important, the process is highly political and conditioned by constellations of power.

We raise these issues because they are part of the very difficult terrain of development and social impact analysis examined by the authors of the chapters in this book. Moreover, some of the differences about the nature of development are reflected in these chapters. There is widespread agreement among our contributors about whom development should reach: Development activities should assist those who have the greatest need. This agreement among the authors does not necessarily reflect the general attitude of scholars and/or practitioners in the development field, nor does it reflect past perspectives on development. Rather, it reflects a growing concern with the actual consequences of development upon different segments (or sectors) of less developed countries.

This concern was reflected in the United States foreign assistance legislation of 1973, known as the New Directions Congressional Mandate. The approach was new because it emphasized income distribution (as well as growth), the participation of intended beneficiaries in decision making, the use of appropriate technology, the use of labor intensive activities (rather than capital intensive ones) in order to generate meaningful employment, and the adaptation of programs to local conditions. In addition, Congress has since added an emphasis upon basic human needs, i.e., nutrition, shelter, health, and education. The New Directions Mandate reflects the recognition that many development activities have in fact undermined the position of the most needy and that these activities often have had vastly different consequences for different sectors of any given country (these might be sex, class, or region). How permanent this governmental concern will be, and whether or not it has fundamentally changed foreign aid programs, remain controversial issues. What does emerge from the most recent studies of development agencies (Hoben 1980; Morgan, this volume) is that in the foreign assistance process, there is no clear place for the beneficiary population to articulate what it wants or how it would like to receive the intended benefits. If the poor are the intended beneficiaries, and we have already emphasized that there is profound disagreement in the development field on this issue, then it is clear that how one conceptualizes poverty and seeks to cope with its causes will affect the outcomes of the recommended programs and strategies. As C. P. Wolf correctly points out, "What the 'problem' is may be a foregone conclusion from a particular standpoint; the task at hand is to open it to question. Upon examination, the 'problem' turns out to be a good deal more complicated, and its identification can vary depending upon who does the defining" (Wolf 1983:20). There are no easy answers here, but there can be no avoidance of the basic issues of development.

The authors of the chapters in this book have examined projects and have asked the planners what people were to benefit from the projects, in what way were they to benefit, what were the actual impacts, and why. The authors show that even if the explicit goal is to "assist the poor," it does not follow that the poor will indeed be assisted. In fact, it has been the experience of many people working in development that a great number of projects and programs have had the opposite effect. The desire to correct the problem has, in part, led to the increasing use of social impact assessment in development work.

The use of social impact analysis in development work derives from a range of sources whose various threads are, perhaps, no longer possible to retrace. In addition, the boundary between social impact analysis, including SIA, and applied social science is not clear. For example, applied social anthropology is almost as old as anthropology itself. One of the early influential anthropologists, A. R. Radcliffe-Brown, envisioned the application of the science of social anthropology to the problems of incorporating the world's different societies into the "modern world." He wrote:

> When we undertake the control and education of a backward people such as an African tribe or the natives of New Guinea, we are attempting to produce or to direct changes in their social integration. Our task is to substitute for the existing social structure some other and more complex structure. If we destroy or seriously weaken the existing structure without replacing it by some other more effective, then we only produce general social disintegration with all its attendant evils. [Radcliffe-Brown 1980:126]

The idea, then, of being able to use an emerging social science to understand and then to change other societies has a long history. Although the language of Radcliffe-Brown is clearly colonial, it is important to observe that many people in less developed nations also link the social sciences with a colonial heritage. This linkage is easy to demonstrate in the passage just quoted, in which the problems are seen to lie in the colonized societies, not in the colonizers. The changes that are required have to be made in the former and not the latter. Although almost fifty years separate Radcliffe-Brown's work from social impact analysis, it is hard not to see some parallels.

> Both among initial beneficiaries and among later, wider populations, durability of project results is largely a matter of how thoroughly the changed activity patterns introduced by the (irrigation) project become incorporated into the social system. The degree of this incorporation is, in turn, largely a

matter of how thoroughly the new rewards, necessary to support the new kind of activity, can become integrated into the control mechanisms of the social system of the people involved. Their social system must become capable of providing the sanctions to support their changed behavior patterns and relationships. [Ingersoll 1977:35]

Whether past or present, the purpose of applied work is to figure out how to design projects, programs, and policies so that they will attain desirable ends. The means that are used, and their acceptance, will be highly variable, depending upon the particular context and society. However, what the ends are can only be a value judgment about what future life should be like. It is this ideological part of all applied work that nonapplied social scientists question. We insist that planned change takes place under an ideology. This is not necessarily either good or bad but an objective fact. Most of the SIA literature that we have read does not include a discussion about an overall perspective of social, cultural, and economic change. In other words, it does not contain a vision of what life is and should be like for the affected populations. It is particularly striking how often outsiders assume that they know the answers to questions concerning the target population, even though the larger goals and contexts may be highly ideological and controversial. The assumption usually made is that since change is inevitable, it can be taken for granted without questioning the direction and forces of change. This perspective fits with a long tradition of applied work in the social sciences, including anthropology and economics, in which the assumption or conclusion has been that what need to be changed are the poor, the powerless, the minorities, and the small communities, not the rich, the powerful, the urban, or the elites.

From our perspective, social impact assessment needs to take into account the fact that class-based power, nested in unequal control of resources, generates and perpetuates poverty. Development projects can lead to a more equitable control of resources and power, or they can have the opposite effect. Subsequently, factors that influence these projects become a critical dimension of social impact analysis. This issue has been raised quite forcefully in recent work on the consequences for women of many development activities (Obbo, Chapter 11).

The task of SIA is to describe and analyze the real or potential effects of proposed projects upon specific groups of people. Although some practitioners of SIA feel the assessment should be restricted to the social human dimension, we feel that interrelationships among the social, economic, and environmental variables constitute a critical dimension of development planning and analysis. For example, in arid regions of the world, the scarcity of irrigation water is regarded as the key bottleneck prohibiting the expansion of agriculture. Yet irrigation requires elaborate social organization and complex maintenance and distribution systems that alter the environment and, in some cases, may destroy the traditional bases of subsistence, such as fish populations in rivers that have been dammed. Where such an effect has occurred, significant numbers of people have had to seek alternative forms of subsistence and have faced declining standards of health and nutrition. It is important to combine the social, environmental, and economic analyses wherever possible, because they are systemically linked.

The aim of social impact assessment, according to C. P. Wolf, "is to predict and evaluate those impacts [what is being done to people] before they have happened" (1983:1). SIA is anticipatory research in the sense that "it seeks to place the expectation and attainment of desired outcomes on a more rational and reliable basis" (1983:1). We have a right in the 1980s to be skeptical of any claims that are made about the ability to predict how groups of organized human beings will react to change, particularly in cases in which the social scientists do not understand the culture or cultures of the populations participating in the project or program. Economic predictions are just as treacherous as social predictions, yet programs are designed with announced expectations that are based on particular theoretical positions. Both economic and social predictions must be treated with a great deal of caution.

The use of SIA in the United States and Canada coincides with the development of environmental impact studies and statements. SIA (along with environmental work) was initially a political response, proposed by a variety of scholars and bureaucrats, to a continuing series of significant and unresolved social problems. These problems were caused by such projects as highway building, dam building, boom-town mining, offshore oil drilling, and the introduction of new technologies. In this context, SIA was designed to make it possible for local populations to have a better understanding of the implications of the projects on their lives and to give them greater control over the social, economic, and natural environments. SIA evolved as an approach that was used by people with very different agendas. In the United States and Canada, it is most often associated with "the evaluation of alternative designs for public construction projects" (Finsterbusch 1980:13). Finsterbusch's chapter titles provide an understanding of the current focus of SIA in the United States and Canada as being on population movement and residential habitat: home and neighborhood, displacement and relocation, community relocation, boom towns, community decline in rural areas, noise impact, leisure and recreation impacts, and unemployment. The purpose of social impact analysis is to affect public policy decisions. How this purpose is accomplished in the United States and Canada is critically different from the way it is accomplished in other nations.

In the United States and Canada, SIA provides a place for "public input." How the affected populations are defined, who are the publics involved, how their inputs are to be obtained, and the results upon policy of those influences will vary (Geisler, Green, Usner, West 1982). One example in this book is Funk's description of the Mackenzie Valley pipeline as the environmental and social impact assessment, combined.

with broad-based public input, led to a postponement of the pipeline. In the international context, we have few reports of comparable experiences. The publics are not well defined, and the processes by which their inputs are sought are not clear. SIA typically refers to the more general study by a social scientist of whether or not a given project or program will do what its sponsors claim and what the other consequences of undertaking such an action will be. There is, though, a commonality that perhaps cannot be too heavily emphasized. It was stated by Dixon about Fairbanks, but it has almost universal application:

> Perhaps the most important lesson that can be learned from the Fairbanks experience [referring to the impact of the Alaskan pipeline] is that unjust and unrealistic expectations were placed on the community. Decisions about projects were made outside the community, but the community had to bear the responsibilities for coping with the consequences of those decisions. The inherent structure of the community meant that it could not cope effectively in many situations. [Dixon 1980:292–293]

But the degree to which the public can express and organize its position with respect to development activities is influenced by specific national and cultural factors.

In this volume, we have emphasized the rural dimensions of development and their social impacts. It should be pointed out that this aspect, of course, does not reflect the full range of work in SIA. However, it does reflect the major emphases of development efforts in the 1970s. Unlike the thrust of the 1960s, the 1970s and the early 1980s saw great emphasis placed upon the interrelated issues of food deficits, rural-urban migration, unemployment, and underemployment in less developed countries (LDCs). Simultaneously, there was a wave of criticism of earlier development efforts for having neglected the people most in need by depending upon gross economic indicators that actually concealed the pauperization or declining living standards of rural populations. The chapters in this volume incorporate many of the criticisms that have been made of development efforts, including the neglect of health, nutrition, and women in development projects. The lack of attention given to rural social differentiation, which blocks the intended beneficiaries from receiving their criticisms, brings us back to the issue of what constitutes development and whether the mistakes of the past can be rectified, or whether they are part of an intrinsic pattern of draining resources and people from the LDCs toward external concentration of power and wealth. We do not try to resolve this issue here, for to do so would take another book. However, in our case studies, we have selected two nations (Mozambique and Nicaragua) that are actively seeking an alternative path of development and have asked the authors to address how their approaches to development influence the basic issues of social impact analysis or assessment? The contribution made by all the chapters is to bridge the levels of analysis that are required in moving from the international to the local level.

We turn now to a consideration of the national political contexts affecting social impact analysis.

The nation-state is increasingly seen by citizens as the vehicle for development. State leaders and bureaucrats throughout the world institute programs and projects in the name of development. Within this context, class interests are played out, giving particular classes or sectors special access to state power and subsequent benefits. The critical importance of the state in defining the nature of the programs and in mediating their impact upon society cannot be understated. As Ben Wisner points out in his chapter, neither SIA nor social impact analysis should or can be separated from the wider economic and political arenas.

Social impact assessment, by its nature, is part of the planning process, a process that is embedded in the political system. Inevitably, projects or programs favor one sector of the society, often at the expense of others. If the people who control the government are threatened by a project, it can easily be stopped at an early stage. If the project threatens the powerless but benefits those in power, it is highly probable that it will be enacted despite dire predictions by a social impact analyst. Efforts to develop appropriate methodologies without confronting the political issues can only legitimize the projects, and ultimately, the status quo. Regardless of the nature of the government, social scientists engaged in SIA must always be aware of their limited ability to influence government policy programs and, more important, of the limited ability of the potentially affected populations to influence the planning process. If there is little popular input in the analysis and planning, then the social scientists are probably only providing "window dressing" for imposed social change.

The importance of the organization of power, its effects on the policy process, and its relevance to SIA are critical issues. In this volume Jack Corbett examines several major Mexican development projects to determine how institutional imperatives facilitate or limit SIA application, and therefore the extent to which SIA is likely to play a role in policy selection and implementation. Mexico has experience with large-scale, integrated development projects, a commitment to social improvement embedded in the history and mythology of the Mexican Revolution, an active and a sophisticated social science community capable of providing SIA, and a centralized decision-making process, which presumably could facilitate the application of social impact assessment and its integration into the policy process. Corbett concludes that while there is an identifiable tradition of social impact assessment in Mexico, other demands on the political system take primacy in the planning and implementation process.

There is ample evidence of government planning projects, implemented under the label of development, that have inflicted serious problems on segments of the populations that were served. The chapters by Dewey, Meehan and Whiteford, and Barlett and Harrison document this process. Meehan and Whiteford show how policies and program that were designed to increase agricultural production (particularly of beef and cotton) in Costa Rica have resulted in greater productivity and exports. At the same time, the standard of living and the community structure of the people in the most productive regions are being destroyed. Dewey examines one of the major development projects in Mexico, Plan Chontalpa. The degrees to which populations were either included in or excluded from this project had a tremendous impact on their social and economic organization, and the consequences of this process were reflected in the deteriorating nutritional status of an important segment of the peasantry. These cases document the negative consequences of government and international programs that are not designed specifically to bring about a redistribution of power within the societies, and consequently do not allow adequate participation by the poor in the decision-making process. Even if social impact studies had been carried out before the programs and policies were implemented, in these cases, it is doubtful that the analysis would have altered the programs significantly.

There is a paucity of well-documented longitudinal studies of development projects and their social impact. Social impact studies are a low priority for most program administrators, who assume that they know the answers to the problems and how to achieve the goals they have defined. Unfortunately, this is seldom the case, especially when the larger goals and contexts are highly ideological and controversial.

There are situations in which SIAs can, and do, play an important role in the creation of equitable and productive development programs and policies. Such a situation is possible when the SIAs are integrated into a political structure that includes the participation of all segments of the society, and when there is an ideological commitment on the part of the government to give local populations a voice in the planning and implementation of any projects that will directly affect them. Within this context, how "local population" is defined and how the interests of the most vulnerable can be protected are critical issues.

The degree to which one group is forced to sacrifice for the "greater public good" is one of the most difficult issues in equitable planning. It is important to examine carefully how and by whom the "greater public good" and "sacrifice" are defined. The mere assertion of public good or national interest will not and should not suffice for the people who bear the social cost of such programs. How SIA can be effected by this issue is developed in the chapter by Desiré Yande Sarr. In this case, the Senegalese Institute for Agricultural Research (ISRA) commissioned a social impact assessment for a proposed project. The purpose of the proposed project was twofold: to increase the use of oxen for all agricultural operations previously done by hand and to introduce new settlers into the region (on land that was previously used for pasture by the local people) in order to increase the agricultural productivity of the area. The chapter examines the way in which ISRA used SIA and the ways in which SIA was used to prevent very expensive mistakes and to formulate more appropriate alternatives.

Funk examines the historic inquiry of the Berger Commission into the consequences of constructing a gas pipeline and energy corridor through the underdeveloped Mackenzie River and delta region. He shows that the political decision to permit native Canadians to participate in the hearings and to play a major part in the discussion of possible consequences had a profound effect on the social impact analysis and its significance to the policy that emerged. The chapter also raises a series of complex issues that are inherent in the SIA process and conceptualization. Central to these issues is the concept of participation, and this issue is a central topic in the chapter by Schwartz and Eckhardt. These authors grapple with the important issue of appropriate units of program design, implementation, and evaluation. They explore the inherent contradiction between project autonomy and heteronomy, which in turn leads them into a discussion of scale and control.

One of the implicit themes in all the chapters is the need to increase the participation of citizens in the design and implementation of projects. Paulo Freire (1970, 1980) and his followers have played an important role in developing participatory research, action, and evaluation programs. Participation has become increasingly important for national or international government development agencies because of the growing recognition that new approaches are necessary. Yet centralized authority and imposed outside experts can threaten many of the strengths of a participatory approach. It has been suggested by some social scientists that the "most critical factor in the success of a development scheme is the degree of political participation in decision making by local beneficiaries" (Lees 1980:375). In all cultures, there are indigenous mechanisms of participation that are critical to an understanding of local-level organizations. These include the traditional means of decision making (at different levels, from the household on up) and conflict resolution. The processes of decision making and conflict resolution are reinforced by culturally defined sets of sanctions and expected patterns of conduct (Ingersoll, Sullivan, and Lenkerd 1981:22). Any project that anticipates local participation must be based on an understanding of these mechanisms and must develop a means for incorporating them from the beginning of the project.

Participation has been defined as "involvement of a significant number of persons in situations or actions which enhance their well being, e.g., their income, security or self-esteem" (Uphoff, Cohen, and Goldsmith 1979:4). The same authors go on to suggest that participation should be viewed not as a single event, but as a process. This process would include the degree of participation by individuals or groups during the different stages of a project (i.e., defining the problem, examining different alternative ways of dealing with problems, developing and implementing the program, benefiting from the project, and evaluating the project). These steps are not unilinear; they feed back into one another and may continue after the project officially ends.

The definition of participation used here is intentionally broad. Implicit, but not stated in the definition, is the understanding that most populations are organized and already have a series of concepts and ideas about what constitutes a good life or moral behavior, why things are the way they are, and how things may or may not be changed. It is the cultural dimension that gives structure, meaning, and significance to who they are and to what they do. Populations selected for programs or projects are not only distinct from other populations within the nation but may be divided into complex constellations based on ethnic, racial, class, sex, or caste divisions. If a particular project is designed to improve the position of a segment of the population, the project must give this population increased access to control of resources.

Women's "participation" has become a major issue. How women are treated, analytically as well as in specific projects, has led to strong and forceful critiques like that of Dr. Obbo (see Chapter 11). She argues for the serious inclusion of women in development (what she terms "modernization") but suggests that this is not sufficient. What emerges, however, is a duality that is not fully resolved. On the one hand, she criticizes Western women (we have some qualms of generalization at this level) for their societally bounded ideologies of gender issues while stating that gender inequality precedes the emergence of capitalism, and on the other hand, she does not accord women (either in the West or in Africa) with having created the means to buffer the exploitation and to influence the people who wield economic and political power.

If a population has enough power, it can set the terms for its own participation, and it can influence the direction of or even stop a particular project that is generated from the outside. To create participation in the absence of such power is a key dilemma for SIA and for development projects. Many development projects are, in fact, undertaken to enhance the circumstances of the powerful, with little concern for the consequences for the powerless. In these circumstances, SIA is ineffective as a means for reform and, as we pointed out earlier, can only serve to legitimize the status quo. In some cases, the explicit goals of projects are to increase the economic viability of a region in which almost everyone is poor without increasing the power of the local elite vis-à-vis the other people in the region. The degree to which this philosophy is adhered to is usually outside the power of the social scientist, although the project impacts can be calculated.

Differences in the amount of control of the basic means of production constitute a key factor that is included in most social impact baseline studies. The chapter by Axinn in this volume examines the significance of social differentiation and introduces an innovative approach for measurement. Using an energy flow approach, Axinn focuses on family farms in Nepal to show how different segments of a small community utilize energy resources distinctively.

One of the major topics of SIA is the impact of new technologies. Technology is never neutral. Some segments of a society, because of their positions of power and their resources, have a distinct advantage over other segments of the same society in the control and/or utilization of new technologies (Vessuri 1980). This process not only has a profound effect at the local level but is also critical to the formation of unequal linkages between nations. The chapters by Robert Stock and John Donahue on access to medical technology are excellent examples of this process.

Kidd and Kumar (1981) have differentiated between the people who view the problem of underdevelopment as one of poverty and others who view the basic problem as one of oppression. They point out that the two views are not necessarily dichotomous but that they are reached from very different assumptions. The people who focus on poverty usually lay the blame for it on the deficiency of the poor and focus their development activities upon programs that are designed to change behavior by teaching the poor new skills or by giving them new information. There is a body of theoretical literature that supports the deficiency approach. In contrast, the people who see oppression as the primary cause of underdevelopment feel that the focus of development activities should be upon breaking the forces of repression. Although few scholars would suggest that the two approaches are necessarily mutually exclusive, in fact many projects have been designed without addressing the issue of oppression and social relationships. This lack can be attributed to the fact that governments often either initiate the project themselves or invite others to design the projects. These governments usually represent the dominant classes and do not want to have the social relationships altered.

The chapter by Barlett and Harrison takes an important step in clarifying the problems inherent in defining poverty and its causes. Structural conditions analyzed within a historical and spatial context form the basis of the model the authors present. The authors proceed to examine the policy implications of their model (a model that was contracted by the United States Agency for International Development [USAID]) on USAID projects in Costa Rica. Their discussion shows both the relevance and the difficulty of incorporating social science analysis into agency or government policy.

Because fundamental reforms have been instituted in socialist countries, the issues of participation are played out in a different context than they are in capitalist countries. National governments still play the central role in implementing projects, and projects do have important social impacts. Therefore, the discussions by Donahue and Wisner of projects in Nicaragua and Mozambique are particularly significant. Their studies of these projects show many similar structural problems that are inherent in programs controlled by the nation-state governments regardless of their ideology. At the same time, there are significant differences between the types and mechanisms of participation.

Ben Wisner challenges the very basis of traditional SIA, suggesting that it plays only an atomized role in project planning and that in the capitalist state, the purpose of project planning is to minimize the risk to capital, not people. Yet socialist states develop their own entrenched bureaucratic interests, which may effectively prevent the participation of larger or smaller sectors of the citizenry in the planning process. This problem raises a series of complex issues about the nature of the state and the planning process regardless of ideological underpinnings.

In examining several cases in Mozambique, Wisner suggests that conflict and power cannot be examined in an ahistorical context. SIA studies have generally been ahistorical, in part because of a question of methods—questionnaires are not very effective instruments for gathering historical materials—but more important, because the historical bias reflects a theoretical perspective that is insensitive to issues of social inequality and class conflict. We feel strongly that social analysis in general and SIA in particular require a historical perspective. Survey research that focuses on individuals lacks a critical dimension, i.e., how individuals relate to each other over time. Long-term patterns of conflict and cooperation can only emerge for the researcher if the class, ethnic, village, and family networks and boundaries are defined, using a methodology that includes a historical component.

The institutional context for development programs becomes even more complicated when international agencies or binational organizations become involved. In a sense, these institutions are restructuring the Third World into their competing domains of influence. The programs of these organizations reflect the policies and ideologies of the major lending nations and have very specific agendas. The World Bank, the Canadian Agency for International Development, USAID, the French Assistance and Cooperation Fund, and a variety of other voluntary and government agencies all claim to be concerned about the social impact of their programs, but they seldom do baseline or evaluation studies. The economic cost-benefit results remain the key factor in their analyses of the success or failure of their projects.

How effective funding agencies are or should be in using social impact assessment is one of the central questions explored by Charles Reilly. Reilly questions what types of information agencies need in order to make their projects more effective in accomplishing the goals of the target population. The case materials are based on reports by the Inter-American Foundation, an organization explicitly organized by the United States Congress to bypass the bureaucratic structure of USAID and to fund grass-roots, locally conceived projects to benefit rural and urban poor. The analysis differentiates between participatory assessment and agency-centered assessment and discusses why both types are important but underutilized.

Whether or not SIA makes a difference remains to be seen and depends upon a number of factors. Some social scientists have claimed success for SIA because they were able to block ill-advised projects; others have argued that SIA has been able to mitigate particularly harmful effects; and others have argued that SIA makes USAID more sophisticated in carrying out U.S. foreign policy, which is against the interests of Third World populations. There is no simple resolution of these related arguments. The reasons lie in the nature and distribution of power. Here, we might only point out the limited potential of social science, especially in cultural situations and contexts outside North America. When the Soviets sent their army into Afghanistan, they did not do a social impact study of the range of impacts such an intervention would have. Likewise, no one is or will be carrying out a social impact study of Israeli intervention in Lebanon. It is not that these instances are not important, but there is a whole range of circumstances under which social impact analysis will not be done or carried out. Many of the most powerful institutions (like the military or giant transnational corporations) do not and will not carry out social impact studies. Who does SIA studies, and under what circumstances, varies from agency to agency and nation to nation. Subsequently, many of the most powerful institutions and their activities are never examined or controlled by the population to be affected.

In this volume, the chapter by Morgan illustrates the pressures and institutional context that can negate the potential influence of social analysis in development projects sponsored by USAID. A key question for those people who are concerned about the transformation process associated with development efforts is whether these efforts are basically perpetuating the existing power relationships and the status quo or whether they are attempting to bring about real change. This becomes a critical issue for the social scientist as well as for the economist when they work in the planning process.

SIA requires understanding the world of the planners and developers and also the world of the host populations. In their study of the use of social soundness analysis in USAID, Ingersoll, Sullivan, and Lenkerd have written: "most social analysts apparently feel that they must examine proposed projects with a very critical eye because they define their role in the project process as being that of the people's advocate: an advocate who must champion the cause of those who may not otherwise have anyone to represent their interests" (1981:47). Most project analysts are performing legitimized advocacy roles of one sort or another. Specialists are called in to assess proposed projects to see if they make sense in terms of economic, technological, administrative, and environmental parameters. The essential task of the social analyst is to make sure that such projects make sense in terms of social parameters, that is the people (Ingersoll, Sullivan, and Lenkerd 1981:47). Implicit in their study is the assumption that the public will *not* have appropriate vehicles to express their thoughts or to organize their response with respect to projects or programs in which they will be involved. Most governments take the view that they represent the views of the population and that no additional mechanisms are required to solicit the views of the intended beneficiaries. This is often far from the case.

Social scientists concerned with the broad issues of development have established their place in the critical tradition of the social sciences. It is recognized that SIA is a product of Western culture, steeped in the positivist tradition, often overstating its scientific strength and efficacy. Sociocultural systems are always in the process of change as new ways of seeing the world and dealing with problems are constantly being created. The transformation processes associated with development efforts are, as we have pointed out, highly dependent upon factors that SIA can not influence. Yet there is a need for a constant analysis of these processes and structures in the hope of not repeating the same mistakes. Despite the promise of SIA, a great deal more needs to be done to make it meaningful to the people whose lives are most affected by the transformation process.

References

Bowles, Roy T.
   1981   *Social Impact Assessment in Small Communities.* Toronto: Butterworths.

Cohen, John, and Uphoff, Norman
   1979   Rural Development Participation: Concepts and Measures for Project Design, Implementation, and Evaluation. Cornell University Rural Development Committee. Rural Development Monograph #2.

Derman, William
   1984   USAID in the Sahel: Development and Poverty. In *The Politics of Agriculture in Tropical Africa,* edited by Jonathan Barker. Beverly Hills, Calif.: Sage.

Dixon, Mim
   1980   *What Happened to Fairbanks? The Effects of the TransAlaska Oil Pipeline on the Community of Fairbanks, Alaska.* Boulder, Colo.: Westview Press.

Finsterbusch, Kurt
   1980   *Understanding Social Impacts: Assessing the Effects of Public Projects.* Beverly Hills, Calif.: Sage.

Franke, Richard, and Chasin, Barbara
   1980   *Seeds of Famine: Ecological Destruction and the Development Dilemma in the West African Sahel.* Montclair, N.J.: Allenheld Osmun.

Freeman, Linda
   1978   The Nature of Canadian Interests in Black Southern Africa. Ph.D. Thesis. University of Toronto.

Freire, Paulo
   1970   *Pedagogy of the Oppressed.* New York: Seabury Press.

   1980   *Education for Critical Consciousness.* New York: Continuum Publishing Corporation.

Geisler, Charles; Green, Rayna; Usner, Daniel; West, Patrick C.
    1982   Indian SIA: Social Impact Assessment of Rapid Resource Development on Native Peoples. Ann Arbor: University of Michigan Natural Resources Sociology Research Lab Monograph #3.

Hoben, Allen
    1980   Agricultural Decision Making in Foreign Assistance: An Anthropological Analysis. In *Agricultural Decision Making: Anthropological Contributions to Rural Development*, edited by Peggy F. Barlett. New York: Academic Press.

Ingersoll, J. P.
    1977   Social Analysis of Development Projects: A Suggested Approach for Social Soundness Analysis. AID Development Studies Program. May.

Ingersoll, Jasper; Sullivan, Mark; and Lenkerd, Barbara
    1981   Social Analysis of AID Projects: A Review of the Experience. AID Contract. Washington, D.C.

Kidd, Ross, and Kumar, Krishna
    1981   Co-opting Freire: A Critical Analysis of Pseudo-Freirean Adult Education. *Economic and Political Weekly* XVCI(1&2): 27–36.

Lappe, Frances Moore; Collins, Joseph; and Kinley, David
    1980   *Aid as Obstacle: Twenty Questions About Our Foreign Aid and the Hungry*. San Francisco: Institute for Food and Development Policy.

Lees, Susan
    1980   Dryland Development. *Human Organization* 39(4): 372–376.

Radcliffe-Brown, A. R.
    1980   Applied Anthropology. First published in 1930; reprinted in *Research in Economic Anthropology: A Research Manual*, vol. 3, edited by George Dalton. Greenwich, Conn.: JAI Press.

Uphoff, Norman; Cohen, John M.; and Goldsmith, Arthur A.
    1979   Feasibility and Application of Rural Development Participation: A State-of-the-Art Paper. Cornell University Rural Development Committee. Rural Development Monograph #3.

Vessuri, Hebe M.C.
    1980   Technological Change and the Social Organization of Agricultural Production. *Current Anthropology* 21(3): 315–327.

Whyte, William F.
    1981   Participatory Approaches to Agricultural Research and Development: A State-of-the-Art Paper. Special Series on Agriculture Research and Extension, ARE no. 1. Rural Development Committee, Cornell University.

Wolf, C. P.
  1983   Social Impact Assessment: A Methodological Overview. In *Social Impact Assessment Methods*, edited by Kurt Finsterbusch, Lynn Llewellyn, and C. P. Wolf. Beverly Hills, Calif.: Sage.

World Bank
  1980   Human Factors in Project Work. World Bank Staff Working Paper no. 397. Washington, D.C.

Part I

Social Impact Assessment and Development Projects

Social Analysis and the Dynamics of Advocacy in Development Assistance

E. Philip Morgan

In 1975, the U.S. Agency for International Development (AID), the principal administrative agent for U.S. bilateral development assistance, mandated a social analysis component to the project preparation and approval process.[1] Although "social soundness analysis" is now a required dimension of project identification and design, its presumed positive effects are not yet apparent on the output side. Postproject impact evaluations reveal that there continue to be negative social effects from AID's development efforts, regardless of project type. Why?

In the process by which projects are identified, framed, approved, and ultimately implemented, important signals identified by preproject social analysis get displaced. This situation occurs because anticipating social impact is only one of several goals or functions served by preproject design analysis. This chapter interprets the role of social analysis in the dynamics of project preparation, identifying structures and procedures that attenuate its influence.

The Problem

An examination of AID's own project impact evaluation reports shows a recurrent pattern of negative social effects, both during implementation and after completion. A few comments will illustrate:

On rural roads in Liberia:

> Though the projects intended to strengthen the capability of local contractors, this has generally not happened. . . . In addition, as the market value of the land for . . . cash enterprises (crops, lumbering, mineral exploitation) has increased, competition for the land and its resources has sharpened. Small farmers who have traditionally farmed the land are the first to lose rights to it. [AID 1980a: 18]

On small-scale irrigation in the Philippines:

The Philippine government has not focused on the debt burdens of the farmers, but rather on increased rice production. . . . Farmers will be unable to pay back loans to Irrigation Service Associations that, in turn, will be unable to repay the government. As farmers fall into debt, it will be harder to borrow money for fertilizer, good seeds, and pesticides. This could lead to a decline in productivity. . . . The social and political implications of such deterioration could be momentous. [AID 1980b: 8]

On rural water supplies in Kenya:

No one consults the community before building the system to find out what the users want in the way of individual connections or Communal Water Points (CWPs) so there is no basis for designing the system to meet the needs of the community. Indeed, CWPs are usually located to discourage their use. . . . CWPs are closed to encourage users to pay for individual service. . . . The cost of installing individual service is subsidized to encourage use yet the bureaucratic procedures required to get a connection discourage potential users . . . [moreover] funds are not available for the portion of the cost subsidized by the Ministry of Water Development. [AID 1980c: 16–17]

On village-level health dispensaries in Senegal:

One third of the [health] Huts in Nioro Department, where most had been open for the longest time [about 9 months], had already closed. . . . It was difficult to face . . . community elders. Their interest in and concern about village health had been demonstrated by their building of the Hut. They told us, with some pride, of communal labor by the village youth and their money contributions to buy doors, paint, extra cement and iron sheets for the roof. They were confused and frustrated because many Huts had closed. If Huts continue to close, as seems probable, the main impact of the project may well be the frustrated expectations of some 800,000 villagers. [AID 1980d: 12]

It must be noted that most AID projects are not *comprehensive* failures, nor is the social impact *always* negative.[2] Although these illustrations are more indicative than selective of agency experience, there are many aspects of project implementation beyond the control of the agency. Contractors fail to live up to their commitments, recipient country governments prove to be less committed to certain social aspects of a project than the AID field mission was led to believe, and so on.

What concerns us here are the internal, organizational reasons for the frequency of negative social consequences in the 1980s, particularly some years after the agency institutionalized social analysis as part of project design. Why, after thirty years of development assistance, is AID still underwriting the construction of roads that have the effect of displacing the rural poor from their land? Why does AID support water development projects in which the public to be served is ignored? What is the point of raising expectations among 800,000 people in remote areas about the availability of health services when even a modest number of installations cannot be sustained? Assuming that these consequences are not by design, where is the organizational learning in development assistance?

Social Analysis and Project Design

In 1975, AID specified guidelines for conducting "social soundness analyses" of potential projects (AID 1975: 5A-1). Three areas of inquiry are to be examined for each prospective project: sociocultural feasibility, potential spread effect, and social impact, or distribution of benefits and burdens among different groups. Sociocultural feasibility requires an examination of local values, beliefs, social structure, and organization in order to determine the compatibility of the project with the perceptions and practices of the target population. Spread effect refers to "the likelihood that the new practices or institutions introduced among the initial project target population will be diffused among other groups" (AID 1975: 5A-1). Social impact assessment requires the identification of groups that would be positively affected by a project, those that would be adversely affected, and in what ways. Participation of the target population in all phases of the project—from identification through implementation—is also to be specified.

This is an abbreviated version of the guidelines, which take up twelve single-spaced pages in the *Project Assistance Handbook*. One could infer that the scope and depth of the social analyses are to be more substantial than cursory. In practice, that has proved to be somewhat at odds with the way the findings are presented and the proviso that "the data should be possible to obtain in two to three weeks" (AID 1975: 5A-12).[3]

How is social soundness analysis reflected in the project preparation and approval process? In the case of the most preliminary stage of project development, the Project Identification Document (PID), the social analysis is essentially presented as a set of questions that are to be answered in a subsequent field analysis done for the final project design, the so-called Project Paper (PP). At the identification (PID) stage, the questions related to the specific project are general and predictable. The social soundness analysis in a PID might therefore be one page, noting that, e.g., relationships between government officials and the *campesinos* will be described, methods of communication and decision making among agricultural-sector officials with regard to implementation will be identified, the impact of the agricultural technology of the project on women will be described, etc.

The actual social analysis is supposed to be done as part of the activity of the Project Paper design team, with one team member being the designated social analyst. Depending on the nature of the project, the social analyst might be an anthropologist, a sociologist, or some other behavioral scientist. The social analyst might be contracted as part of the design team or separately.

In the final PP, a summary of the social analysis takes up three to five pages, and it is included in a section along with the other subproject analyses: e.g., technical analysis, institutional analysis, economic analysis, financial analysis, and environmental analysis. The full text is to be included in an appendix, along with the full narratives of the other analyses.

The writing of the first draft of the PP may be a joint effort on the part of the members of the design team, but it is also not uncommon for one member of the design team to integrate the rough drafts of the respective separate analyses into a single draft narrative. Usually the team leader takes this responsibility unless another of the analysts proves to be a more able and willing writer. Thus, the social analysis, as with any other separate analytic component, might be well presented and balanced with the other analyses or not, depending on who does the writing.

Moreover, the final packaging of a PP for review and approval in Washington is done by a design officer in the AID field mission. The design officer has considerable discretion. He (rarely she) edits, synthesizes, and summarizes large parts of the various analyses in order to make the overall PP narrative succinct, balanced, and complete in terms of the agency's format and statutory requirements.

Some Analyses Are More Equal Than Others[4]

Only 25 percent of those projects examined in a recent review of social analysis in AID's project design were influenced by the social analysis component (Ingersoll, Sullivan, and Lenkerd 1981: 2). There are a number of practices that diminish the value and influence of social soundness analysis in AID's project preparation. The Ingersoll study is helpful in identifying the variable quality of the social analyses themselves. Many social analysts do not critique the basic goals, assumptions, or logic of the project (p. 62); instead, they tend to emphasize benefits more than to ascertain the costs of project effects (p. 36). There is no standard format for writing the social analysis (p. 55).

Often the social analyst does not interact with the technical analysts sufficiently to afford an integrated, comprehensive perspective. This situation has resulted in the social component's standing alone in the project summary; it does not appear to inform, or be informed by, the other analyses. It has been observed that the social analyst is often called in only after the major features of a project have already been determined (Ingersoll, Sullivan, and Lenkerd 1981: 51). This problem might reflect scheduling problems; it also suggests an attitude about priorities among the respective types of analysis on the part of the AID field mission staff or the regional bureau in Washington recruiting the design team. As with environmental impact analysis, there is sometimes a last minute, perfunctory quality to the social analysis (Morgan 1980: 5).

Qualifiers and caveats included in the full narrative of a social soundness analysis are sometimes missing in the PP summary. The discretion accorded design officers in editing and balancing the final PP submission is thus a two-edged sword: It guarantees a succinct, spare document; it can also obscure potentially important project deficiencies.[5] The Ingersoll study reported that AID mission staff and design team leaders respond more positively to social analysis when it reinforces the positive aspects or probabilities of success of a project than when it reveals doubt about its potential social impact (Ingersoll, Sullivan, and Lenkerd 1981: 45).

Other indicators of design team dynamics suggest an implicit hierarchy of analyses for the mission submitting the PP. Veteran technicians, whether AID personnel or outside consultants, are most likely to be the leaders of the design team, and prejudice is sometimes manifest in attitudes toward social scientists, especially anthropologists, by veteran field technicians. Anthropologists are perceived by some as naysayers when it comes to the effects of social change on traditional cultures, and they are accused of emphasizing the negative, rather than the positive, effects. Moreover, field people want the social analyst to tell them on the spot what incremental adjustments in the project design would mitigate a possible negative effect (rather than reconsider the project in any fundamental sense). If the social analyst cannot give a firm recommendation, field staff members become frustrated.

Since many anthropologists are women, they report a residual sexism in which the social analyst is not made to feel a full member of the team. Condescension toward or a reluctant tolerance of the female analyst whose contribution must be included sometimes characterizes team relationships. Although the trend is still impressionistic, this effect appears to be mitigated when the anthropologist is an internal agency specialist as opposed to a temporary outside consultant (Ingersoll, Sullivan, and Lenkerd 1981: 57).

Project Development as Advocacy

However, there are more fundamental reasons why social analysis gets displaced in project preparation, and it is necessary to look at the purposes that are served by the preparation and approval processes. Analysis for the better "design" of projects is only one purpose, although it is the most manifest. The various analytic components of project preparation also serve the purpose of advocacy. In fact, the multistage project development procedure is essentially an advocacy process, inextricably tied to internal agency dynamics between the field missions and Washington headquarters.

An AID field mission formulates projects that are many months, frequently several years, in preparation. Project ideas and proposals are the product of some synthesis of overall U.S. aid policy objectives and the development plans and objectives of the recipient government worked out over time, albeit sometimes discontinuously because of changes in government on both sides. By the time a project gets to the PP stage, the recipient government knows about it and has already invested enough time and other local resources to have a stake in it. In summary, Project Papers in particular already represent a de facto commitment. Therefore the AID mission director, because of local pressures, is interested in expediting the review and approval processes to whatever extent possible.

Project preparation also represents commitments of money. For agency, especially mission, planning purposes, a project is earmarked for a given fiscal year. If projects are held up during the approval process because of doubts reflected in the various analyses, moving large amounts of money through the pipeline is interrupted. This situation can negatively affect Washington's perception of the mission as an efficient programmer of agency funds, which can be crucial to the mission's future credibility in securing funds to execute the program proposed in its annual budget submissions.[6]

The mission director's mobility within the agency, and that of his or her immediate staff, depends upon his or her productivity in terms of project approvals, pipeline commitments, and projects that are actually being implemented. Mission directors and mission staff are rotated frequently enough that most are not around when project impact evaluations are done. Certainly there are interim evaluations, which might reflect badly on a mission staff if projects are not going well, but by and large, organizational output for a mission staff tends to be defined more in terms of moving projects to the implementation stage than in successful project performance or outcomes.

Consequently, mission staffs are project advocates; it is in their interest to get projects approved and show movement both to the government of the country in which they are located and to Washington. The incentive is to promote the sound aspects of proposed projects, not risk delays in project approval by emphasizing caveats turned up in the social analysis.

In Washington, the AID bureaucrats also want to be perceived as facilitating project development, not inhibiting it. It is important not to be the bottleneck in what is already a lengthy process. Therefore, the respective regional bureaus (Asia, Africa, Latin America, Near East) also have an interest in moving money. The rate of spending affects funding levels from year to year from bureau to bureau.

As a large, complex organization, AID experiences the usual tensions between field operations and headquarters. Each locus has a different scope of responsibilities. Washington has overall responsibility for approval and oversight; at the same time, the regional bureaus are to support and backstop field operations. The horizons of a field mission are more narrow. In the relations between Washington and the field, it must be remembered that the mission is an island of considerable authority. If the signals are clear from the field that a mission director wants a particular project, he or she will usually get it approved. Delays in approval result in complicated and sometimes fractious cable exchanges, which delay the start-up of a project.

This is not to say that project review panels in Washington are casual and uncaring about the quality of the analysis presented in the PPs. However, their workload is such that not every criterion of the elaborate PP can be evaluated with equal weight. Reviews will also vary with the technical skills and special competencies of the people who make up the review panel for any given project or set of projects. Consequently, the accountability for the cash flows usually ends up being the most carefully considered factor. The social analysis might raise red flags to the careful reader, even if they have been softened, but that warning may not provide cause for holding up approval if the technical analyses are judged to be adequate.

The upshot of the advocacy function of project preparation and approval is "overdesign," both in terms of preprogramming and optimism. Preprogramming, or "premature programming," as a type of overdesign refers to confident statements about the distribution of benefits, economic return, positive institutional outcomes, and replicability sustainability— all supported by detailed implementation schedules as if the uncertainty characterizing any development activity had been accounted for in advance planning.[7]

To the extent that the advocacy purpose of project development is well served by the positive impression conveyed by quantitative measures of inputs delivered, return on investment, number of beneficiaries in the target population, and so forth, social analysis is at a disadvantage. Sociological and/or anthropological observations that point to potentially negative impacts through verbal, impressionistic narratives cannot compete with the seemingly scientifically grounded economic and technical analyses, however false the latter may prove to be. Doubts, which cannot be conveyed with the same aura of empirical evidence, get downplayed almost by default in a contest in which confidence exudes from numbers.

Thus, as used by the people promoting a project, the design criteria themselves have the effect of substituting aspiration for probability very early in the game. Projects are approved on the basis of the confident estimates presented along a range of output criteria, many of which prove faulty during the course of implementation. The agency's own evaluation teams have observed, "AID analysis in project papers has been overly and unnecessarily optimistic and has resulted in unrealistic expectations for performance" (AID 1980b: 1).

The Future

Is there any prospect that social analysis will get better, or be better used, during the Reagan administration? Can we anticipate changes that might reflect agency learning and that, in turn, might result in more positive social impacts?

The Ingersoll study offers suggestions on how social analysis might be improved through revised guidelines (Ingersoll, Sullivan, and Lenkerd 1981: Appendix 1). It also provides a thoughtful framework whereby the social analysis component of a project should be evaluated during the Washington-based review exercise (Appendix 2). As the study revealed a lack of consensus and consistency in the preparation of, as well as in the evaluation of, social analysis, the recommendations are based on the reasonable assumption that a certain amount of standardization of format and procedure will be at least modestly helpful.

However, to the extent that advocacy remains a function of project development, it is unlikely that social analysis will play a more influential role than it presently does. Precisely because advocacy is an implicit, or a latent, function of project preparation and review, rather than explicit, altering that fact is not readily subject to revised guidelines or exhortation by memorandum. As we have seen, the advocacy purpose of project development derives from the incentive structures that move mission staff members, the consultants that are engaged, and certain elements within the central bureaucracy. Therefore, unless the incentives that motivate agency personnel are changed, a more objective application of design criteria is unlikely.

To be sure, AID has begun to place more emphasis on implementation and evaluation, as opposed to front-end planning, in recent years. A state-of-the-art review of the literature on "implementation" was commissioned in 1979 (Ingle), and implementation and evaluation are receiving substantially more attention in the agency's in-house training activities. One of the most effective and thoughtful of agency contractors has urged the substitution of a "development benefits delivered" incentive for the current "funds obligated" incentive (Mickelwait, Sweet, and Morss 1979: 230). This suggestion implies a greater concern with the long-run consequences of projects. Accordingly, the new AID administrator has said the impact evaluation program will continue (AID 1981: 1).

From this greater emphasis on implementation and evaluation, we might infer a gradual shift of informal signals to mission staff members. Doing more with less, a slogan now frequently heard in the agency, might mean that more emphasis will be placed on project outcomes. This change could, over time, supplant the present incentives to move money at the expense of socially desirable consequences.

At the same time, the administrator has said some things about changes in emphasis that are less encouraging. A recurrent theme in AID under the Reagan administration is the same as one propagated in domestic policy: Economic efficiency is a value to be reasserted. The AID administrator had noted that the agency will emphasize activities with direct results for increased productivity and incomes (AID 1981: 1). Economic feasibility tests will be more rigorous, i.e., more attention will be paid to the internal rate of return on investment when assessing potential projects, and emphasis will be on the "lowest cost solutions" to the greatest number of beneficiaries. In terms of agency personnel, and by extension agency incentives, this emphasis will mean more technical and professional expertise in macro- and microeconomic analysis.

Consequently, the slogan Doing more with less could mean giving even more weight to technical analysis in project development, which would put social analysis at an even greater disadvantage. The administrator has said that issues of equity and distribution will not be abandoned in agency programming during his tenure. However, unless agency procedures are changed in ways that downplay the advocacy function of project analysis and substitute overall quality for quantity, reorganizing and changing guidelines for social analysis will prove cosmetic. So long as the present reward system remains intact, the impact evaluations will continue to report negative effects.

Progress in social problem solving requires some combination of formal, technical knowledge with the "ordinary" knowledge that reposes in the community with the problem.[8] Formally packaged information and analysis are most useful when they interact with socially derived knowledge (Lindblom and Cohen 1979). Parameters of AID programming such as participation, decentralization, environmental impact, and social soundness are indicative of agency learning to the extent that they reflect tentative attempts to interactively capture local knowledge. If agricultural, rural development, nutrition, and population programs are to remain the "centerpiece" of agency policy, as the administrator has said, social analysis must be central to project formulation *and* implementation. Good social analysis is probably the most interactive of all the analytic components involved in project development.

Reestablishing a rationalist (as opposed to an interactive, incrementalist) approach to agency programming would be regressive on any organizational learning curve where social change is an objective. This analysis suggests that upgrading technical, economic analysis is likely to have an effect opposite to that intended. What is required is a posture of "doing less with more," with "less" referring to the number of projects and countries of activity and "more" meaning, not more money, but money that is more concentrated on experimental ventures to enhance agency learning and improve future prospects for positive social, as well as productivity, outcomes.

Notes

The author is grateful for cooperation received from many AID officials and the opportunity to learn agency procedures while directing a Cooperative Agreement between AID and the National Association of Schools of Public Affairs and Administration.

1. "Development assistance" as used in this chapter refers to concessional lending, grants, and technical assistance. In AID nomenclature, "impact evaluation" is an ex post procedure that examines performance and impact along a range of

criteria, one of which is social. "Social soundness analysis" is ex ante, along with economic, financial, and technical analyses, which, collectively, inform project design.

2. The candor of these evaluations suggests that whatever the reasons for the recurrent, unanticipated social consequences of many projects, people within AID would like to do better. This fact must be acknowledged because the publication of negative findings cannot help the agency in its annual requests for appropriations from a reluctant Congress.

3. The guidelines are currently being revised.

4. The analysis that follows is based on the author's experience in managing a contract with AID for a professional society, discussion with AID officials both in Washington and in the field, and the examination of project documents. In addition, the analysis was aided by a study by J. Ingersoll, M. Sullivan, and B. Lenkerd on "Social Analysis of AID Projects: A Review of the Experience," prepared for the agency's Office of Policy and Program Coordination in June 1981, in which 48 sets of project documents were examined and for which interviews were held with 35 "producers and consumers of social soundness analyses in AID" (p. 1 of draft manuscript).

5. A member of the design team for an agricultural services delivery project in Ghana reported that the PP did not have a social analysis section when it was first submitted. Later, during the actual review, a social analysis was included, but certain of the awkward and critical statements about the project were missing. Ingersoll (Ingersoll, Sullivan, and Lenkerd 1981: 41) also reports such occurrences as well as pressures applied to social analysts by mission staff or other team members to soften or alter their criticism about potential social impact.

6. The bureaucratic effects of programming large amounts of money through a development agency are well described by Tendler (1975).

7. There is an ample literature on this phenomenon as it relates to decision making in complex organizations. It begins in the 1950s with James Thompson and is applied to development organization in the 1960s and 1970s by Martin Landau, William J. Siffin, and Russell Stout, Jr. The most comprehensive bibliography can be found in Stout (1980).

8. The work of David C. Korten (1980) is an excellent start.

References

Agency for International Development

1975   *Project Assistance Handbook, No. 3,* Chapter 5, Appendix A. September.

1980a   "Impact of Rural Roads in Liberia." Project Impact Evaluation Report no. 6. June.

1980b   "Philippine Small Scale Irrigation." Project Impact Evaluation Report no. 4. May

1980c   "Kenya Rural Water Supply: Program, Progress, Prospects." Project Impact Evaluation Report no. 5. June.

1980d   "Senegal: The Sine Saloum Rural Health Care Project." Project Impact Evaluation Report no. 9. October.

1981   "Administrator Sets Policy Guidance." *Front Lines* 19(9), May, p. 7.

Ingersoll, J., M. Sullivan, and B. Lenkerd
   1981   "Social Analysis of AID Projects: A Review of the Experience."
            Draft. June.

Ingle, M. D.
   1979   *Implementing Development Programs.* Washington: Agency for In-
            ternational Development. January.

Korten, David C.
   1980   "Community Organization and Rural Development: A Learning
            Process Approach." *Public Administration Review* 40(5), September/
            October, pp. 480–512.

Landau, M.
   1970   "Development Administration and Decision Theory," in E. W.
            Weidner, ed., *Development Administration in Asia*, pp. 73–105.
            Durham: Duke University Press.

Landau, M., and R. Stout, Jr.
   1980   "To Manage Is Not to Control: Or the Folly of Type II Errors."
            Public Administration Review 39, March/April, pp. 148–156.

Lindblom, Charles, and David Cohen
   1979   *Usable Knowledge.* New Haven: Yale University Press.

Mickelwait, D. R., C. F. Sweet, and E. R. Morss
   1979   *New Directions in Development: A Study of U.S. AID.* Boulder,
            Colo.: Westview Press.

Morgan, E. P.
   1980   "Managing Development Assistance: Some Effects with Special
            Reference to Southern Africa." *SADEX* 2(1), January/February, p.
            5.

Stout, Russell, Jr.
   1980   *Management or Control: The Organizational Challenge and Or-
            ganizations, Management, and Control: An Annotated Bibliography.*
            Bloomington: Indiana University Press.

Tendler, J.
   1975   *Inside Foreign Aid.* Baltimore: Johns Hopkins University Press.

Thompson, J., and A. Tuden
   1959   "Strategies, Structures and Processes of Organization Decision." In
            James D. Thompson, ed., *Comparative Studies in Administration*,
            pp. 195–216. Pittsburgh: University of Pittsburgh Press.

2
Who Learns What, When, How? Development Agencies and Project Monitoring

Charles A. Reilly

Introduction

Who gets what, when, how? was the query that guided Harold Lasswell's study of values and political influence (Lasswell 1966), and his question applies very well to an examination of the activities of international funding organizations. Lasswell framed political inquiry in terms of distribution of resources, influence, and ultimately power within a society. Development agencies operate between societies and are sometimes assessed on the basis of who gets what. Given the extent of human need and the scarcity of available resources (including that elusive commodity called "political will"), a more pertinent question before development donors is, Who learns what, when, how? or What have you learned that has made a positive difference in poor people's lives?

This chapter examines some approaches to learning tested by the Inter-American Foundation (IAF), a small agency created by the U.S. Congress in 1971 to find new ways to channel U.S. aid to grass-roots organizations of the poor in Latin America and the Caribbean. The chapter is also a commentary on what Peter Dorner calls the

> basic division of labor in the entire developmental enterprise. There is the world of physical work and action; there is the world of ideas—the intellectual enterprise; and there is the world of public decision-making—the public policy enterprise. These are not isolated activities; they are closely linked and interdependent. . . . a recognition of the role and importance of these different functions—as well as their limitations—should be sufficient ground for approaching this complex task of development with a sense of humility. [Dorner 1983:297]

Although some people asked whether any U.S. government agency could be expected to promote social transformation in the area, the IAF track record over thirteen years has led many Latins to answer affirmatively.

Another question to be addressed is how the IAF as an organization is structured for, and has succeeded in, learning from its performance? The problem is not limited to development assistance agencies, of course. As Alice Rivlin put it, "neither social service delivery systems nor government programs are organized to generate information about their effectiveness" (Rivlin 1971:64).

An introductory discussion of what I mean by "learning," and how it relates to social impact analysis is in order. "Learning" is here understood as the acquiring of knowledge and skill about development programs and projects. I use it as a generic term that embraces knowledge and information acquired both by funding agencies and by "client" groups. From the perspective of the development agency, the emphasis is on determining through observation, inquiry, and research what is going on in a project. From the client or local organization's perspective, learning derives from project activity, experience, and praxis. Learning may be carefully codified and recorded, or it may reside in individual and collective memories that are never set to paper.

Social impact analysis, as I understand it, attempts to bridge agency and client learning agendas by using various tools of social science research for social problem solving. Knowledge and action are to be grounded in real life changes for specific populations, whether the purpose is improved decision making (funder), improved project activity and outcomes (client organization or beneficiary), or improved social impact analysis and an expanded knowledge base (academic practioner). Actions are assessed and justified by reference to their consequences for concrete populations. Although changes in social structures and institutions may be sought, they have no intrinsic value. The bottom line in assessment, evaluation, or social impact analysis will be the effects of action on human populations. Men and women are indeed the measure.

Organizational learning requires a system of monitoring, or generating and recording information on what happens in the observed world. Monitoring demonstrates the need for action and the kind of action needed and assesses the effects of action. The sequence is important: Project appraisal refers to ex ante analysis and decision making, and project evaluation refers to ex post assessment. In the appraisal phase, the information includes a diagnosis of the situation, an estimate of the likely outcomes of intervention, and a normative assessment that leads to decisions on preferences for intervention or passivity. Underlying these functions (and often a hidden agenda) is the existence of a value system, or preference structure, that informs decisions, as well as the genuine capacity to alter the existing or anticipated state of affairs (knowledge, willingness, and resources come into play here). The second use of information, the assessment of outcomes or effects of action (evaluation), is linked to improving performance efficiency and accuracy by relating the costs, benefits, and results of action to the purposes sought by the action. Information about the effects of action is also essential for building theory, i.e., supporting knowledge claims establishing the patterns that link actions to consequences under specified limiting conditions. The entire package, then, includes description, forecast, theory, preference, choice, and action.

The following elements will be required for a fully developed monitoring approach:

> adequate monitoring depends on identification of (a) the normatively significant dimensions of the conditions of life of a specific target population, (b) the environmental factors that influence the situation, (c) the kinds of changes that can be presently induced in that situation, (d) the preferred outcome from among a real range of possibilities, (e) the intervention strategy that will achieve that outcome at least cost (not just monetary), and (f) the linkage between action and consequence that allows improvement in both the pursuit of purposes and the purposes pursued. [Meehan 1982:8]

In short, learning within a development organization means identifying the people it is supposed to assist (Latin American and Caribbean poor) and the channels or organizations through which such help can be processed. It must specify what to do to obtain desired results, i.e., what works under what conditions, and trace the effects of such help and such organizations on people's life conditions. The Inter-American Foundation was set up to be such an organization.

The Inter-American Foundation

The Inter-American Foundation was created as an alternative approach to foreign aid. In the late 1960s, some members of the United States Congress recognized that U.S. aid was not reaching the people who really needed it; that "trickle down" was taking too long; and that aid "carrots" were being dangled in an offensive, manipulative manner. Thus, in 1969, Congress, through an amendment to the Foreign Assistance Act, created the Inter-American Social Development Institute (the name was changed in 1971 to the Inter-American Foundation) with the rather broad mandate to find new ways to channel U.S. assistance to the poor of Latin America and the Caribbean. IAF was created as a relatively autonomous member of the development assistance establishment; an unusual government-to-private-sector link between U.S., Latin American, and Caribbean peoples; and an exceptional attempt to more directly channel aid funds for social problem solving. (Although part of the foreign aid establishment, the foundation's serving as a mechanism of revenue transfer to poor people has domestic relevance as well.)

IAF was an expression of congressional discontent with top-heavy, bilateral governmental approaches to foreign assistance and the failure of Alliance for Progress programs to effectively reach the poor. The multiplication of military, authoritarian regimes in the region confirmed the "antistatist" attitude of some congressional advocates, and skepticism and cynicism abounded at home and abroad by 1970. Gone was the heady enthusiasm of the 1960s. The "great society" had foundered, the "war on poverty" had ended.

The original congressional mandate included the general goal of improving life conditions for the poor of Latin America and the Caribbean through supporting self-help efforts, furthering broader participation of the people, and encouraging the development of democratic institutions. Fifty million dollars were set aside for the new agency, and a board of directors was established, with four of its seven members' being drawn from the private sector. Three additional principles of operation distinguished the new agency from prevailing policy and practice: First, IAF would be independent of U.S. foreign policy machinery to the fullest extent possible; second, it would assist indigenous nongovernment organizations; and third, it would respond to requests for assistance and not formulate or design overall country plans.

From 1971 through 1983, the foundation made grants totaling $153,700,000 to projects or programs in Latin America and the Caribbean. The original congressional appropriation has been supplemented in recent years by up to $16 million annually, drawn from the Social Progress Trust Fund through the Inter-American Development Bank. Unlike most development assistance agencies, IAF has generally responded to Latin American and Caribbean program designs rather than initiating projects itself. A rough functional breakdown indicates the range of programs funded.

Among the organizations engaged in providing goods, services, and human development assistance to the poor, there are local, regional, and national level groups that focus on marketing, agricultural production, banking and credit, housing, fishing, food processing, health care, consumer goods, counseling, education, technical training, community centers, day-care operations, performing arts and cultural awareness programs, and various combinations of these activities. Changes in existing institutional arrangements are sought through legal aid programs, lawyers' associations, curriculum reform, organizations concerned with education and the dissemination of information, cooperatives, and a range of multipurpose community organizations. Dissemination of information has involved activities as diverse as publishing, radio and television broadcasting, the performing arts, conscientization, program evaluation, meetings and conferences, education and training, and academic research and analysis. These organizations have operated under highly varied conditions in virtually every country in Latin America and the Caribbean.

Not surprisingly, suspicion was rife among Latin Americans about the advent of a "change-oriented" U.S. government agency—Project Camelot was one of many notorious U.S. government initiatives that had poisoned the atmosphere. Over the years, this suspicion has receded considerably, and a fairly unique relationship has developed between grantees and the small foundation staff based in Washington. It is a partnership, but one that places the major responsibility on the grantee. IAF provides resources, freedom of action, flexibility with respect to contractual relations, and often crucial moral support. The grantee must provide the idea; plan, staff, and operate the program; maintain a responsible and accountable relationship with its membership; satisfy its own government's requirements; and provide basic information on program outcomes, learning, and auditing to the foundation. Such was the political and administrative setting when IAF began. What was the status of academic disciplines relating to development when IAF opened its doors?

Development Theories and Praxis

Development theories abounded in and across disciplines. The yawning gulf between such theories, models, and paradigms on the one hand and development assistance practice, programs, and policies on the other seemed wider even than the gap between human need and available resources. Economics enjoyed a monopoly position. Guillermo O'Donnell has observed that the "optimists' equation"—that from economic development (read "growth") would flow all manner of good social, cultural, and political things—was quite patently off the mark. Increased authoritarianism was the more prevalent outcome of delayed development and import-substituting industrialization (O'Donnell 1973). Determinisms of left as well as right found a home in economic-based theories. Monetarists and Marxists, achievement-motivated individualists and multinational globalists, imperialists, "dependentistas" and conspiratorialists—the dogmatics abounded. Whether "development of underdevelopment" or a developmental "paradigm surrogate," causality by long distance was the explanatory fashion.

Latin American intellectuals were rapidly producing their own ideological and theoretical frameworks, and there was a growing number of "postideological pragmatists" who were well aware of the facts and mechanisms of domination and exploitation, but equally convinced that intramural academic debate would not reverse them. Fortunately, too, some Latin theorists pointed out the interpenetration of elites between center and periphery, clarified the history and structures of "associated, dependent development," and demonstrated that highly discriminatory, nondistributive development really was occurring. The fact of growth without equity was recognized and recorded.

Sociological traditions eddied around tradition-versus-modernity dichotomies, with some people acknowledging the presence of "transitionals." Industrialization ranked as the number-one promoter of change. Implicit was the assumption that the routes already traveled by North Atlantic nations would be smoothly replicated, with but minor detours and variations in scale or pace. Different starting points, the prior distribution of resources, and the impact of technological breakthroughs were much too casually disregarded.

Political paradigms were soon forthcoming. Although rhetoric, even preferences, echoed the pluralist dream, some people opted for "order and state building" before change, since chaos must first be banished. Gradually, a world view crossed by but two development paths (pluralist and Marxist) admitted a third possibility, as Barrington Moore, Joan Linz, Philippe Schmitter, and others took a second look at Europe and the apparent "elective affinity" between late capitalist development and authoritarian regimes, especially in the Iberian-Mediterranean south. A corporatist structuring of society became the third development path, and more often than not, the military became its executors. Much of this literature was characterized by a static appraisal of corporatist institutions—so separating state and society, and so mythologizing the powers of preemptive co-optation, that change appeared quite impossible. Spain, then Portugal, gave evidence that the paradigm was not absolute, that unanticipated processes and unnoticed space within society and even within the regimes might permit democracy to function, if not flourish.

Finally, a plethora of cultural and historical explanations of backwardness were trotted out to dismiss those people who had not yet properly modernized. Iberian stereotypes and Catholic authoritarian predispositions became fasionable explanations in some quarters, as well as the more blatant racial and ethnic biases projected toward native American, Afro-Brazilian and Afro-Caribbean populations. For such observers, acculturation; more middle-class folk; and a homogeneous, global consumer society were the prescriptions. Causal connectors, links in the chain from grand theories to concrete responses to Lenin's query, What is to be done? were slow to appear.

But were there no translators of grand paradigms? The 1960s did see some attempts to link social science and development in a more fruitful manner. Albert Hirschman, who contributed considerably to the effort, had this to say:

> I believe the countries of the third world have become fair game for the model builders and paradigm molders to an intolerable degree. I would suggest a little more reverence for life; a little less strait-jacketing of the future, a little more allowance for the unexpected, and a little less wishful thinking. I am not unaware that without models, paradigms, ideal types, and similar abstractions, we cannot even begin to think. But cognitive style, i.e., the kinds of paradigms we search out, the way we put them together, and the ambitions we nurture for their powers—all this can make a great deal of difference. . . . The open endedness of history is the despair of the paradigm-obsessed social scientist. [Hirschman 1970:335]

To overambitious paradigms and underambitious measurement should be added the indiscriminate prescribers who broadcast remedies irregardless of environment, local priorities, perceived needs of the poor, etc. Paul Streeten has isolated problems at another level of analysis: "The danger of social science research that attempts to emulate the 'hard' sciences is that it focuses on the measurable and neglects the rest. Some of the most important obstacles to the eradication of poverty and the promotion of greater equality lie in areas in which measurement is still very difficult or perhaps impossible" (Streeten 1974:48). Another tendency, labeled by Charles Lindblom and Stephen Cohen the "mistaken pursuit of authoritativeness," pointed out the limitations of social science, the high cost of conclusiveness, and alternative sources of information available to policymakers (Lindblom and Cohen 1979).

One final complication was the considerable gap between such frameworks for macro political-economic analysis and the generally micro universe of development praxis. Research tends to be skewed upward to focus on state more than society, on military preponderance more than local initiative, on authoritarian control rather than peasant resistance, on top-down rather than bottom-up development. If the micro and macro have been successfully integrated in economic theory (a dubious proposition), they have not been successfully joined in either political or developmental literature. (Guillermo O'Donnell has lately turned his attention to the micro-macro bonds within the political democratization processes of his native Argentina [O'Donnell 1983].)

The academic disciplines linked to development were in some disarray, but there is another rationale for foundation involvement. A foundation enjoys a comparative advantage over universities, think tanks, and other information agencies precisely because of its operational nature and the field-based content of its learning. The operational nature of such an agency makes it possible (though it does not guarantee) that its learning can be highly purposive and directional, since that learning can flow directly back into decision making. And frequent contact with the field affords healthy opportunities for a reality testing of development ideas.

IAF and Learning—Constraints and Critique

The foundation set out to find and fund innovative projects—to discover who was doing different activities in the nongovernment arena. Learning was not the primary agenda at the outset. But IAF does not make sense simply as a funder—the need in the region is too great, and the funds are too few. IAF has little purpose if it is merely a token gesture, even though its government-to-people dimension makes it unique in the U.S. government aid portfolio. IAF has demonstrated that it can find, and fund, organizations of the poor in Latin America and the Caribbean, which was one portion of its congressional mandate. But learning-while-funding continues to be more a challenge than an accomplishment.

A number of constraints have reduced the learning yield. Some constraints stem from the "legitimate paranoia" of Latin Americans who question data gathering by any U.S. government agency. Others derive from self-imposed limitations on foundation management, which has struggled to keep the ratio between funding activities and administrative costs in the 10–14 percent range—an administrator's ideal, but hardly realistic if the sort of learning sketched out here is to be derived from the operation. The "responsiveness" tenet that guided foundation activities for many years (and, in fact, replaced internally defined purpose and direction) also discouraged concentrating learning. A more recent tendency of an agency under siege has been to substitute public relations and defensive debate for project-generated learning. Shared with all development and domestic programs were the problems of establishing institutional memory despite personnel changes and the tendency to create an unviable ménage à trois among agency, grantee, and evaluator. Similarly, the inviting of outside evaluators to do post hoc reviews of projects with inadequate baseline data yielded limited knowledge. Perhaps the most thorny issue that has impeded a more comprehensive learning yield within the foundation has been the reluctance to implement an "experimenting" approach to project selection. Although quite understandable if construed as a laboratory exercise with human subjects, it shouldn't be offensive to enunciate assumptions, build rationales, announce hypotheses, and pose questions to be answered through funding a concrete activity.

If the IAF's potential as a learning operation about what works in development at the local level has not been fully realized, this fact should not serve as a pretext to eviscerate the organization and prevent it from achieving that original purpose. Surrendering the learning-through-funding quest to ideologues who already have their answers would be as much a travesty of the original purpose as relinquishing bipartisan support and opting to serve short-term foreign policy goals.

The questions remain. Can a small government agency efficiently and effectively learn through funding? Can it convincingly demonstrate what helps Latin America's poor people to better their lives? The answers will depend on a reaffirmation of the purpose and direction of the agency and a reallocation of staff priorities to incorporate the learning thrust.

From Theory to Praxis

A number of IAF accomplishments are evident. Especially important has been the demonstration that a U.S. government agency can contribute to improving the lives of, and even empowering to a limited degree, some poor people of these countries. Important too have been the delineation of the characteristics of effective grass-roots development organizations and the beginnings of a theoretical apparatus for learning about development.

The foundation early adopted a praxis approach to learning, derived from its experience working in partnership with Latins and Caribbeans. Rather than grand sociological, economic, or political interpretations of change, a problem-attacking, self-limiting, locally defined cognitive style began to evolve. At first, quite simply and appropriately, the foundation aimed at improving the quality of its own funding decisions.

Although IAF rejected sweeping paradigms, it began to evolve its own theoretical apparatus, the core of which is quite simple. During its first years, IAF developed a basic pattern or set of characteristics of organizations that clearly and directly obtained desired results in projects. The elements of the pattern include strength of commitment to assisting the poor; evidence of self-help efforts and potential risk; equitable distribution of benefits; concern for full human development, including participation in organizational affairs; accountable relationships to the beneficiaries; flexibility; and reliance on democratic procedures. The organization also had to enter into a firm partnership with the foundation. The theory asserts that the extent to which the conditions included in the basic pattern are fulfilled determines the quality of results achieved. If all requirements are met, one would expect significant and fairly rapid accomplishment; if some of the elements were missing, expectations would lower and, at some point, the organization would be expected to fail. The test of the theory is the relationship between satisfaction of requirements of the pattern and the accomplishments of the organization—measured in terms of the production of goods and services and human development.

The ideal typical grass-roots or primary organization and the secondary or intermediary development organizations were assessed in terms of their "vital signs":

1. The organization must have a genuine commitment to improving the life conditions of the very poor, and its actions must be endorsed by the beneficiaries.
2. There must be efforts at self-help and some measure of risk or commitment.
3. The organization's benefits should be fairly distributed, and organizational purposes should go beyond strictly economic improvement. There must be accountability between the organization and its beneficiaries, with mechanisms to ensure such accountability and control. "Participation" is no panacea (indeed, the rhetoric of participation in development has sometimes eclipsed the need for managerial competence).
4. There should be evidence of flexibility in the program; an ability to make changes in organization, purposes, and operating procedures in order to achieve objectives.
5. In secondary organizations (networks that serve the primary groups), similar criteria apply. Ultimately, their performance too, as in the case of primary groups, is assessed by the effects of action on individual beneficiaries.

Thus, IAF came to insist that development assistance must go beyond physical and economic improvements in society to incorporate a substantial element of human improvement, that physical capital must be augmented by social capital, and that neither economic nor human improvement could be achieved reliably without meaningful individual initiative, participation, and commitment to the enterprise. These criteria imply an overall strategy of action that is almost diametrically opposed to the centrally planned, top-to-bottom mode of operation that characterized most development assistance strategies.

Attempts were made along several related tracks to identify the "social gains" produced by the project activity. It was important to learn the extent to which beneficiaries in a project obtained information, resources, experience, and other direct opportunities for increasing their own human capital. What leverage was generated by the project in relation to both public and private sources of support, and to what degree was such leverage diffused within the organization? What was the range of choices generated by the project activity, and what was the effect of the project on the public status and private self-esteem of the beneficiaries? Such output and outcome information is, of course, most signficant, and still elusive. What were some of the instruments for obtaining such information?

Approaches to Learning

Over the years, IAF has employed some conventional and has evolved some unconventional ways to learn from projects. Even though the "learning" cart stayed behind the funding horse, some useful approaches still evolved. Just as social scientists spun their wheels for many years on the "fact-value" debate, so in the business of development and social analysis much time has been lost because the division of labor and learning noted by Dorner (1983:297) has been ignored. It makes a difference if the learning is done by poor people, development practitioners, donor agencies, local or national government officials, social scientists and consultants, or the development community in general.

In the following pages, I will describe some learning approaches employed by the Inter-American Foundation, emphasizing the distinction between the learning that accrues primarily to the poor people and their "promoters" and the learning that centers primarily in the donor agency for its own purposes and publics. Although learning that accrues to each of these publics may well benefit the other, a great deal of conceptual and organizational confusion derives from assuming that any and all lessons learned will be equally relevant to all parties concerned. For example, there is good reason for a peasant to know that the cost of agricultural inputs quite exceeds eventual earnings, but the cost-benefit analysis that led to that conclusion is aimed primarily at a donor agency and its resident economists. A tidy multiple regression on wage differentials over time may titillate a development economist, but it won't do much for a peasant or an unemployed slum dweller.

Evaluation as practiced in IAF, and many an agency, has all too frequently taken on the complexities of a ménage à trois, usually with heavy adversarial overtones between evaluator and evaluatee. The "responsive" posture taken by IAF during its early years helped reduce the levels of tension found in such organizational evaluation—since the planning function as well as programmatic direction and activities were generated from within the local organization—but that tension was resolved at considerable cost to IAF's organizational purpose.

From the perspective of donor agencies, one further tension must be recognized: the very frequent use of evaluations for accountability, for enhancing the agency's own institutional credibility, for expanding its clientele, and for good old-fashioned public relations. Such diversified approaches to the use of learning tend to distort, endanger, or drown the more prosaic "improve decision making" and "expand the knowledge base" rationales for learning within agencies. Public relations, evaluation, appraisal, and monitoring are not the same—although they may all share a common information base.

Finally, no apologies will be tendered for methodological diversity in the following approaches to monitoring. As the projects, programs, and activities vary widely, so too do the efforts to monitor and learn from them. Methodologies should be explicit and reliable. Conclusions should be validated and, to the degree possible, generalizable. The dilemmas of the world of development permit neither tidy nor heremetically sealed laboratories. Methodological purity should not impede experimentation within the learning process itself.

Following are some brief sketches of approaches to learning. First, the primary subject or agent is the beneficiary group (I'll call this client-centered learning) followed by a series aimed primarily at improving the information and decision making of the donor agency (which I call agency-centered assessment). These approaches to learning do not exhaust the IAF knowledge-producing functions. There is a large fellowship program, for instance, which supports field research throughout Latin America, and there are many grants to research organizations and individual scholars on problems related to the poor, which are not included in this review. The approaches here are highlighted either for their novelty or because there is little literature that attends to them at present.

Client-Centered Learning

Chronicle. One of the simplest and lowest cost approaches to learning is the chronicle. There is a rich lode of chronicles in Latin America dating back to the conquest (and through painting and stone carvings, to pre-Columbian eras). For our purposes, the chronicle consists of a diary of events related to a set of project activities, which is maintained by a member of a project. Such a simple narrative record can capture on a daily or a weekly basis the principal events of the project's life span. One such chronicle kept by a small cooperative of Indian carpenters in the Tarascan highlands of Mexico, for example, summarized the history of the cooperative, served as the basis for self-criticism and congratulation, and finally, systematically compiled important events which were then incorporated into reports to the donor agency.

Such chronicles can be very realistic accounts of a project's ups and downs, and, among other benefits, they can show how project people generally view their experience as the movement from one set of problems to another, a cycle of continuous problem attacking and occasional problem solving. Such a sequential narrative has a tone that is quite distinct from, and superior to, the oversimplified success-failure dichotomy that is often employed in "external evaluation." The chronicle serves as a document for self-criticism for the proponents and as an interesting and very-close-to-the-events source of data for donor agencies. Its cost is generally measured solely in the time devoted to preparing it. One of the principal shortcomings I have seen in such an approach is the problem of perseverance—the novelty of the method and the enthusiasm of a newly commenced (or newly funded) project is not easily sustained. Although chronicles will vary widely in content, quality, and quantity of information, they can be unsurpassed in terms of their immediacy. The chronicle approach can be enriched by external catalysts (see the section later in this chapter on oral histories).

"Musical Chairs" Learning. Another relatively uncomplicated, low-cost approach to facilitating project learning is what I call "musical chairs" learning for project activists, which recognizes and takes advantage of the wide range of experience, maturity, and knowledge among development practitioners. Such an exchange can be especially useful for groups with similar functional specialties but at different stages of organizational evolution. For example, a group of people involved in furniture cooperatives may benefit greatly from visiting and working with people running similar enterprises. A number of production cooperatives in Mexico sent members to other cooperatives for a few days, and in some cases for a few months, to pick up skills and accelerate organizational learning. (I have always found it remarkable that donor agency professionals and academic program evaluators, among the most peripatetic of men and women, are slow to facilitate such practical learning among their clients.) The accelerated learning prospects of such exchanges and the natural skill acquisition of such work/study have been too seldom realized. On the negative side, it is often difficult for key project leaders to "get away," so some encouragement and incentive may be required from the donor. The broker role of donors comes into play here as well, through linking groups and organizations that might benefit from such exchanges.

"Consultations." An expansion and variation on the musical chairs approach that has been quite fruitful in IAF experience has been the use of consultation—generally of persons representing organizations involved in a similar functional area (rural development projects, for example) or of organizations in the same geographical region with different, but complementary functional specializations. Using this method, the exchange of information could be organized to reach a wider audience. Since 1975, such consultations have permitted informational exchange and opinion sharing that transcend day-to-day operational problems for activist and

funder. One such exchange, almost lost in institutional memory, brought peasant leaders from several Latin American countries to California for a series of meetings with farmworkers and agricultural cooperative members. Among the unanticipated outcomes of that session was to hear Latin Americans chide U.S. farmworkers for their "excessive dependency" on federal funds and the absence of "self-reliance strategies." The pitfalls of such an approach sometimes derive from a "show-and-tell" competitiveness, but this problem can be corrected through planning and well-structured working agendas.

Participatory Evaluation. Among the most promising approaches to client-centered learning, more complex and sophisticated than the preceding examples, is participatory evaluation. As the name suggests, the learning emphasis lies with the project participants, sometimes with an external facilitator. The exercise attempts to encourage people actively involved in a project to continuously assess their own experience, develop habits of self-criticism, and link learning immediately to program operations. Most proponents of this type of evaluation have been influenced by Paulo Freire and his conscientization methodologies, sometimes blended with a smattering of social science techniques (Freire 1970). Some people have adopted this approach following negative experiences with academic evaluators, whose assessments are often regarded as being too distant or dilatory for practitioners. Undoubtedly, some of the advocates of such participatory learning are unable to accept pertinent criticism from outsiders, so this methodology must be taken with more than a few grains of salt. Learning derived from participatory evaluative exercises is destined principally for the practitioners themselves and many of the Latin American organizations that have pioneered in this approach tend to be nongovernment voluntary organizations, which prefer such an assessment approach to the more traditional evaluations (de la Rosa 1982).

Participatory evaluation efforts in Latin America resemble "action research" approaches adopted by some social scientists in the United States, which "aim to contribute both to the practical concerns of people involved in an immediate problematic situation and to the goals of social science by joint collaboration within a mutually acceptable ethical framework" (Rappaport 1972).

Agency-Centered Assessment

As in the case of client-centered learning, agency approaches can range from very brief, narrowly defined, relatively superficial, and inexpensive methods of gathering information to the more opulent ends of these continua. Cost, time, depth, and scope may be determined by the agency's needs at any moment for improving its decision-making capability, demonstrating its accountability to the source of its funds, establishing its credibility, or communicating with its own clientele. Therefore, there is a wide range of approaches to monitoring projects and assessing social impact. Budgetary and staff constraints as well as contextual realities prevent an in-depth monitoring of every project. Although the agency will require some lowest common denominator of information on every project it supports, it is more important to identify the projects that deserve more intensive monitoring. And clearly, these should be identified at the outset, the assumptions and hypotheses underlying them should be articulated, questions to be answered through the project should be posed, and arrangements for systematizing baseline information on the project should be made. In the following pages, I list a number of tested approaches, beginning at the less complex and less costly end of the scale.

Rapid Appraisal. The Institute of Development Studies at Sussex has documented a number of interesting experiences of "rapid rural appraisal," a frequently used method of gathering data prior to project funding decisions but less frequently applied to the assessment of project outcomes (Institute of Development Studies 1981). It is the latter application that interests me here. The IAF has had positive results from both staff and external consultant rapid appraisals—generally consisting of intensive field observation of projects over a brief period of three days to one week. Such field reviews are generally prefaced by a study of pertinent documents on program objectives, contain anthropological participant observations, and conclude with short and focused reports on project outcomes. Such a rapid review can be open-ended, aiming at a general assessment of project performance and outcomes and enriched by the questions, rationales, and hypotheses that motivated the funding of the project in the first place. Crucial to the exercise is the framing of such "originating questions" or hypotheses by the agency prior to funding.

This approach lends itself to a second "quick and dirty" variation, occasioned by program concerns, or red flags, that lead the agency to dispatch an observer to review problems internal to the project or that stem from broader, contextual changes affecting program performance. The nationalization of banks or the creation of new state-sponsored development programs, for example, radically revised availability of agricultural credit in Mexico and occasioned such reviews or appraisals.

A variation on this approach was tested in 1978 and 1979 when a group of staff members and consultants decided to fund a number of community-based programs in São Paulo, Brazil. Project review and funding decisions were made within one week, and staff members constructed brief profiles of these projects in order to trace project outcomes. Monitoring visits one year later tracked the performance of the projects—most of them community organized and controlled and concentrated on single-service activities such as day care centers and local clinics. Unfortunately, the experiment was neither adequately recorded nor replicated, and—as occurs too frequently—emphasis was placed on the novelty of the funding mechanism rather than on the potential for learning.

Case Studies. Next in ascending order are project case studies, which may be narrowly focused snapshots and single disciplinary in character or may include multiple disciplinary teams for both synoptic and sequential views of project performance and outcomes. Such case studies generally include extensive fieldwork as well as both archival and contextual reviews. Typically, a case study evaluation might include an agricultural economist, an anthropologist, and a political scientist or sociologist, according to the breadth of the project to be examined. Case studies may be project or program specific, or they may include a range of projects grouped together by sectoral categories More rarely, country-level case studies have been carried out. During 1982, for example, twenty-five projects were reviewed by outside evaluators (although I lack information as to how such studies currently influence internal decision making). Albert Hirschman visited a number of IAF projects during that same year, and his reflections on grass-roots development resulting from those visits have been published (Hirschman 1984).

Sectoral Reviews. Development projects may be concerned with a number of very specific issues and themes—health, rural credit, irrigation, marketing, etc.—and even a small learning/development agency must try to make sense of its experience in aggregated as well as in project specific terms. Hence, the value of sectoral reviews, which may span many regions or many countries and attempt to make sense of the funding experience. Such reviews may interact with the development literature but also with other government, nongovernment, and international development organizations. Obviously, sectoral reviews may be much more costly and ambitious than the other approaches, especially if they include extensive fieldwork. More frequently, such reviews have been limited to agency archival research and, as such, are subject to the limitations of available documentation. These reviews have generally been assigned to external consultants known for their expertise in a particular discipline or topic. Although, as defined by development economists, the sectors may be very broad (rural development, public health, legal aid, etc.), a far more fertile use of such studies can be made by narrowing the focus—e.g., the role of day-care centers in low income urban communities. Judith Tendler's study of cooperatives in Bolivia is an excellent example of such a study (Tendler 1983).

Oral Histories. One further instrument, this one borrowed from the anthropologist and the historian, is the oral history. In this approach, overall project assessment derives from the effort to elicit from project proponents, members, local observers, and even adversaries their own interpretation of what is going on in a particular community and project locale. Project oral histories permit greater space for local people to articulate their own reality and perceptions of the project and they often relativize the funders' tendency to believe that life begins with external funding. In one oral history, for example, it became clear to the anthropologist who conducted the exercise that a local community was strongly divided into two camps—pro and con a project activity and its leaders. The lines of cleavage within the community traced back to events some forty years previous, a fact that would have been quite inaccessible to the short-term visitor (Wasserstrom 1985).

Conclusion

Gunnar Myrdal wrote that both knowledge and ignorance are opportunistic (Myrdal 1973:159), and it seems that historically, much U.S.-based social science research vis-à-vis development flowed from excessively detached observers. Raw data, like minerals, were mined and refined, exported, processed and marketed, but few, if any, of the profits were repatriated. The level of analysis was skewed upward. It focused on state more than on society; on macro more than on micro problems. Tradition was viewed negatively, and modernity was depicted as desirable.

IAF has offered an alternative for funding and learning. It has facilitated problem solving and interdisciplinary approaches through fellowships for field research in Latin America and the Caribbean, which have become the largest funding source for U.S. field research in the region and have considerably increased the information base. IAF has encouraged grantees to find ways to document and share their own learning, quite beyond the basic common denominator of information required by the foundation to satisfy its own accountability needs. "Standard" evaluations have drifted in and out of fashion within the foundation—at times regarded as reified and useless, at other times expected to yield extraordinary amounts of wisdom, if not data. IAF has experimented with self-evaluations and with academic and technical specialists' appraisals, and it has offered grants to selected project participants to reflect and write up their own experiences for broader audiences. The musical chairs approach has speeded up the pace of organizational learning, and consultations have pooled program experience and institutional feedback in the field. For most of the first decade, the people actively involved in projects were the window into local social processes; more recently, IAF has multiplied studies and supported research institutions to clarify the situation and context of the poor in the region.

Lasswell asked, Who gets what? I've added, Who learns what? The learning enterprise is a complicated one—applied epistemology is not everyone's piece of cake—and learning outputs are "in areas in which measurement is still very difficult" (Streeten 1974:48). It will be both ironic and tragic if IAF should fall captive to a predetermined and imposed world view in the name of learning. Inquiry would cease and neither of the above questions could be answered. But if IAF can survive partisan and ideological intrusions, maintaining its independence from short term foreign policy manipulation, it may yet make the funding-learning nexus work. Doing so could benefit its clients, the foundation itself, and concerned people throughout the Americas.

References

de la Rosa, Martin, and Jorge Fuentes Morua, eds.
1982   *Encuentro Nacional Sobre Investigacion Participativa en el Medio Rural.* Morelia, Mexico: IMISAC.

Dorner, Peter
1983   "Development Dilemmas and Paradoxes." In *Population Growth and Urbanization in Latin America,* J. Hunter and S. Whiteford, eds., pp. 293–310. Cambridge: Schenkman.

Freire, Paulo
1970   "Cultural Action for Freedom." *Harvard Educational Review* 40(3): 452–477.

Hirschman, Albert O.
1970   "The Search for Paradigms for Understanding." *World Politics* 22(3): 329–338.
1984   *Getting Ahead Collectively.* New York: Pergamon Press.

Institute of Development Studies
1981   "Rapid Rural Appraisal." *IDS Bulletin* 12(4).

Inter-American Foundation
1983-84   *Grassroots Development: Journal of the InterAmerican Foundation.* Rosslyn, Va.
1984   "The InterAmerican Foundation: Report of the Evaluation Group." Internal report. Rosslyn, Va.

Lasswell, Harold
1966   *Politics: Who Gets What, When, How?* Cleveland: Meridian.

Lindblom, Charles, and Stephen Cohen
1979   *Usable Knowledge—Social Science and Social Problem Solving.* New Haven: Yale University Press.

Meehan, Eugene
1979   *In Partnership with People.* Washington, D.C.: GAO.
1982   "Monitoring." Mimeograph.
1983   *Economics and Policy-Making: The Tragic Illusion.* Westport, Conn.: Greenwood Press.

Myrdal, Gunnar
1973   *Against the Stream.* New York: Pantheon Press.

O'Donnell, Guillermo
1973   *Modernization and Bureaucratic Authoritarianism: Studies in South American Politics.* Institute of International Studies. Berkeley: University of California Press.
1983   "Democracia en la Argentina: Micro y Macro." Working paper. Notre Dame: Helen Kellogg Institute for International Studies.

Rappaport, R.
1972   Cited in Peter Clark, *Action Research and Organizational Change.* New York: Harper and Row.

Reilly, Charles, and Eugene Meehan
  1983   "Local-Level Development in Rural Latin America." In *Progress in Rural Extension and Community Development*, G. Jones, ed. London: John Wiley.

Rivlin, Alice
  1971   *Systematic Thinking for Social Action.* Washington, D.C.: Brookings Institution.

Streeten, Paul
  1974   *The Social Sciences and Development.* Washington, D.C.: IBRD.

Tendler, Judith
  1983   *What to Think About Cooperatives.* Rosslyn, Va.: IAF.

Wasserstrom, Robert
  1985   *Grassroots Development in Latin America and the Caribbean: Oral Histories of Social Change.* New York: Praeger.

3
Mexico: The Policy Context of Social Impact Analysis

Jack Corbett

Practitioners and scholars of social impact analysis commonly justify their efforts on the grounds of policy relevance, i.e., "to facilitate decision making . . . [and] to improve the design and administration of policies in order to ameliorate the disbenefits and to increase the benefits" (Finsterbusch 1977: 2). A standard theme in social impact assessment (SIA) literature is its utility for identifying the outcomes and consequences of government action. Whatever the specific goals, issues, focus, or methodology of social impact analysis, the common thread running through such studies is a desire to improve the quality of policy outputs, "to place the expectation and attainment of desired outcomes on a more rational and reliable basis" (Wolf 1981: 9). These affirmations of policy relevance rarely make explicit the linkages between information generated through SIA and political institutions, system priorities, organization behavior, decision-making styles, and other aspects of the policy process. Instead, they become imbedded in assumptions about the context or setting of SIA utilization and therefore become part of the conventional or taken-for-granted wisdom of the field, e.g., Burch and DeLuca 1984; Finsterbusch 1980; Finsterbusch, Llewellyn, and Wolf 1983; Soderstrom 1981; and Tester and Mykes 1981. A quick review of two such assumptions may clarify this point.

Implicit in the "policy relevance" justification is the assumption that policy is knowledge driven, i.e., that policymakers seek to channel improved personal or institutional knowledge into more effective policy. More timely, accurate, and complete knowledge improves policy quality, most frequently by reducing unanticipated adverse consequences or by identifying the most attractive cost-benefit mix. Such information should enter the policy process as early as possible, hence Wolf's characterization of social impact assessment as "*anticipatory* research" (Wolf 1983: 15, emphasis in the original). This knowledge-driven model of the policy process directs attention to the methodology of data gathering, analysis, decision selection, and information dissemination. It does not, however, deal with the "whys" of policy choice. If policies turn on private ambitions, group competition, external pressures, or some other motive, then the prospects that SIA has a significant place in policy formulation are correspondingly diminished.

The second assumption holds that public officials, sensitive to the political repercussions of policy failures or misjudgments, will utilize SIA to avoid or limit potential problems. In essence, this assumption suggests a norm of accountability, with an implicit indication that decision makers respond as necessary to avoid electoral challenges, litigation, unfavorable media coverage, or other adverse reactions. It requires a political system that is open to public participation and prepared to absorb criticism and controversy. Llewellyn, for example, suggests that "agencies must also contend with better informed and more politically active publics" (Llewellyn 1983: 11), a perspective applicable to Canada or the United States but largely outside the experience of the Third World. To the extent the public does not have the capacity to enforce accountability, or to the extent the political system insulates key actors from the consequences of social impacts, the prospects that SIA will be a meaningful factor in policy selection or implementation decline accordingly. When the consequences become the responsibility of another agency, administration, or office holder, social impact analysis becomes less significant as a policy tool.

To justify social impact analysis through its policy relevance is to acknowledge its linkage with all those complexities, conflicts, and uncertainties that are so common in the political world, and to underscore the necessity for understanding its place in the policy process. Assumptions based on models drawn from SIA utilization in Canada or the United States may be misleading or totally irrelevant in Bolivia, India, Zaire, or other Third World countries. Before presuming its ready application elsewhere, therefore, SIA specialists need to develop a clear appreciation of the policy context into which SIA must fit and any special circumstances likely to constrain or enhance its use.

Mexico as a Case Study

Mexico offers an interesting opportunity to explore the relationships between SIA and a Third World political system for several reasons. First, Mexico has a history of large-scale development projects in which the use of social impact analysis would appear to be quite appropriate. From major irrigation works in northwestern Mexico to several river basin development projects (Barkin and King 1970), the Ciudad Sahagun industrial center, and the petrochemical facilities of the late 1970s, Mexico has accumulated considerable experience with large public sector projects designed to have a major impact on regional economies. Second, through its ownership of or financial participation in most key industries, the national government commands excellent leverage over development decisions that in countries with more extensive and independent private sectors would be in the hands of autonomous entrepreneurs. In theory, such leverage reduces the prospect that public sector/private sector bargaining will compromise the public good by permitting adverse social impacts.

Third, the Mexican Revolution incorporated a strong commitment to the ideals of social justice and progress, both powerful ideological justifications for attention to social impacts. Fourth, Mexico's large, sophisticated social science community includes a sizable cadre with the requisite skills for social impact analysis. Finally, the political system itself, with its centralized decision making, extensive bureaucracy, and substantial organizational capabilities, would appear to have significant potential for integrating SIA into the policy process. Given this apparently favorable setting, it seems reasonable to examine the policy system's receptivity to insights supplied by social analysis and the extent to which it is shaped or dominated by other considerations.

At the outset it should be noted that in Mexico, social impact analysis has not been institutionalized to the degree that it has been in Canada or the United States, i.e., it is not grounded in law or doctrine, nor is it supported by formalized arrangements for debate, exchange, and professional interaction, e.g., meetings or a self-conscious literature. Preproject forecasting, or social impact assessment as it has come to be called, is not a major decision tool. The more inclusive notion of social impact analysis is used here precisely because most studies facilitiate or monitor work in progress (Molina 1976, Toledo 1982, Villa Rojas 1955, Zapata et al. 1978) or are retrospective or evaluative studies (e.g., Barkin 1978, Ewell and Poleman 1981, McMahon 1973, or Revel-Mouroz 1980). Their significance lies, not in immediate feedback for decision input, but in better understanding and interpreting the results of past or present projects with the hope of shaping future government planning.

Structure and Process in the Mexican Political System

A detailed, comprehensive review of the Mexican political system is beyond the scope of this chapter—people wishing such accounts will find numerous sources available (e.g., Cornelius and Craig 1984, Fagen and Tuohy 1972, Grindle 1977, Levy and Szekely 1983). In any event, familiarity with the formal structure is less important than understanding the unwritten rules and priorities of the political game, for these determine system attention to and concern for social impact analysis. This section will examine four aspects of the system that have a special bearing on the utilization of SIA in Mexico.

Centralization

All students of the Mexican political system, foreign and domestic, concur on the high degree of centralization in public sector decision making. By statute and by virtue of his control over the political apparatus, the president of Mexico concentrates enormous authority in his own hands. The president dominates the Partido Revolucionario Institucional (PRI), the "official" political party, and through it controls the selection of candidates at the federal, state, and local levels. He also controls an elaborate organizational communications network that reaches from party headquarters into almost every corner of political life. As head of the executive branch, the president not only determines policy and budgetary priorities but also exercises direct appointment or veto power over thousands of positions in the bureaucracy and government-owned enterprises (Cornelius and Craig 1984: 428). Fagen and Tuohy note that presidential power is exercised with "minimal reference" to the judiciary and legislature (1972: 20). A dramatic expansion in the public sector during the past two decades has somewhat reduced direct presidential oversight, but careful use of trusted advisers and two key ministries, the Secretary of the Presidency and the Secretary of Programing and Budgeting, assure overall compliance and control.

In theory, such centralization could work to the advantage of social impact analysis, for its acceptance as a decision tool at the top of the administrative hierarchy should lead to rapid promulgation throughout the system. In practice, however, it is difficult to compete for the attention of high-level decision makers and to convince them that SIA merits adoption, particularly given its mixed reception in developed countries. Given the centralization of decision authority, it is difficult to find someone at intermediate levels with sufficient autonomy and motivation to give SIA a try. Whatever the long-term benefits, in the short term, SIA may delay projects or increase their complexity by identifying potential problems. There is also the awkwardness that is inherent in using a procedure that might call attention to flaws in or undesirable consequences of projects or policies approved by the highest authority, an act readily construed as organizational disloyalty. Unless SIA receives sanction at the highest levels, then, its use in a centralized system is likely to be limited and tentative.

Authoritarianism

There is also widespread agreement regarding the authoritarian nature of the Mexican political system (e.g., Brandenburg 1964, Gonzalez Casanova 1970, Reyna and Weinert 1977, Smith 1979). Some observers trace it to the merging of the Hispanic and Indian traditions, and others see it as a calculated means of curtailing postrevolutionary political competition. An emphasis on control, reinforced by widespread patterns of symbol manipulation, co-optation, and patron-client relations, supports the view that communications move primarily from the top of the political hierarchy to the bottom, with only a limited, fragmented, and episodic flow in the other direction. Gonzalez Casanova, noting "the violent offense taken by the authorities when confronted by individuals or groups of inferior status who protest and demand instead of supplicate," regards depersonalization, coercion, and other mechanisms of subordination as persistent elements of the contemporary Mexican political system (1970: 102–103).

This authoritarian orientation is inconsistent with the notion of public participation's being regarded as an integral aspect of social impact analysis (Tester and Mykes 1981). Public involvement in SIA opens the door to dissent and opposition to government policy, neither of which is likely to find favor in a regime based on control and mobilization by political elites. Without making the normative argument that democracy is a prerequisite for comprehensive SIA, governments that are apprehensive about the broader political implications of public participation will be reluctant to adopt it except in a narrow and technocratic sense.

Proyectismo

A third significant dimension of the political system has come to be known as *proyectismo* (Poleman 1964), *plazismo* (Fagen and Tuohy 1972), or a "public works mentality" (Corbett and Hammergren 1980). The essence of the public works mentality is a strong, uncritical commitment to the construction of civic improvements such as fountains or plazas, hence *plazismo*, or to major investments in developmental infrastructure, e.g., dams or irrigation districts. Such projects are justified on the basis of their contributions to local or national pride, as a means of meeting a critical need, or as catalysts for economic growth. Such projects are very attractive to political leaders, as they offer broad visibility, the opportunity to be seen acting for the common good, and a relative immortality—the Papaloapan Project, initiated under President Miguel Alemán, commemorates his role with the Alemán Dam, Alemán Reservoir, Ciudad Alemán, and other, lesser facilities named for him (Poleman 1964). Such projects also offer individuals who are in a position to take advantage of them opportunities to profit personally from construction contracts, real estate investment, and other inside dealings (Graham 1968: 26–28). These mixed motives create a powerful bias supporting *proyectismo*. They also encourage project development to move rapidly, as leaders cannot expect their successors to support inherited projects at the cost of their own priorities. Within five years of President Alemán's retirement, many elements of the Papaloapan Project had been canceled or curtailed, and its budget was reduced to planning and maintenance (Poleman 1964).

Conflicts between *proyectismo* and SIA are readily apparent. The need to put projects in place during an officeholder's term is critical, as the Mexican Constitution's prohibition on reelection to the same office assures continuing turnover. In addition, it removes the prospect of electoral accountability, although the political dominance enjoyed by the PRI makes that point somewhat moot. Nor is there a strong incentive to consider a "no build" option; as elsewhere the decision favoring the project is a given, and SIA serves primarily to facilitate or make minor operating adjustments in its implementation. The Papaloapan Commission, charged with overseeing the Papaloapan Project, included an Office of Social and

Economic Research, but its purpose was to smooth resettlement of thousands of Mazatec Indians displaced by construction, not to raise fundamental questions regarding the project itself (McMahon 1973, Partridge and Brown 1983, Villa Rojas 1955). More recent studies by the Centro de Ecodesarrollo of petroleum development criticized Petroleos Mexicanos, the research sponsor, for its insensitivity to the social impacts of its projects in Tabasco (Toledo, ed., 1982; Toledo 1983). There is no indication, however, that this criticism has influenced operating policy.

Bureaucratization

The high level of bureaucratization found in the Mexican political system is both a legacy of its historical development and a result of the postrevolutionary expansion of the role of the state. The bureaucracy defines its role in terms of paternalistic supervision and control, not public service. Rigidity, delay, disinterest, and other much-lamented attributes plague the people needing assistance, though frequently assistance will be forthcoming through personal relations, petty corruption, or exceptional efforts by the dedicated. In addition to its slow pace, the bureaucracy is noteworthy for its tendencies toward secrecy and labyrinthine complexities. Agencies have few obligations or motivations to provide information about activities and plans to outsiders, including other government departments. Information is a commodity to be traded, not shared. This situation creates serious management problems, even for top decision makers, for departments tend to become bureaucratic islands, living largely independently. To assure the degree of coordination that large development projects require, there is a strong inclination to create new agencies, which duplicate the activities of those already in existence. Creating new agencies is often easier than trying to arrange cooperation among numerous existing units, but the history of such bodies, from the Papaloapan Commission to the Sistema Alimentario Mexicano, indicates that a great deal of organizational energy will be consumed in bureaucratic turf battles. Established departments resist the surrender of program operations, budgets, or clients that constitute a bloc of political support.

The high degree of bureaucratization confronts social impact analysts with several challenges. Of these, the penchant for secrecy and hoarding of information is perhaps the most serious. Unless the analyst can convince the bureaucrat that SIA will be beneficial, not theatening, there is little that can be offered in exchange for access to data. There is an element of circularity here, for without data, it is difficult to demonstrate applications that are useful to the agency (assuming they exist), yet without such demonstrations, the formal and informal organizational codes of behavior will hamper access to information. One solution to this situation lies in a successful response to the second challenge, namely, finding a strong organizational base or sponsor. Analysts operating outside the bureaucratic system need some influential support to legitimize their efforts and to assure cooperation. In its impact study, the Centro de Ecodesarrollo makes explicit reference to the indispensable endorsement by Jorge Díaz Serrano, then-director of Petroleos Mexicanos (Toledo, ed., 1982: 17). Without clearance and assistance from the highest levels, effective SIA becomes problematic, and to obtain that support, decision makers must regard SIA as (1) nonthreatening or (2) favored by the powerful. In situations in which numerous organizations pursue over-lapping responsibilities, the early stage of working through the networks of contacts and interests can be a major drain on the analyst's time and resources.

None of the constraints or limitations described here are unique to the Mexican political system, as even a cursory review of SIA literature from developed countries will reveal. The point is that the convergence of these structural factors creates a climate that is unreceptive to SIA, a climate reinforced by the norms and rules of the bureaucratic process. These norms and rules center on the management of career advancement in an organizational environment that is marked by insecurity, uncertainty, and the primacy of personal relations.

Article 83 of the Mexican Constitution prohibits reelection of the president, a safeguard against self-perpetuation in power that has the indirect effect of promoting a massive personnel turnover at the upper and middle levels of the bureaucracy at the beginning of each presidential term, or *sexenio* (Grindle 1977: 41–69). Each incoming president attempts to protect his political base and to assure policy compliance by putting in place decision makers and advisers in whom he has confidence, and who are committed to him. To anyone aspiring to a career in the public bureaucracy, these patterns of circulation and replacement have two significant implications. First, there is a continuing need to build extensive networks of exchange and obligation that may be tapped for information and assistance (Carlos and Anderson 1981). These networks reduce vulnerability by providing advance warning of shifts in policy or political fortunes and in bolstering the probability of successful relocation after each change in administration. Second, it is critical to demonstrate personal loyalty to the president or a chief subordinate, which frequently involves participation in a *camarilla*, or political clique, that supports and is assisted by a powerful political figure (Cornelius and Craig 1984: 431; Grindle 1977; Smith 1979). These cliques or factions compete for presidential favor, power, and access to resources. Loyalty involves not only direct support but also avoiding actions or decisions that might embarrass one's patron or superiors.

All of these factors have direct relevance for social impact analysis in terms of the behavioral patterns they engender. Several observers have suggested they lead to a distinct operating style, and Peter Smith has attempted to distill such behavior into "rules of the game" (Smith 1979: 242–274), a rational approach to surviving within the bureaucratic system. Such rules include "don't rock the boat," "avoid mistakes," "work fast," "pass difficult decisions to your superiors," and "keep making friends." There are others, and together they promote "conservatism and detachment from the substance of public policy" (Fagen and Tuohy 1972: 26). Conservatism means supporting the political system and the status quo while detachment from policy means giving first consideration to personal and political benefits. Fagan and Tuohy go on to note that this style places a low value on planning and expertise, as "people move so fast through a series of posts that have little in common (except their political characteristics and possibilities) that few careerists develop any substantial attachment to or base of knowledge about a given domain of public policy" (p. 28). Although this characterization may not have universal application (for a different view see Greenberg 1970), it suggests that decisions are made, not on the merits of the policy alternatives, but on their career implications for bureaucrats and the patronage opportunities available to *camarillas*.

These patterns of behavior are inconsistent with social impact analysis. In the short run, SIA slows, not accelerates, project development, an attribute that is unlikely to recommend it to a policymaker struggling to complete a project before the next election or rotation of officeholders. Although SIA might help avoid embarrassing mistakes, circulation from position to position reduces the prospect that the individual initiating SIA will be there to reap any potential benefits. There are few systemic rewards for successful technical innovation, but there are clear disadvantages associated with delay, controversy, or embarrassment, even if in the long run these lead to corrective measures that enhance policy implementation. To the extent that SIA identifies flawed plans or thinking, it calls attention to errors by decision makers, exposing individuals, agencies, or *camarillas* to criticism. In addition, social impact analysis may make explicit likely winners and losers from a given project, crystallizing opposition in a system that is poorly equipped to accommodate it. Although it is possible to make strong developmental arguments for the use of social impact analysis, the would-be innovator needs to sell its value on political, not technical, grounds, a challenge made even more difficult by the paucity of successful precedents.

Agricultural Development as a Case Study

As noted earlier, the social impact analysis literature on Mexico consists overwhelmingly of concurrent or evaluative studies rather than preproject assessments. In the absence of such assessments, the most productive approach to SIA would be to search for examples of institutional learning in which experience from early projects would appear to have influenced the design, management, and implementation of later efforts. Evidence of such learning would suggest that some of the concerns regarding the inhospitable atmosphere of bureaucratic norms and behavior for SIA were misplaced. Conversely, repetition of flawed or ineffective policies would indicate that either such learning did not occur or that such weaknesses were not accorded much importance. Career interests, insulation from political pressures for accountability, and bureaucratic routines would undermine systematic incorporation of institutional learning into the policy process.

If evidence of an increased utilization of social impact analysis is going to appear anywhere, one would expect to see it guiding policies toward colonization and development of tropical lowlands in southeastern Mexico. Since the 1940s, the region has been the focus of a series of plans and projects to stimulate settlement and agricultural production. Presidents since Avila Camacho have called for a "march to the sea," anticipating that successful colonization of the relatively empty tropics would both relieve demographic pressures on the densely populated farmlands of central Mexico and make a substantial contribution to Mexico's agricultural output. In addition, colonization projects would also help resettle the thousands of people displaced by flood control projects and reservoir construction along the region's major rivers. River basin commissions, loosely patterned after the Tennessee Valley Authority, were created to promote an integrated approach to regional development, including construction of dams, roads, and other physical infrastructure; encouraging commercial agriculture; and meeting such social needs as disease control and government services. A substantial literature (e.g., Barkin 1978, Barkin and King 1970, Ewell and Poleman 1981, McMahon 1973, Poleman 1964, Revel-Mouroz 1980, and Rodríquez Castro 1979) examines aspects of three decades of development activity, so this review simply asks whether there is evidence that project design, management, and implementation have improved across time.

The Papaloapan Project, the first of three to be discussed here, took its name from the river basin that would be the center of its activities. Established by President Miguel Alemán in 1947, shortly after he took office, the Papaloapan Commission quickly emphasized high visibility investments, e.g., flood control, highways, and new agricultural colonies. The colonies were not only expected to accommodate settlers brought in from elsewhere in Mexico, but to resettle more than 20,000 Mazatec Indians displaced by the construction of the Alemán Dam and the Alemán Reservoir. Although basic data on regional hydrology, potential agricultural productivity, and other key topics were unreliable or inadequate, pressure to complete major works by the end of Alemán's term in 1952 led the commission staff to suspend or disregard basic research (Poleman 1964: 103). The resettlement program, which was poorly organized and funded despite repeated pleas by the anthropologists guiding it, became a hurried rescue effort as the reservoir filled more rapidly than anticipated (Partridge and Brown 1983: 350). Delays, land speculation, and other unforeseen problems resulted in hurried resettlement in areas that lacked support services and had limited agricultural potential.

Other colonization efforts also encountered difficulties. Colonists inexperienced in tropical agriculture discovered (1) that much of the information necessary for successful adaptation to new settings and practices was unavailable and (2) that the commission's management style emphasized paternalism and tight control by administrators. This concentration of decision making within the commission bureaucracy disregarded both the lack of appropriate knowledge among administrators and the variations in individual settler circumstance, initiative, and experience. Poleman observed, "For all the influence his skill and aspirations could have over the management of his plot, the enterprising colonist might almost have been a laborer working on a plantation managed by the Commission" (Poleman 1964: 139). The administration of President Adolfo Ruiz Cortines, taking power at the end of 1952, shifted commission priorities from construction to agricultural credit and services, but the paternalism and inadequate information base continued to plague operations. The Papaloapan Commission managed to transfer responsibility for the Mazatec resettlement imbroglio to the newly created Instituto Nacional Indigenista (National Indigenous Peoples Institute). Although efforts to improve colony viability continued for several more years, by 1957—a decade after its creation—the Papaloapan Project was in decline, and the commission had been reduced to caretaker status.

Although the foregoing comments are largely critical of the commission, it should be noted the commission improved life in the Papaloapan Basin through better flood control, sanitary conditions, and communications. The key point is that many of the criticisms of the commission are readily associated with aspects of the political system discussed earlier: *proyectismo*, paternalism and bureaucratic centralism, authoritarianism, displacement of responsibility, and lack of systematic planning. As the first such project in the region, these weaknesses could be more readily accepted if there were evidence that the lessons learned improved subsequent projects.

Although the second case, the Chontalpa Plan, also originated with river basin development, several aspects of the setting were different. The Chontalpa region was already experiencing spontaneous and directed colonization, negotiations with the Inter-American Development Bank for funding required planning studies, and there was less rush to complete the project, which was envisioned as a multiphase effort that would span more than a decade. Initiated in 1966, the Chontalpa Plan included replacement of subsistence and small-scale agriculture with capital-intensive production geared to national and international markets, concentration of the population into twenty-two service centers, compulsory sale or exchange of land to permit tenancy changes, and expansion of communications, flood control, and drainage. All of these and other changes required careful coordination and continuing cooperation by numerous government agencies, a challenge traced by Barkin (1978) and Rodríguez Castro (1979). The multiphase approach permitted some experimentation, such as an agricultural research station and a pilot resettlement community, and made it easier to alter the project in the event it proved necessary.

Although the Grijalva Commission had carried out several studies prior to activating its plan, these had emphasized physical rather than social engineering. The literature does not reveal evidence of feasibility research or impact assessments for the relocation and retraining of thousands of small-scale producers. Armed resistance to the plan emerged in 1967, as local political bosses and landlords attempted to capitalize on the dissatisfaction associated with abrupt, obligatory relocation or collectivization, and the tone of the commission's management became increasingly bureaucratic and authoritarian. Barkin notes that all key production decisions were concentrated in the hands of agronomists, bankers, and marketing specialists while the *campesinos* provided nothing but raw labor under the supervision of a variety of government functionaries (Barkin 1978: 80–81). Despite agreements between the Rio Grijalva Commission and federal agencies, within a few years the agencies were downgrading or ignoring their commitments (Rodríguez Castro 1979). In 1972, under President Luis Echeverría, a special agency was created to oversee coordination, but by 1976, the Chontalpa Plan was years behind schedule, far over budget, and redefined to emphasize cattle and sugarcane production. In January 1977, shortly after taking office, President Jose López Portillo abolished Echeverría's coordinating agency, and the entire plan entered still another round of review and modification.

Twenty years after construction of the Alemán Dam, the Papaloapan Commission received permission to build another, Cerro de Oro, as a flood control project on the Papaloapan River. This dam also displaced several thousand families, most of them Chinantec Indian. The commission selected Uxpanapa, a dense, sparsely populated rain forest in the state of Veracruz, as the primary resettlement site. Drawing from its earlier experience, its resettlement policy included prompt indemnification for losses, infrastructure development, and an agricultural experiment station. This policy proved to be exceptionally expensive and could be justified only by organizing resettlement around capital-intensive, mechanized agriculture geared to meeting growing shortfalls in national food production (Ewell and Poleman 1981: 121). Over 200,000 acres were to be cleared, mostly by machine, and the land was to be brought under cultivation as quickly as possible.

As noted above, the Papaloapan Commission modified its approach to resettlement to reflect earlier experience, a modification consistent with the idea of institutional learning. Ewell and Poleman (1981: 121) believe it responded to the failures and criticisms of the Mazatec resettlement in the 1950s, but in other respects, evidence of such learning is rather sparse. Just as happened twenty years earlier, the quickly prepared, superficial agricultural productivity estimates for Uxpanapa proved to be excessively optimistic as soil conditions were generally less fertile than anticipated, agricultural experiment data were limited and unreliable, and mechanization proved more difficult than expected. Commission personnel could not speak Chinantec, so they encountered the same communications problems non-Mazatec speakers had encountered during the Alemán resettlement. As in Chontalpa, the commission emphasized central control over planting decisions and resource allocation, reducing settlers to the de facto status of agricultural laborers and leaving them vulnerable to lapses in management effectiveness. Despite problems elsewhere—brought on by paternalism, bureaucratic rigidity, and technocratic authoritarianism—many of these same patterns and practices dominated the commission's approach to the Uxpanapa settlers.

Such a quick summary of the three cases does not do justice to their complexity, nor to the changing contexts of public policymaking. The case material available suggests that whatever the marginal improvements in its handling of resettlement, the Papaloapan Commission was unable to overcome the fundamental problems associated with the ethos that guides bureaucratic behavior. In a broader sense, neither the Chontalpa nor the Uxpanapa colonization efforts examined the central assumptions driving project management, including the malleability of physical and social systems and the persistent misjudgments of the capacity of authoritarian decision makers to command cooperation and compliance from colonists. Poleman's early work (1964) demonstrated pitfalls in this approach, but to no avail, as outsiders challenging the commission in Uxpanapa found themselves excluded from any meaningful contribution (Ewell and Poleman 1981: 128). Indeed, despite repeated failures, the commitments to centralized control and capital-intensive commercial production appear to be articles of faith. To the extent that existing studies serve as substitutes for systematic social impact analyses, they suggest that the primary explanation for the persistent mismatch between grand plans and modest accomplishments may be found in the nature of the bureaucratic system itself. If this assumption is correct, it is not difficult to see why social impact analysis is not used more widely.

It should be noted that although this discussion focuses on SIA in relation to decision making and administration in agricultural development, other focuses are also possible, even within the confines of the three cases discussed. Social impact analysis could be used to explore the consequences of resettlement and colonization on cultural identity (McMahon 1973; Partridge, Brown, and Nugent 1982; Partridge and Brown 1983); it could also be used in an examination of the integration of small-scale producers into the national agricultural economy (Barkin 1978, Ewell and Poleman 1981). Some people fare reasonably well, but others, pressed by credit burdens, the uncertainties of the marketplace, and shifting government priorities, find themselves incorporated into a rural proletariat. The questions and issues raised here represent only one of several ways SIA could be employed for agricultural, resource extraction, or other development projects.

Social Impact Analysis and
Public Policymaking in Mexico

The foregoing may help to explain why, despite the nominally favorable setting, formal social impact analysis along the lines of Canadian or U.S. models has made little impression on public policy in Mexico. Opportunities to use it are not limited to tropical agriculture; the Las Truchas steel complex (Zapata et al. 1978), petroleum-led urbanization and industrialization along the Gulf coast (Toledo, ed., 1982; Toledo 1983), major tourist resorts such as Cancún and Ixtapa, the port complex at Salina Cruz, and other major construction projects (e.g., Molina 1976) offer settings in which to test or revise the argument advanced here. In the real world of Mexican policymaking, social impact analysis offers only marginal contributions to political accountability and to the knowledge base used in policy choice.

Accountability

The political dominance of the PRI and the control capabilities of the federal government assure policymakers they will not be subject to demands for political accountability through the electoral process. There may be concern that poor policy choice will generate embarrassment or even turbulence, but it is not necessary to use SIA as an early warning device. Occasionally, an affected party may seek a writ of *amparo*, or judicial protection, but the lack of class action suits and the political power of the executive render the judicial system an improbable source of demands for accountability. Armed protest, as in the Chontalpa case in 1967, is more likely to stimulate repression than policy change (Rodríquez Castro 1979: 54–59), and imprudent acts may lead to the replacement of public officials, but political implications, not social impact analysis, are the determining consideration.

Policy-Relevant Knowledge

More important than the limitations on accountability, however, is the marginal role for social impact analysis in shaping choices within the Mexican policy system. Its use, although sometimes unstructured, in project monitoring and evaluation suggests it may be accorded some long-term, technocratic value; establishment of agricultural experiment stations in Chontalpa and Uxpanapa may reflect lessons learned from poor agricultural performance in the Papaloapan Project. But many other lessons, including ecological constraints on the rapid transformation of a tropical rainforest to commercial agriculture, problems in the centralization of decision making, and the need to avoid excessive organizational complexity, remain unappreciated or ignored. The Papaloapan Commission's difficulties in managing indemnification of the Mazatecs in the 1950s may have been avoided with the Chinantecs in the 1970s, but the more serious matter of substituting bureaucratic knowledge for the experiental knowledge of peasant farmers has not been resolved (Ewell and Poleman 1981: 182). Given the current configuration of policymaking in Mexico, SIA may be accepted when it improves the quality of technical operations, but on those occasions when it collides with deeply rooted bureaucratic norms, organizational turf, or career ambitions, there is little reason to expect that a new social technology will displace powerful traditional concerns.

Political Implications of Social Impact Analysis

Perhaps the fundamental issue centers around the normative notions of participation and responsiveness, notions that are often unstated but are generally implicit in discussions of social impact analysis. The principles that people affected by large-scale projects have a right to participate in decisions affecting them and that they have legitimate expectations for responsiveness from the people responsible for such projects run through much of the literature. In Mexico, these ideals clash with a political system that is based on centralized control, broad restrictions on citizen involvement in the policy process, and a political culture stressing passivity and an acceptance of higher authority. To the extent that SIA is envisioned as a narrow, technical process facilitating organizational problem solving and efficient management, it is not inconsistent with a centralized, authoritarian system. But to the extent that social impact analysis incorporates participation and responsiveness as constituent elements, it raises the specter of a challenge, not merely to specific projects, but to the political system itself. Once conceded for some groups in some situations, how will the system manage the inevitable demands that these same principles be extended to other groups and situations?

In addition, SIA often makes explicit who will benefit and who will lose from a given project or policy. Given the serious tensions in Mexico over the persistence of deep social and economic inequities, many of which are the consequence of government policies, SIA could aggravate conflicts over distributive politics. Toledo (1983) discusses conflict between federal agencies and communities in southeastern Mexico, noting that the latter believe the ecological basis of their way of life is being systematically destroyed to provide the resources to sustain the interests of powerful constituencies in central Mexico. Effective citizen participation in politics and social justice were central themes in the Mexican Revolution, and seventy-five years after the start of the Revolution, those aspirations remain largely unfulfilled for many Mexicans. To the extent that policymakers perceive social impact analysis as a potential contributor to, rather than an ameliorator of, tension and stress within the political system, the prospects for its widespread use will remain limited.

Notes

Research for this study was part of a larger project carried out while the author was a Mellon Summer Research Fellow at the Institute of Latin American Studies at the University of Texas at Austin. The support of the Mellon Foundation and the Institute of Latin American Studies is gratefully acknowledged.

References

Barkin, David
    1978   *Desarrollo Regional y Reorganización Campesina.* Mexico, D.F.: Editorial Nueva Imagen.

Barkin, David, and Timothy King
    1970   *Regional Economic Development in Mexico.* Cambridge: Cambridge University Press.

Brandenburg, Frank R.
    1964   *The Making of Modern Mexico.* Englewood Cliffs, N.J.: Prentice-Hall.

Burch, William R., Jr., and Donald R. DeLuca
    1984   *Measuring the Social Impact of Natural Resource Policies.* Albuquerque: University of New Mexico Press.

Carlos, Manuel L., and Bo Anderson
    1981   "Political Brokerage and Network Politics in Mexico." In *Networks, Exchange, and Coercion,* edited by David Willer and Bo Anderson. New York: Elsevier.

Corbett, John G., and Linn Hammergren
    1980   "Public Policy-Making at the Local Level in Mexico and Peru." *Compatative Urban Research* 7(3), pp. 27–48.

Cornelius, Wayne R., and Ann L. Craig
    1984   "Politics in Mexico." In *Comparative Politics Today,* edited by Gabriel A. Almond and G. Bingham Powell. 3d ed. Boston: Little, Brown and Company.

Ewell, Peter T., and Thomas T. Poleman
    1981   *Uxpanapa: Agricultural Development in the Mexican Tropics.* New York: Pergamon Press.

Fagen, Richard R., and William S. Tuohy
    1972   *Politics and Privilege in a Mexican City.* Stanford: Stanford University Press.

Finsterbusch, Kurt
    1977   "The Potential Role of Social Impact Assessments in Instituting Public Policy." In *Methodology of Social Impact Assessment,* edited by Kurt Finsterbusch and Charles P. Wolf. Stroudsburg, Pa.: Dowden, Hutchinson and Ross.
    1980   *Understanding Social Impacts.* Beverly Hills, Calif.: Sage Publications.

Finsterbusch, Kurt, Lynn G. Llewellyn, and Charles P. Wolf, eds.
    1983   *Social Impact Assessment Methods.* Beverly Hills, Calif.: Sage Publications.

Gonzalez Casanova, Pablo
1970   Democracy in Mexico. New York: Oxford University Press.

Graham, Lawrence S.
1968   Politics in a Mexican Community. Gainesville: University of Florida Press.

Greenberg, Martin H.
1970   Bureaucracy and Development: A Mexican Case Study. Lexington, Mass.: Heath Lexington Books.

Grindle, Merilee S.
1977   Bureaucrats, Politicians, and Peasants in Mexico. Berkeley: University of California Press.

Levy, Daniel, and Gabriel Szekely
1983   Mexico: Paradoxes of Stability and Change. Boulder, Colo.: Westview Press.

Llewellyn, Lynn G.
1983   "Introduction." In Social Impact Assessment Methods, edited by Kurt Finsterbusch, Lynn G. Llewellyn, and Charles P. Wolf. Beverly Hills, Calif.: Sage Publications.

McMahon, David F.
1973   Antropología de una Presa: Los Mazatecos y el Proyecto del Papaloapan. Mexico, D.F.: Instituto Nacional Indigenista.

Molina, Virginia
1976   San Bartolomé de los Llanos: una urbanización frenada. Mexico, D.F.: CISINAH.

Partridge, William L., and Antoinette B. Brown
1983   "Desarrollo Agrícola entre los Mazatecos Reacomodados." América Indígena 43(2), pp. 343–362.

Partridge, William L., Antoinette B. Brown, and Jeffery B. Nugent
1982   "The Papaloapan Dam and Resettlement Project: Human Ecology and Health Impacts." In Involuntary Migration and Resettlement, edited by Art Hansen and Anthony Oliver-Smith. Boulder, Colo.: Westview Press.

Poleman, Thomas T.
1964   The Papaloapan Project. Stanford: Stanford University Press.

Revel-Mouroz, Jean
1980   Aprovechamiento y Colonización del Tropico Humedo Mexicano. Mexico, D.F.: Fondo de Cultura Economica.

Reyna, Jose Luis, and Richard S. Weinert, eds.
1977   Authoritarianism in Mexico. Philadelphia: Institute for the Study of Human Issues.

Rodríquez Castro, Ignacio
1979   El Ejido Colectivo como Agroempresa. Mexico, D.F.: Instituto Nacional Indigenista.

Smith, Peter H.
  1979   *Labyrinths of Power.* Princeton: Princeton University Press.

Soderstrom, Edward J.
  1981   *Social Impact Assessment.* New York: Praeger Publishers.

Tester, Frank J., and William Mykes, eds.
  1981   *Social Impact Assessment: Theory, Method, and Practice.* Edmonton,
            Alberta: Detselig Enterprises.

Toledo, Alejandro
  1983   *Como Destruir el Paraíso: el Desastre Ecológico del Sureste.* Mexico,
            D.F.: Océano.

Toledo, Alejandro, ed.
  1982   *Petroleo y Ecodesarrollo en el Sureste de México.* Mexico, D.F.: Centro
            de Ecodesarrollo.

Villa Rojas, Alfonso
  1955   *Los Mazatecos y el Problema Indígena en la Cuenca del Papaloapan.*
            Mexico, D.F.: Instituto Nacional Indigenista.

Wolf, Charles P.
  1981   "Social Impact Assessment." *IAIA Bulletin* 1(1), pp. 9–17.
  1983   "Social Impact Assessment: A Methodological Overview." In *Social
            Impact Assessment Methods,* edited by Kurt Finsterbusch, Lynn
            Llewellyn, and C. P. Wolf. Beverly Hills, Calif.: Sage.

Zapata, Francisco, et al.
  1978   *Las Truchas: Acero y Sociedad en México.* Mexico, D.F.: El Colegio
            de Mexico.

4
Social Impact Assessment and Agricultural Projects: A Case Study in Ndiemane, Senegal

Desiré Yande Sarr

Why have so many development projects failed and continue to fail in Africa? Although some people would blame the problems on a congenital African incapacity to change, the answer rests with the nature of the structural relationships, which in turn are reflected in the projects themselves. We need to question the objectives of the projects and the methodology used to reach those objectives. This process then raises a series of questions that must be asked before a project is implemented. Representing a framework for a social impact assessment, the key questions are:

1. What are the project's goals?
2. By whom and for whom is the project being implemented?
3. Who chose the target population?
4. Will the target population participate in determining the objectives?
5. Who will benefit and who will suffer from the project?

All of these issues should be raised in a preproject analysis along with the gathering of social, economic, and ecological data about the region. The project should be designed to incorporate the values and needs of the people involved, through their participation. Such a design will lead to projects with objectives that are relevant to the local population, which enhances the possibility of project success. Yet there are many problems to complicate the process.

In this chapter, I will describe and discuss a feasibility study of a major project, Management of Alluvial Soils in the Ndiemane, which I participated in while working for the Senegalese Institute for Agricultural Research (ISRA). The discussion will highlight the social impact assessment issues that emerged as the project was designed and implemented.

Management of Alluvial Soils in the Ndiemane

The zone of Ndiemane is located in the Department of Bambey (in the region of Diourbel) in central northwestern Senegal. It is part of the "groundnut basin," which, since the colonial period, has been the site of an extensive export monoculture—the cultivation of groundnuts. As a consequence, the area devoted to producing subsistence food has been sharply reduced, and the soils have deteriorated badly. Population growth and the expansion of livestock have further intensified the demographic pressure on the land. Almost 100 percent of the population of the five villages in the zone depends on agriculture, raising millet for subsistence and groundnuts for exports. In addition, there are two other important agricultural activities: vegetable cultivation and livestock.

The project emanated from the preoccupation of the Senegalese government with rural regional development. Originally, the project was designed to encompass an area of 10,000 hectares of nearby uncultivated land that the villagers used intensively during the rainy season as grazing land for their livestock. Although funded by USAID, the project's structure and organization was at the discretion of the regional administrative authorities. When the project was conceived in 1968, it had a double objective: (1) to increase agricultural production, especially of grains, in order to resolve the food shortage in the zone and (2) to resettle 2,500 to 3,000 villagers from the zone's periphery, where the demographic pressure was intensifying. To accomplish the first objective, the project had two thrusts: to encourage the use of oxen to replace manual labor and to drill wells so there could be large-scale irrigation during the dry season. In 1969, a demonstration group was created in the zone, and ten farmers from the village of Ndiemane were chosen to use the new technique (oxen). In 1969, the first well was drilled near the village of Ndiemane on the project's periphery, but it was not equipped. Furthermore, project plans were drastically altered by the regional government that same year.

Instead of helping the local villagers by allocating land to those who needed it, the new proposal was to settle in the zone 300 young farmers (ages fifteen to twenty-five) who had already received training in an agricultural school. Each would receive from 8 to 10 hectares and credit for equipment. To accommodate these settlers, the government planned to create a basic infrastructure—health centers, schools, cooperatives, etc.—claiming that the local people would benefit from these facilities as well. The governor's new plan, although backed by the prefect of the Department of Bambey, was not supported by the development societies (SAED, SODEVA, and SODEFITEX) or ISRA. The people representing these societies felt the local population was being excluded in the project's planning and implementation, so without abandoning their arguments, the regional authorities agreed that a survey should be conducted in order to gain a better understanding of regional agriculture and social organization. This information was then to be used in designing the final project. ISRA was appointed to conduct the investigation, and I, as a sociologist, was assigned to do the field survey.

I began with the assumption that if the project were to be viable, a better understanding of the social, economic, and ecological relationships was needed. Such a preoccupation led me to consider the following: the demographic problem, land utilization, land tenure procedures, crop composition, extra-agricultural activities (handicrafts, small commercial activities, animal fattening), social services, road traffic, levels of living, agricultural inputs and services, and livestock and environmental effects. I found it necessary to answer to the following questions:

1. To what extent was the population in the different villages aware of the project and its orientation?
2. How important was the demographic pressure?
3. Would the people in the zone accept the fact that people from different regions would be given land while they themselves lacked it?
4. How would giving developed land to young fifteen-to-twenty-five-year-old farmers fit with the social reality that men of the same age still work in their father's fields?
5. Why set agricultural school training as a condition when the ratio of literacy in the zone is less than 3 percent (Koranic school excluded)?
6. To what extent was there a land shortage in the zone, and why confiscate land from those who owned it in favor of immigrants?
7. Why was the indigenous population generally excluded from training in new agricultural techniques?
8. What are the economic activities of production in the zone, and how could this project affect them?
9. How would the different segments of the population be affected (men, women, young men old enough to have their own fields?)
10. How would livestock be affected by cultivation in the zone?
11. How would the people in the villages react to the project?
12. What factors do they consider to be priorities that the project should help to resolve?
13. What positive impact do people anticipate?

I hoped that the answers to these questions would help determine how realistic it would be to keep the project focused on the local population, instead of following the orientation desired by the governor. I was also convinced that the best answers would be found only by including the local population directly in my investigation.

Methodology

Because of its proximity to the National Center for Agricultural Research of Bambey, the zone of Ndiemane has long been the object of study. Thus, reports on soils, climate, varieties of crops, demography, and production were available. In addition, I was provided with the plans of the project since its inception in 1968. I spent two months reading what had been written about the zone and visiting villages for informal discussions and observation. These activities significantly helped me construct a questionnaire for my future investigations.

Time constraints imposed by the report deadline made it impossible to conduct exhaustive work in all five villages. For this reason, I chose to sample one-quarter of the households in three of the villages. In the other two villages, Ndiemane and Battal, all of the households were included in the sample because the villages were located on opposite sides of the project zone and because they were the first villages settled in the zone.

For four months, the field staff conducted both formal and informal interviews at different social levels, including the leaders of each village. We discussed with both young and mature men and women what they believed the major problems to be, their proposed solutions, how they viewed the project, how they would like the project modified, how they could participate in the project, and how they thought it would affect their situation. The research took nine months altogether.

Data and Discussion

Two types of soil are found in Ndiemane: a sandy soil suitable for groundnut growing and alluvial soils suitable for sorghum but very difficult to work by hand. According to a report published by ISRA, oxen-pulled equipment greatly facilitated work in alluvial soils. As the reports on the follow-up of indigenous farmers' using oxen showed very positive results, I concluded that the technological innovations that had been proposed required no formal training.

Rainfall in the zone varies between 450 and 600 mm. For this reason, almost all farmers in the zone cultivate a native variety of millet that has a 75-day cycle and needs a minimum of 300 mm. of water. There is also a variety of groundnut that has a 90-day cycle and needs a minimum of 400 mm. of water. As sorghum has a cycle of 120 days and requires 550 mm. of water, its cultivation decreased with the reduction of rainfall in the zone. As a result, the zone that was peripheral to the project, where crop rotation had been practiced before, was no longer being cultivated.

Tables 4.1 and 4.2 demonstrate the current land shortage for the villagers and indicate that the current organization of agricultural and livestock production would be dramatically affected by the introduction

TABLE 4.1
Population characteristics of study zone

POPULATION	NDIEMANE	BATTAL
Total population	1114	1892
Male	542	934
Female	572	958
pop < 20 years	56.55%	52.9%
*Active population NN		
(National specification)	591	958
Number of compounds	86	122
**Number of independent households	137	226
***Number of dependent households	43	89
Average pop/compound	12.9	15.5
Average pop/independent households	18.13	8.3
Active population/compounds	6.83	8.1
Active population/households		
Independent	4.3	4.4

*NATIONAL Specifications for labor units		
Male	8-15 years	0.5
	15-60 years	1
Female	8-15 years	0.25
	15-60 years	0.5

** Independent households: Independent unit of production within a compound but economically independent

*** Dependent household: Family unit still economically dependent on the head of the compound

of a new population in the area. These consequences alter the availability of land for both agriculture and herding. Considering the data collected, one finds a discrepancy between what is foreseen for the future new settlers and the realities of people now living around the zone of project. How rational will it be to give 8 to 10 hectares to new settlers when farmers in the zone now own an average of 1.56 hectares? What effect will the increased population have on the land? Farmers themselves give

TABLE 4.2
Land utilization and cattle herds

	Ndiemane	Battal
Total cultivated area in hectares	974.65	1,498.03
Available cultivated area per person	.87	.79
Available cultivated area per labor unit	1.65	1.56
Cattle	476	443
Cattle sent on transhumance	243	271

the response to this question: "All that we will have to do will be to migrate during the rainy season to the northeast, to the zone of Terres Nueves." In fact, this movement already exists. Young men, usually those of marriageable age who no longer have enough land to cultivate for their own needs, leave the village for the six months of the agricultural season. They go to eastern Senegal where they are given land and shelter in return for their labor. But the women, who also suffer from the demographic pressure on land, do not have this option. Instead, they work for their own needs on the fields given to them by the household head. When land is scarce, the size of the fields given to women or to very young men is further reduced.

Another important point concerns the number of livestock in the region. P. Pelissier speaks of the three important roles of animals: social, economic, and agricultural.[1] Animals confer a meaningful social status on the owner as well as making it possible to satisfy different social obligations in cases of marriage, birthday, circumcision, or death. The economic role of animals is to provide the major form of saving for the farmer, and finally, animals ensure the fertility of the soil. Even since the introduction of chemical fertilizer, some people continue to use manure to fertilize their fields.

The importance of the animals explains why people in the peripheral villages said: "If you develop this zone, where are we going to graze our animals? What is going to happen to us if we don't have these animals? We are now sending animals to rainy season pasture where most of them die." Elderly people described to me the time when the forest of Kob O Ran was a place where animals from the zone as well as from distant areas were herded to graze. If, as planned, the new settlers were to be given forest land, many residents expressed their concern that one day they would be forced to get rid of this livestock. It appeared that extensive breeding of livestock was coming into conflict with population growth, which was creating conflicting pressures on the land. Any plan for the region has to balance these two processes in order to avoid creating a sudden disequilibrium.

In terms of agricultural techniques, there is a trend toward the use of ox-drawn cultivation in the villages. The follow-up study of the farmers who used this method of cultivation shows positive results, but many of the farmers lack the new technology. If they had the money, most farmers would purchase oxen and adequate equipment.

In the study, I was also concerned with the infrastructure available to farmers living in the zone, realizing that the introduction of new techniques alone could not bring major improvements in living standards if other components such as health care and water availability were ignored. The zone of Ndiemane lacks basic infrastructures. The villagers have to walk to Bambey (6 km.) to get medical care, and they have to walk about 7 to 10 km. to sell their peanuts in the nearest cooperative or a weekly market. There is only one public school (with two classes) and no private schools. In each village, however, there is a Koranic school that the people built themselves to have their children taught Islamic principles. Only the village of Babak, which is equipped with a solar pump, has water during the dry season. All the other villages have traditional wells where women draw water from 25 to 30 meters. These wells are without water from the end of April until the beginning of the following rainy season which means that sometimes the women must walk more than 4 km. carrying water on their heads.

To the farmers in Ndiemane, their livelihood is based on three components: land, water, herds. During the interviews they were preoccupied with the following questions:

1. Is it true that the government plans to give our land to people who come from outside our zone?
2. Are we at least going to benefit from the canals that will be installed?
3. What are we going to do with our livestock once Kob O Ran no longer exists?

When asked what Kob O Ran represented to them, the villagers' answers reflected the various roles that the forest played and still plays in their lives. Thus, old men would always say:

Look at this house, all the material, the wood which constitutes the scaffolding, the straw which covers it: I took them from the forest of Kob O Ran. If I want milk I just ask my son to go to the herd enclosure. If I needed money to buy something, I knew that my herd was not far and that I could use it at any time. But these animals need to graze; if there is no forest, we will not be able to keep them.

"What are we going to cook with?" ask the women since the firewood now comes from the forest. "Is the project going to provide villages with water?" And the young men argue, "Give us this land and provide us with the same facilities as those which will be given to future settlers, and we will show you that even without formal training we can perform the same activities."

I have tried to show throughout this chapter that the project can only succeed if it responds to the needs and desires of the villagers in the zone. Indeed, a political orientation that neglects the local population would create a disparity between a disadvantaged local population and a privileged segment of the external population, which would unavoidably compromise the project's chance of success. Only by considering the water shortage, demographic pressure, the socioeconomic role of animals, and the lack of basic infrastructure will the migration from rural villages by young men in search of land for cultivation be arrested.

Integrating the local population into the project involves three different thrusts. First, in order to increase agricultural production, the population should be trained in new agricultural techniques. Second, land should be given to those people who lack sufficient land for cultivation in addition to subsistence production because farmers should have the option of selling part of their produce. A cooperative should be created, since in Senegal, the cooperative is the only institution that buys the production of farmers and provides them with credit. This cooperative should be open to all individuals, not just to the men who head the unit of production. In addition, roads should be constructed, as otherwise transport during the rainy season is impossible. Third, the project should be concerned with *overall* development in the zone—economic, social, and ecological—and respect the relationships among these elements. This consideration means improving living conditions (creating schools, health centers, wells, etc.) as well as recognizing the importance of leaving some grazing space for animals. Only by this orientation will the conditions that prevail in the zone be ameliorated. It is still too early to evaluate the importance of the social impact study because the project has not been completed, but the original project has been significantly revised in light of the analysis and now incorporates many of the suggestions and concerns of the people.

Notes

1. Paul Pelissier, *Les Paysans du Senegal: Les Civilisations agraires du Cayor à la Casamance* (Saint Yrieix, France: Fabrègue, 1966).

Part II

Issues of Scale and Context

5
International Development Projects, Communities, and Social Impact: Some Critical Notes

Norman B. Schwartz
Kenneth W. Eckhardt

Introduction

This chapter examines some of the local-level factors that influence the social-cultural impact of development projects. Despite the immensity of local-level change and development, little of this knowledge has been codified. There are few, if any, generally accepted scientific models of how the local development process works. In one sense, almost anything one might say about the topic already has been said, but at the same time, it has not yet been put together. As Penny observes, "there is not yet any agreed-upon framework of development theory" (1973:5).

The abundance of case studies, information, and ideas coupled with the lack of central theory affect social impact assessment (SIA) methodology and may be responsible in part for the fact that, with few exceptions, even the most contemporary and useful SIA methods resemble checklists of the type found in the Human Relations Area Files' *Outline of Cultural Materials* (Murdock et al. 1971) or Spicer's "Suggestions for Study" (1952:91–92). Although Finsterbusch is no doubt correct when he writes, "As an area of applied social science, SIA was born with the National Development Policy Act (NDPA) in 1969" (1980:14), SIA-like checklists have a much longer history. In any case, the point—too obvious to dwell upon—is that the type of SIA method used in any particular study does or should depend on the social-cultural level and characteristics of the group at which a project is aimed. Better theory, or at least more agreement about the nature of local-level units of development, should enhance SIA methodology, and the reverse is also true.

The theme we wish to explore is based on the fact that many, perhaps most, contemporary international development projects are designed for local, usually rural, communities (see Bowles 1979; Bryant and White 1980:14,46; Foster 1973:182–183; Schwartz 1978). As a consequence, certain areas of SIA are based on sociological and anthropological conceptions of community "vitality" (Bowles 1979), "cohesion" (Finsterbusch 1980), "well-being," and so forth and how to enhance them. This approach to development and to SIA raises two immediate concerns. First, there is concern about whether and in what circumstances the community is the appropriate unit for development projects. Second, in "an era of aggressive penetration efforts by the national government and an expanding web of economic relationships," which make it impossible to study the local community apart from "its broader setting" (Corbett and Whiteford 1983:9), there is a need to refine cross-culturally useful methods for examining local-national linkages, although doing so, in turn, may create political problems for SIA.

SIA, Community, and Social Science

In theory, SIA, or what USAID calls "social soundness analysis," does not set policy for public agencies; rather, it evaluates alternative ways to implement policy and assesses the alternatives "in terms of their estimated consequences" for specifically identified peoples and groups (Finsterbusch 1980:13; see also Cochrane 1979). It is, as Bowles puts it, an assumption of "social responsibility" on the part of public agencies and, as a result, almost always calls for "extensive public participation" (Bowles 1979:17,43; see also Carpenter and Matthews 1980:8, Hoben 1980:356,365). In particular, SIA is concerned with the impact of a planned change or intervention on a group's "quality of life," that is, its traditions, social relationships, and institutions (Bowles 1979:9), and also in some cases with what is now commonly called "growth with equity" (see Ingersoll 1977:201).

The impacts, for historical reasons, tend "to be catalogued under the concept of community cohesion" (Finsterbusch 1980:75). Thus, although a project may be designed, for example, to increase farm productivity or to facilitate access to markets, the primary aim of SIA is "the positive adaptation of . . . the community" to the external intervention (Bowles 1979:44). The SIA should "protect individuals, households, organizations, neighborhoods, and communities—from adverse consequences of public actions" (Finsterbusch 1980:14). It is not enough that a project be technically and economically sound, for "it is important to remember that homes and neighborhoods (i.e., communities) provide not only shelter and services but also social and psychological functions for their residents" (Finsterbusch 1980:69; see also Bowles 1979:38, Ingersoll 1977). In short, SIA assumes, among other things, that social scientists can make predictions, that community is an empirical reality, and that it is a positive context for human activities and experiences—something to be protected, maintained, and enhanced.

It may be noted that the main thrust of SIA resembles what Spicer (1952) once called the anthropology of "human problems in technological change," standard community development (see for example Brokensha and Hodge 1969, Wilkinson 1979), and, of course, the United States' new directions legislation. SIA and development social science also share a generally similar outlook; giving the same positive emphasis to local-level participation in decision making, microanalysis, fitting technical and economic development projects to the specific contours of local society and culture for both moral and practical reasons, assessing ways to minimize the potentially disruptive, latent consequences of planned change, and preserving local institutions and values. Perhaps more explicitly in social science than in SIA, there is also a stress on growth with equity and on aiding the "poor majority," that is, the rural poor, in developing nations, but SIA easily incorporates these standards. Last, at least some of the SIA and some of the scholarly literature place a similar importance on the local community as the arena for and the object of development.

One of the important local-level factors that influences the sociocultural impact of a development project, then, is the nature of the target community, particularly the degree of its cohesion or solidarity (although its social formation is also important). In order to assess impact, it is necessary for SIA and for some types of development social science to frame adequate definitions of the key terms. Although there are as many meanings of community as there are of culture or society in the literature, Finsterbusch finds it possible to "provide a working definition," immediately adding that "impact assessors also need an intuitive grasp of the social phenomena to which the terms point" (1980:76). We can, he says, "consider a territorial unit a community only if it involves some undefined amount of social interaction among its members, some undefined degree of solidarity, and some undefined amount of member identification" (p. 76). This situation implies that socioterritorial units larger than small rural towns or urban microneighborhoods are "inappropriate units for measuring project impacts on community cohesion" (p. 76).

Community cohesion is also difficult to measure, although its presence often is said to characterize technically and socially successful development projects (see Schwartz 1978:238). Community cohesion refers to activities within the unit that tie people together in positive ways and enhance personal identification with the group. It "is advanced by high prestige, attractive activities, cooperative and voluntary relationships, and abundant provision for individuals' needs" (Finsterbusch 1980:77–78, see also Redfield 1955:3–12). In measuring cohesion, it is necessary to locate the boundaries of the community, particularly as they are understood by its members, recalling that folk conceptions of the boundaries may not coincide with the administrative divisions. Solidarity may be measured by the ratio of social interaction inside and outside the community, intimacy scales, participation in local collective activities and use of local facilities, identification with the locale, and shared meanings and values.

Cohesive neighborhoods or communities are critical sources of personal security, of aid in life crises, of status and psychological satisfaction, and of social control as well as an arena for the socialization of children. The cohesive neighborhood, much like the well-bounded or corporate community studied by anthropologists, serves as a reference group for its members (see Rubel 1977), i.e., it is the critical location for personal pain as well as pleasure. "If, then, a community manages a homogeneity of people and values, a territorial integrity, and a reasonable degree of stability, some of the necessary conditions for community cohesion are satisfied" (Greisman 1980:12).

Bowles, who relies equally on anthropological and sociological literature, is explicit about the preceding thesis. He argues that to develop a "conceptual framework" for SIA (in his case, to deal with towns in the Canadian North), one must assess local social vitality, economic viability, and political efficacy (1979:52). His discussion of "vitality" is most interesting. SIAs, he says, should forecast the ways in which technical-economic projects can respect, strengthen, or at least refrain from weakening "community vitality." The latter has nine characteristics that are similar to those marking cohesive urban neighborhoods (Bowles 1979:67–68). A "socially vital community" has (1) many collective events with (2) high degrees of member participation. In addition, (3) the events are internally organized and controlled; (4) routine services and (5) life crises supports are provided for by internal, informal social networks; and (6) few people are sociometric isolates. There also are (7) stable structures of internal "governance," (8) the community can respond collectively to intrusions, and (9) people gauge the latter in collective as well as in personal terms. Each trait can be scored independently, but one assumes they may be mutually reinforcing.

"In the ideal case, the community will act as a unit and will be sufficiently effective to force those who control the impacting events to be responsive to community wishes" (Bowles 1979:67), a possibility, one must add, more easily conceived of in some national political systems than in others. Bowles cautions that "the statement that 'the vital community will successfully control the patterns of impact' must be treated as an hypothesis, not as a proven theorem" (1979:68). Less in doubt is the fact that Bowles and many other social scientists favor such communities and, when push comes to shove, are willing to bet that the hypothesis is sound.

In summary, the argument outlined here is that one, some policymakers believe that development programs should be designed to materially (technically and economically) benefit the communities or individuals for whom the local community is the relevant and critical arena of operations. Two, a socially vital, cohesive community is better able to utilize, cope with, and perhaps even control the impact of a project (whether aimed directly at it and/or its members or not) than a community that lacks vitality is. Three, some projects should be planned to enhance or generate community vitality and the involvement of community members in locally sponsored as well as in project-sponsored activities. Four, SIAs should recommend to policymakers and change agents ways to respect and work through the institutions of the vital community.

Furthermore, behavioral scientists possess the techniques to measure cohesion, and even if precise prediction is impossible, they can make reasonable estimates about how projects will affect communities and suggest ways to avoid negative technical, economic, and social consequences. SIAs focus on the social side of events, but since technology, production, individual decision making, and so forth are institutionally, culturally, and politically embedded processes (see for recent examples, Bennett 1980, Foster 1973, Jedlicka 1979, Morss et al. 1976, Saint and Coward 1977, Spicer 1952, Vessuri 1980), this is an appropriate emphasis. Without making any simplistic cause-and-effect arguments, it is still the case that rural development, maintenance of sound ecological conditions, equitable distribution of benefits, and so forth are primarily social and cultural and sociopolitical rather than strictly technical-economic processes. What assessors call community vitality, neighborhood cohesion, devolution of power, and so on are *exactly* what social scientists, whether of the functionalist persuasion or not, have been describing and analyzing for some time, although for reasons other than SIA. With some adjustments, and probably as much in professional identity and imagery as anything else, standard social science methods and studies can make important contributions to SIA and social soundness analysis (see Brokensha 1980).

The most significant effect social scientists have had on development thinking has come through microanalytic research (see Epstein 1976). For example, there is now some agreement across disciplinary lines that successful rural development strategies require a complete understanding of the variable, microlevel social organization of food production. The strategies, however, must be tailored to fit specific local sociocultural and ecological conditions (Saint and Coward 1977). This is the point in Bowles's concluding statement:

> The most general point deriving from this review is that a thorough knowledge of community social and economic patterns and a well informed understanding of the contribution of each aspect of community life to social well-being, is necessary if new projects are to be established without unacceptable costs to the communities and their members. [Bowles 1979:140]

At the same time, there may be an unfortunate side effect to the insistence that development plans must be solved in specific sociocultural contexts, and to its corollary that instead of a few large-scale projects, it is more effective and just to have many smaller ones custom fitted to the sometimes surprisingly diverse range of local circumstances found within even relatively narrow geocultural boundaries. The lesson may be that given this diversity, there are only a few cross-culturally valid guidelines for SIA.

Incorporation and Development

There is, nevertheless, at least one point of general significance concerning local-level development. Social scientists and other scholars working overseas take more seriously than a previous generation did the idea or observation that what goes on inside a community is partly or even largely determined by what goes on outside it, at macrosocial political and economic levels. Platitude this concept undoubtedly is, but it was so lightly regarded in many early community studies that, in retrospect, it seems clear that interests other than science were being served. In any case, over and beyond saying that specific community projects must be linked to national development plans, the problem is to conceptualize how local and nonlocal levels are linked. The connections are critical aspects of the local level factors, which influence the sociocultural aspects of development projects. Although, as in the instance of the impact of projects on communities, there are many first-rate case studies, there are fewer (middle-range) theories that help predict outcomes. Indeed, at this stage of the game, it would be useful to have, if not exactly a theory, then at least some conceptual scheme with which to organize what is otherwise an unmanageable mass of heterogeneous information. Therefore, we wish to report briefly on the framework Corbett and Whiteford (1979) are building to deal with local-national relationships. Although they concentrate on postrevolutionary Mexico, their ideas may have general utility and implications for SIA.

They begin by noting that in the twentieth century, the state has changed from a "passive institution with limited responsibilities centered on system maintenance to an activist institution continuously mobilizing and allocating resourcs in pursuit of a broad array of societal goals" (Corbett and Whiteford 1979:1). The state is expected to engage in social and economic development designed, in rhetoric if not in fact, to benefit all citizens. While doing so, political leaders must take care that "demands made upon the government will not outstrip its ability to respond, and that decisions made at the center will be carried out" (p. 1). Political stability, in other words, hinges on the degree to which government and politically relevant institutions have the capacity to contain and manage the demands that are stimulated by "social mobilization" and "political participation" (Huntington 1968).

In order to ensure political stability while generating and guiding development, the state must build contacts with all its citizens.

> The organizational requirements of an activist government foster a need to develop a communications and compliance network by penetrating all sectors and aspects of society, particularly where its authority and capabilities traditionally have been weak. Thus, penetration, often in the form of organizational and institutional linkages, serves both control and developmental functions. [Corbett and Whiteford 1983:1]

Parenthetically, one implication here is that there is a thin line between the state's encouraging local-level participation in development projects and state co-optation of local leaders. The recommendation that "indigenous leadership therefore can be the crucial link in organizing the community" for participation in projects (Bryant and White 1980:28) also can become a way to penetrate/control the community, thereby weakening just that vitality and local empowerment SIA assessors believe it best to maintain or enhance.

Corbett and Whiteford analyze "penetration" in three "categories." One, "cultural penetration" refers to the processes of (moral) homogenization by which "dominant sector values and behavior" are inculcated in everyone. An example would be campaigns to teach Indians Spanish, something that imparts skills necessary for individual modernization (which some people regard as an antecedent step to development) and also "acculturates" Indians to national values. Two, "institutional transformation" refers to the "capturing" of traditional institutions for purposes of national integration. Thus, the state may extend its control over local government budgets or use indigenous market systems "as a means to distribute manufactured goods to them [the indigenous population] and to tie them more tightly to the case economy," thereby undercutting "traditional community autonomy" (Corbett and Whiteford 1983:9). Three, "structural penetration . . . means the creation of new structures supporting integration," although this may not be their manifest function. In fact, the types of structures cited are overtly designed for local and regional development—services, infrastructures, organizations (including *ejidos*), and political parties. The authors note that the various forms of structural penetration may enhance "the quality of life, e.g., health care or a higher standard of living," or "the loss of autonomy may expose groups of communities to a degradation in the quality of life and a condition of permanent dependency. . . . Integration can bring either substantial benefits or dismal exploitation" (1983:16).

By shifting attention from project-community connections to state-community linkages through the (always?) double-edged mechanism of development projects, Corbett and Whiteford remind us again of the awesome complexities of implementing socially sound programs. At first glance, several of the examples they give seem to satisfy at least some of the SIA standards as given by Finsterbusch and Bowles, although Corbett and Whiteford may not agree. For example, in the case of Oaxaca, the central government has often worked through indigenous community government institutions, thereby permitting "external actors to draw upon the legitimacy of tradition" (Corbett and Whiteford 1983:9), i.e., the state has done precisely what some political scientists (e.g., see Ebel 1969) and many anthropologists recommend be done as a way to ease the burdens of change for local groups. As a result, the local authorities in Oaxaca are less concerned now with "internal system maintenance" and more involved in "managing relations with external government actors" (Corbett and Whiteford 1983:20). Local-level freedom of action has been reduced, and the role of political brokers moving between community and central state arenas has been enhanced. In general, institutional transformation, i.e., building on local institutional precedent, has weakened community cohesion and whatever "vitality" once existed. Structural penetration has compounded the problem. Although the process has brought visible material benefits to the people of Oaxaca—"new roads, schools, power lines, and water systems" (1983:11), and more—these have not been equally distributed and have further eroded local-level sociocultural integration and power.

The point is that even had the projects been better planned, they generally are located in communities that, given their size and resource base, are inherently unable to avoid being overwhelmed by the administrative-political apparatus that normally accompanies projects. In the process of fulfilling technical and economic goals, project personnel also help "integrate" the community into national social and political structures in ways that readily undermine community vitality. When, in addition, there are several loosely coordinated agencies operating in the same community, each is likely to build its own clientele, increasing the erosion of local cohesion (see Corbett and Whiteford's comments on dependency and patronage in Oaxaca. The process is not necessarily intentional, although there are historical instances in which it obviously has been (see Wrong 1979:171–178).

To use the example from our own research, the Panamanian government and several international development groups believe that in order to improve the lot of the *campesinos* ("peasants") in the interior of the country, the latter must be drawn into nucleated settlements and taught the routines of cooperative self-help—to this end, they receive aid and guidance from several agencies. Each extension agent builds his own network of *campesino* clients, but the networks do not coincide, rather they often work at cross-purposes, and the intended community unity is shattered in the making. Without assuming that there is inherent magical virtue in "the little community" as described by Redfield (1955), the point remains that whether planned from the top down or the bottom up, most development projects increase local-state linkages, and local-level units may not be able to maintain any sort of integrity in the process. In dealing with these connections, SIAs require the sort of analytic scheme outlined by Corbett and Whiteford.

It may be objected that the Oaxacan and Panamanian cases are simply instances of bad planning, that the issue is an empirical and not a theoretical one. In this context, an entirely different sort of example, drawn from U.S. experience, is instructive. In much the same spirit as the new directions legislation (Foreign Assistance Act of 1973), federally sponsored community development corporations (CDCs) were designed to "reduce local economic dependency and increase individual and community power" (Stein 1973:243). Stein, an advocate of CDCs, reports that a community supermarket in a small southern city has been quite successful in several ways. The four-year-old (in 1973) venture was controlled by the "low-income constituents" of its service area, participants were accorded genuine respect and encouragement, and the supermarket was an economic success. Several factors account for this outcome. The organization managing the business was "built on an ongoing and useful indigenous community institution (NOC), which provided both initial credibility and strong links to the community" (exactly what Bryant and White 1980, along with others, recommend for the successful management of "peasant participation in rural development"), the prior indigenous institutions provided a sophisticated and involved group "available for early support," and the area "included a sufficient group of committed, influential and knowledgeable black citizens to help forge links between the low-income community and other important groups (OEO, city government, private foundations, and so forth)" (Stein 1973:256). Stein notes, however, that "it continues to be difficult to avoid co-opting community representatives" into the business side of the supermarket "as against its social and community purposes" (1973:254). In this case, the danger is not co-optation into nonlocal power structures but, rather, co-optation into larger economic structures and patterns, with an attendant decrease in community participation and perhaps finally (although Stein may disagree), a loss of community control.

In spite of the differences, the CDC situation has some significant similarities to Panama's attempts to improve economic conditions for peasants and to empower them. Thus, in one province, the government built a large sugarcane mill which was destined to become a cooperative, and linked it to a land distribution plan. The mill has been responsible for many economic advances in the country's standard of living, although the new forms of mill and farm production also have broken down old forms of peasant "communal integration" (Gudeman 1978:158–159). More to the point, Gudeman states that

> the mill itself, however, has been caught between the pressures of having to follow two, sometimes incompatible, paths. The original government was based in part on the ideas of *campesino* (peasant) betterment, of co-operatives, and of the devolution of economic and political power. Social not economic impulses lay behind the project. On the other hand, the mill must succeed economically, for a major portion of the investment funds has come through Wall Street. The quickest way to turn a profit and repay the loans was for the mill to centralize and assume complete control over production. From its inception the mill has embodied contradictory forces. At the moment, the balance has tipped in the direction of pursuing the "more economic" path. [Gudeman 1978:162]

Even without Wall Street, it is difficult to see how the dilemma could have been resolved. There was no way the peasants, drawing on local resources, could have built the mill, and without business, a "devolution of economic and political power" would have meant sharing an empty cupboard. At the same time, profitable business management of the mill quickly undercut the initial plans for local empowerment.

The aims of SIA, social soundness analysis (SSA), and developmental social science are to help structure projects that respond to people's needs, are compatible with local socioecological conditions, yield evenly spread material and access benefits, and enhance community cohesion. The CDC supermarket and the Panamanian sugercane mill were fairly well designed to and were certainly intended to realize most of these goals, but they have had more economic than social success. To say that bottom-up planning would have helped in the Panamanian case overlooks the fact that it was present in the supermarket situation and misses the point that, however planned, projects link up local and nonlocal institutions and forces. What this situation underscores is that planners, particularly those concerned with overseas rural settlements and communities, must come to terms with two commonly found, critical local-level factors. First, in even outwardly cohesive rural villages, there are important differences of will, interest, and power, although, as Friedmann comments in referring to Asian development plans, "the concept of the village community sharing common interests apparently dies hard" (1981:254). It hardly needs to be stressed, given the accumulated evidence, that projects frequently either threaten existing village arrangements, and thus are strongly resisted by at least a portion of the population, or they intensify preexisting inequalities. Second, taken one by one, most rural settlements, however cohesive they may be, lack the power and homogeneity to withstand the community-fragmenting mechanisms of activist states and the equally divisive or contradictory demands of successful project or business management.

In short, analytic frameworks, like Corbett and Whiteford's, that systematically examine local-level units in the context of more inclusive political (and economic) structures are necessary for SIA. The suggestion that emerges from their use is that in principle few, if any, communities can maintain their cohesion or other characteristics deemed socially sound by SIA under the impact of development projects. With or without strategies for participation, local control, bottom-up planning, etc., the outcome is likely to be the same. Development projects, and particularly those designed for groups without access to the levers of economic power, imply some form of vertical integration—links to large and powerful (in relation to the community) agencies that are external to the local unit—and this integration has negative consequences from the perspective of social soundness analysis, as the evidence from Mexico (Corbett and Whiteford 1983), Panama (see above), India and Pakistan (Friedmann 1981), and elsewhere demonstrates. Development projects trigger a process that eclipses the institutions of small communities, socially vital or not.

If this interpretation is generally correct, then SIA must focus attention on structures that stand between the state (or change agencies) and the local units. The starting point for SIA, therefore, is not the impact of a project on a community or its individual members, but an analysis of government and politics at the intermediate levels between state and community. When the appropriate mediating institutions (or processes) are absent, they should be built before the implementation of development projects for local units. (At the same time, we are bothered by the thought that were SIAs to follow this line, assessors would not be permitted to operate in most countries, but this is the subject for another discussion.)

Social Networks and SIA

Before saying something more about mediating structures, we want to discuss briefly another side of the issue regarding which sociocultural units are the appropriate ones for local-level development projects. It is worth recalling that community, as commonly defined in social science and donor agency literature, is irrelevant to the social organization of some groups. Hence, to say, for example, that the absence of cooperative community-based organizations hinders successful project work is off the mark and may distract from the discovery of groups through which development can proceed.

Latin American cities provide one illustration of what is meant here. Lomnitz notes that Cerrada del Condor, a shantytown in Mexico City similar to some other poor urban places in Latin America (see Peattie 1968, Whiteford 1976) and the United States (see Alinsky 1971), "cannot be said to constitute a community in any formal or informal sense" (Lomnitz 1977:184). The apparent inability of the shantytown residents to organize themselves for sustained corporate action has been attributed to their heterogeneous origins, residential and occupational mobility (Lomnitz 1977:185), the divisive influence of external social work agencies (Roberts 1973), and the numbing effects of poverty. "These factors," Lomnitz says, "are assumed to interfere with the development of the sufficiently broad basis of confidence and cooperation needed for the existence of a community of local interests." But, she continues, "the mistake of all 'organizers' from the outside is the assumption that the shantytown represents a community, when it is actually an agglomeration of [mainly extended family] networks" (Lomnitz 1977:185). Although attempts to organize projects on the false assumption that a community is present invariably fail, organizations that "arise directly from the network structure, such as the local soccer teams, are stable and enjoy a broad participation on the part of the settlers" (Lomnitz 1977:186). In this situation, an organizer has two choices. One may try, following Alinsky, to "unify diverse local interests" into a cohesive bloc that can become the foundation for projects, or for bargaining with external agencies (see Reitzes 1980:51). Or, as may be sounder in the long run, the organizer can tie projects to the existing network structure. For better or worse, the latter procedure rarely has been tested in Latin American neighborhoods of the type Lomnitz describes.

In a more general way, Frantz argues that development projects (in particular those of the community development type) encounter difficulties with "acephalous, non-corporate, and impermanently settled" social systems (Frantz 1981:211). These characteristics are commonly found among groups "whose productive regimes depend primarily upon hunting, gathering, nomadic pastoralism, shifting horticulture, and migratory urban/labor" (p. 211). Interestingly, Lomnitz depicts the shantytown settlers of Cerrada del Condor as urban collectors and hunters, and many of the groups Frantz lists are organized in terms of nonterritorial social networks similar to those described by Lomnitz. Frantz demonstrates that most of the social and economic development that has occurred in the Mambila grasslands district of Nigeria has derived from the generally voluntary bonds between and within networks based on ethnicity, not from central government or donor agency planning.

Nor is the Mambila district unusual in sub-Saharan Africa. Citing a wide range of African studies, Frantz contends that many varieties of development have been initiated and carried through by individuals, action-sets, and social networks that are distinct from the territorially based social groups, including communities, through which governments typically act. The nonterritorial, noncorporate groups have conceived new ways or modified old ones to maintain or increase their material and social well-being, although they have rarely been the units around which projects have been planned.

One type of action-set, the faction, is almost universally regarded as an obstacle to successful community development. At times, the evaluation may be correct, yet the faction is one perfectly sound base for the organization of political activity (see Sharma 1978:229), and, in the right circumstances, it can generate evenly distributed technical and material improvements in a settlement (see Schwartz 1969). Despite the evidence, project planners will go to some lengths, at least in the Guatemalan and Panamanian cases, to avoid working officially with this type of indigenous action-set. The fascinating thing is that the same development agency people who sidestep the factions when on project business work through them when pursuing their own private ends. They tend to explain project failures partly or wholly in terms of an alleged inability on the part of the peasants to get together for joint action, citing the presence of factions as evidence of this deficiency but all the while using them as the relevant units of social and political organization when their personal interests are at stake. Although we do not know of any cases in which it has been done, an assessor might recommend that the social units through which people are mobilized for political and private ends also be activated for project goals, putting aside for a time concerns about the value or need for community cohesion (see Paul and Demarest 1981). At a minimum, this tactic would be "compatible," to use a favorite SSA word, with local circumstances in many societies.

Mediating Structures

In an early draft of this chapter, we attempted to outline some local-level factors that shape the impact of international development projects on target groups. More specifically, we attempted to see if there were any clear associations between different types of (a) local. social systems, (b) situational factors, and (c) rural development projects. In addition, and in line with SIA, it was important to look at how projects affected all that is implied in the phrase "growth with equity."

Although the attempt was too ambitious, one factor seems to emerge clearly from the literature—whatever else is going on, a rural development (or some other) project that attempts, for example, to increase farm production and also to assure "growth with equity" depends for its success in some measure on some form of client control and participation. As Whiteford comments, there is a "repeated failure of development programs to increase the standard of living of the poor precisely because they neglected to include the poor in the planning and implementation" of the program (1981, personal communication). Yet what also emerges from the literature is that even under what appear to be relatively favorable circumstances, community control of projects has often meant "slicing up a pie baked by someone else, with the community receiving the smaller slice" (Lancourt 1979:173). The literature indicates that what begins as the empowerment of local groups and small communities readily becomes negative structural penetration, institutional transformation, and increased inequality. Local-level empowerment by itself is inadequate to realize the intended goals, and it must be combined with some form of regional heteronomy, some structure that mediates between central state institutions and small communities so that members of the latter can participate in projects without self-defeating consequences.

The suggestion is that SIA must take up the issue of mediating structures prior to any concern with the local-level factors influencing the impacts of projects on people, and this method of operation transforms assessors into policymakers rather than evaluators of alternate ways to implement policy (cf. Finsterbusch 1980 and Bowles 1979). Although this transformation calls for future discussion, in the remaining space it seems preferable to say something more about mediating structures.

Friedmann's "agropolitan district" is a good illustration of such a structure (in another context, see Berger and Neuhaus 1976). He asks how "rural development (RD) in the agrarian market economies of Asia" may be accelerated in ways that conform to SSA standards (Friedmann 1981:232). The evidence from Asia demonstrates that strictly technical programs and/or those based on the individual farm, village, or growth center have failed, and will continue to fail, because they ignore political problems and also because the units involved are too weak to resist traditional elite domination. In this context, growth may occur, but without equity. Hence, RD depends on the prior solution of sociopolitical organizational problems, mainly those related to the devolution of power. "It used to be thought that political organization, territorialism, and local self-governance were merely ideological issues. . . . In opposition, I would maintain that rural development . . . requires the empowerment of the people" (Friedmann 1981:261).

To carry out this task, Friedmann proposes that power be devolved from the central state to an agropolitan district assembly, which, in Asia, would govern a territory containing several dozen villages and some 50,000 people. Importantly, a unit of this size has a sufficiently large internal market, service population, and ecologically diverse resource base to permit economic self-reliance and to make economic planning efficient. The assembly would be composed of officials elected from small villages and cohesive neighborhood clusters of some 500 people and also delegates from functional organizations. The very size, complexity, and novelty of the assembly would prevent elite control and at the same time permit the expression and reconciliation of diverse functional and class interests. In the process, although Friedmann does not say so explicitly, the assembly could become an arena in which coalitions of the poor and the nonpoor could be built so that RD activity avoided the functional equivalent of "welfare backlash" (see Korpi 1980), something that is badly missing from many "growth with equity" and basic human needs programs. In addition, while the districts obviously could not always prevail in disputes with the central government, the latter would be unable to simply ignore the will of the former in formulating development policy.

The scale and composition of the assemblies also allow for democratic participation in government, or at least they provide for close ties between officials and local groups. Thus, they constitute a political authority that is genuinely "capable of speaking for and acting on behalf of local people" rather than an "administrative convenience" for the state, i.e., a negative form of structural penetration (Friedmann 1981:248–249). The agropolitan district is "the lowest territorial unit in which the state is linked directly through its several institutions and agents" (p. 251) and structurally situated so that it can hinder the state from eclipsing local communities. Given the authority Friedmann proposes for the assembly (e.g., to raise revenues from within the district, to plan development programs, to approve projects, to contract with private and public agencies, etc.), it could generate a greater equalization of access to the bases of social and productive power and become relatively self-reliant in bottom-up planning and economic management. RD could be accelerated in ways that meet local needs, evenly spread access to social power, and are compatible with local social and ecological conditions.

Friedmann proposes a suitable unit for RD and perhaps for development in general. For one thing, international donors and national planners may not be able to effectively fine tune projects at levels much lower than the district, whereas an agropolitan district assembly may. Its members are in close, continuous contact with local populations, and they have the requisite experience to understand local needs and conditions. They also are dependent upon local populations and organizations for social approval and political support in a way that central state agency bureaucrats are not, and so they have the motives as well as the means to grasp grass-roots "felt needs." Second, distributing power to units as small as villages or rural neighborhoods seems utopian for reasons noted in previous sections. On the other hand, Friedmann's design relates these units to the state through a mediating structure that permits both state and community to participate in development and shields the latter from the former. It also gives local elites and the poor at least one immediate common interest—the assembly and, through it, the district. There is at least some chance that the familiar coalition of local elites and state bureaucrats acting against the interests of the poor will be broken up by new groupings that represent the poor by representing the district. Finally, Friedmann's plan underscores the point that poverty and the like are not major problems in development as such; rather, creating access to the social bases of power is the issue. Although this access will not by itself solve RD and other economic problems, it does make their solution a real possibility. When access is more evenly distributed, then providing assistance for increasing productive capacity can occur without unwanted and undesired consequences for increased stratification and similar phenomena.

Friedmann notes that for the sake of efficient RD planning, there also may be a need to create regional bodies that subsume the agropolitan districts. The regional assembly would have autonomous powers corresponding to those of the districts but proportionally greater in scope and depth. Such an assembly, of course, can reduce the "potential independence of the district" and "recentralize" it at higher levels (Friedmann 1981:252). The problem here resembles the balancing act between local, intermediate, and national groups of which Lancourt speaks. More than that, it begins to suggest that a structural escalation of power is built into contemporary political processes (see Adams 1970).

There are other, more immediate questions about Friedmann's proposals. For example, they require the presence and/or training of strong leaders drawn from local communities, something that may not be so easily achieved (see Wrong 1979:151–153). At the same time, it should be noted that this problem also confronts more conventionally designed programs (see for example, Austin and Zeitlin 1981:143). Further, the very nature of an assembly with its cross-cutting alliances may attenuate the expression of otherwise useful (for the poor) social class conflict. Or interdistrict and interregional conflicts may call forth central state intervention with all that implies for recentralizing power. Similarly, second-generation routinization of assembly action could make that body just the sort of administrative "convenience" it is designed not to be, and with that, "local empowerment" could become a code phrase for state and bureaucratic neglect. Most of all, there is the question of whether any national elite would have the will to carry through such a plan. The devolution of power may be a necessary precondition for RD, but who gives power away? Friedmann contends (1981:257) that the alternatives—continued underdevelopment of radical land distribution through internal revolution or external pressure—may make his option reasonable for elites, but it does seem utopian to believe that this line of reasoning will carry much weight with most of them. Notwithstanding this problem and more, Friedmann usefully shifts attention from local communities to one form of a mediating structure, the agropolitan district assembly.

It may be out of place for social scientists who are theoretically committed to cultural relativism to find virtue in egalitarian programs. It is not so much that they cannot solve all the problems of RD or anything else by themselves, but that they generally come from certain types of industrialized nations and are or may be ethnocentric. Cooperation in power may be a necessary precondition for forms of growth that, in the first place, are rooted in the experience of a limited number of societies. Still, the problems of development do seem as much, if not more, political than anything else—technical, economic, social, or cultural. As far as one can judge from the history of the impact of international development projects on local groups, the question is not simply who needs or who gets what, but rather who has the power to decide such matters. For reasons of technical efficiency and humane development, it seems best that the people have that power.

References

Adams, R. N.
  1970   *Crucifixion by Power: Essays on Guatemalan National Social Structure, 1944–1966.* Austin: University of Texas Press.

Alinsky, Saul D.
  1971   *Rules for Radicals: A Practical Primer for Realistic Radicals.* New York: Random House.

Austin, J. E., and M. F. Zeitlin
  1981   Concluding Remarks. In J. E. Austin and M. F. Zeitlin, eds., *Nutrition Intervention in Developing Countries: An Overview,* pp. 137–145. Cambridge Mass.: Oelgeschlager, Gunn and Hain.

Bennett, J. W.
  1980   Management Style: A Concept and a Method for the Analysis of Family-operated Agricultural Enterprise. In P. F. Barlett, ed., *Agricultural Decision Making: Anthropological Contributions to Rural Development,* pp. 203–237. New York: Academic Press.

Berger, P. L., and R. J. Neuhaus
  1976   *To Empower People: The Role of Meditating Structure in Public Policy.* Washington, D.C.: American Enterprise Institute.

Bowles, R. T.
1979   *Social Impact Assessment in Small Canadian Communities.* Peter-
            borough, Can.: Trent University, Department of Sociology.

Brokensha, D.
1980   Rural Roads Evaluations: Social-economic Impacts. Paper presented
            at the Annual Meeting of the American Anthropological Association,
            Washington, D.C., December 5, 1980.

Brokensha, D., and P. Hodge
1969   *Community Development: An Interpretation.* San Francisco: Chandler
            Publishing Company.

Bryant, C., and L. C. White
1980   *Managing Rural Development: Peasant Participation in Rural De-
            velopment.* West Hartford, Conn.: Kumarian Press.

Carpenter, R., and W. Matthews
1980   NEPA: Environmental Innocence Abroad. *East-West Perspectives*
            1:6-11.

Cochrane, G.
1979   *The Cultural Appraisal of Development Projects.* New York: Praeger
            Publishers.

Corbett, J., and S. Whiteford
1983   State Penetration and Development in Mesoamerica, 1950-1980. In
            Carl Kendall, John Hawkins, and Laurel Bussen, eds., *Heritage of
            Conquest Thirty Years Later,* pp. 9-33. Albuquerque: University of
            New Mexico Press.

Ebel, R. H.
1969   *Political Modernization in Three Guatemalan Indian Communities.*
            New Orleans: Middle American Research Institute, Tulane Uni-
            versity. Reprinted from Publication no. 24.

Epstein, S.
1976   The Ideal Marriage Between the Economist's Macro-approach and
            the Anthropologist's Micro-approach. In G. Cochrane, ed., *What
            We Can Do for Each Other: An Interdisciplinary Approach to
            Development Anthropology,* pp. 29-42. Amsterdam: B. R. Gruner
            Publishing Company.

Finsterbusch, K.
1980   *Understanding Social Impacts: Assessing the Effects of Public Projects.*
            Beverly Hills, Calif.: Sage Publications.

Finsterbusch, K., and C. P. Wolf, eds.
1977   *The Methodology of Social Impact Assessment.* Stroudsburg, Pa.:
            Dowden, Hutchinson and Ross.

Foster, G. M.
1973   *Traditional Societies and Technological Change.* 2d ed. New York:
            Harper and Row.

Frantz, C.
1981   Development Without Communities: Social Fields, Networks, and
          Action in the Mambila Grasslands of Nigeria. *Human Organization*
          40:211–220.

Friedmann, J.
1981   The Active Community: Toward a Political-Territorial Framework
          for Rural Development in Asia. *Economic Development and Cultural
          Change* 29:235–261.

Greisman, H. C.
1980   Community Cohesion and Social Change. *Journal of the Community
          Development Society* 11:1–17.

Gudeman, S.
1978   *The Demise of a Rural Economy: From Subsistence to Capitalism in
          a Latin American Village.* London: Routledge and Kegan Paul.

Hoben, A.
1980   Agricultural Decision Making in Foreign Assistance: An Anthro-
          pological Analysis. In P. F. Barlett, ed., *Agricultural Decision Making:
          Anthropological Contributions to Rural Development*, pp. 337–369.
          New York: Academic Press.

Huntington, S. P.
1968   *Political Order in Changing Societies.* New Haven: Yale University
          Press.

Ingersoll, J.
1977   *Social Analysis of Development Projects: A Suggested Approach for
          Social Soundness Analysis—Aid Development Studies Program.* Wash-
          ington, D.C.: AID. May.

Jedlicka, A. D.
1979   The Acquisition and Use of Technological Knowledge by Mexican
          Farmers of United Resources. In J. H. Street and D. D. James,
          eds., *Technological Progress in Latin America: The Prospects for
          Overcoming Dependency*, pp. 121–128. Boulder, Colo.: Westview
          Press.

Korpi, W.
1980   Approaches to the Study of Poverty in the United States: Critical
          Notes from a European Perspective. In V. T. Covello, ed., *Poverty
          and Public Policy*, pp. 287–314. Cambridge, Mass.: Schenkman
          Publishing Company.

Lancourt, J. E.
1979   *Confront or Concede: The Alinsky Citizen-Action Organizations.*
          Lexington, Mass.: D. C. Heath and Company.

Lomnitz, L. A.
1977   *Networks and Marginality: Life in a Mexican Shantytown.* New
          York: Academic Press.

Morss, E. R., J. K. Hatch, D. R. Mickelwait, and C. F. Sweet
1976   *Strategies for Small Farmer Development.* 2 vols. Boulder, Colo.:
         Westview Press.

Murdock, G. P., C. S. Ford, A. E. Hudson, R. Kennedy,
L. W. Simmons, and J.W.M. Whiting
1961   *Outline of Cultural Materials.* Vol. 1. New Haven, Conn.: Human
         Relations Area Files. Fifth printing 1971.

Paul, B. D., and W. J. Demarest
1981   Health Programs, Local Politics, and Community Participation: A
         Guatemalan Case History. Paper presented to the Society for Applied
         Anthropology, Edinburgh, Scotland.

Peattie, L. R.
1968   *The View from the Barrio.* Ann Arbor: University of Michigan
         Press.

Penny, D. H.
1973   Development Studies: Some Reflections. In T. S. Epstein and D.
         H. Penny, eds., *Opportunity and Response: Case Studies in Economic
         Development,* pp. 1–10. New York: Humanities Press.

Redfield, R.
1955   *The Little Community: Viewpoints for the Study of a Human Whole.*
         Chicago: University of Chicago Press.

Reitzes, D. C.
1980   Saul D. Alinsky's Contributions to Community Development. *Jour-
         nal of Community Development Society* 11:39–52.

Roberts, B. R.
1973   *Organizing Strangers: Poor Families in Guatemala City.* Austin:
         University of Texas Press.

Rubel, A. J.
1977   "Limited Good" and "Social Comparison": Two Theories, One
         Problem. *Ethos* 5:222–238.

Saint, W. S., and E. W. Coward, Jr.
1977   Agriculture and Behavioral Science: Emerging Orientations. *Science*
         197:733–737.

Schwartz, N. B.
1968   Goal Attainment Through Factionalism: A Guatemalan Case. *Amer-
         ican Anthropologist* 71:1088–1108.
1978   Community Development and Cultural Change in Latin America.
         In B. J. Siegel, A. R. Beals, and S. A. Tyler, eds., *Annual Review
         of Anthropology* (Palo Alto, Annual Reviews) 7:235–261.

Sharma, M.
1978   *The Politics of Inequality: Competition and Control in an Indian
         Village.* Honolulu: University Press of Hawaii.

Spicer, E. H., ed.
    1952   *Human Problems in Technological Change: A Casebook.* New York:
                Russell Sage Foundation.

Stein, B. A.
    1973   The Centreville Fund, Inc.: A Case Study in Community Economic
                Control. *Applied Behavioral Science* 9:243-260.

Vessuri, H.M.C.
    1980   Technological Change and the Social Organization of Agricultural
                Production. *Current Anthropology* 21:315-327.

Whiteford, M. B.
    1976   *The Forgotten Ones: Colombian Countrymen in an Urban Setting.*
                Gainesville: University Presses of Florida.

Wilkinson, K. P.
    1979   Social Well-Being and Community. *Journal of Community Devel-
                opment Society* 10:5-16.

Wrong, D. H.
    1979   *Power: Its Forms, Bases, and Uses.* New York: Harper and Row.

6
Social Impact, Economic Change, and Development—With Some Illustrations from Nepal

George H. Axinn
Nancy W. Axinn

There are four main aspects of social impact analysis and development discussed in this chapter. These ideas are methodological rather than theoretical, they are at the micro- rather than the macrolevel of analysis, and at best, they may provide some additional categories for people concerned with the social impact of development activities.[1] The four main ideas are (1) impact analysis as evaluation, (2) the need for depth description, (3) analysis via energy transformation, and (4) the recycling ratio in social impact analysis. Then follows a discussion of the potential use of the recycling ratio in social impact analysis, focusing on farming systems research, agricultural extension education, and international development assistance, and the chapter concludes with brief statements on further research opportunities and the limitations of the materials flow and energy transformation approach. Throughout, we refer to evidence we gathered in Nepal.

Impact Analysis as Evaluation

To measure the impact of any particular set of activities upon a group of human beings is an evaluative process. It calls for judgments to be made on the basis of the values of the people who make the judgments, which requires both descriptive and analytic tools. To do well requires both descriptive and analytic tools.

In many ways, the depth and accuracy of the description determine the quality of the evaluation. Unfortunately, the scholarly community, particularly in North America, has tended to devalue descriptive research in favor of studies of trends, comparative studies, and experimental research. Too often, they have undertaken to compare phenomena over time or in different locations, but because the phenomena have been less than adequately described in the first instance, everything else that follows has corresponding shortcomings.

The quality of description, particularly the description of human groups, may be directly related to the empathy of the observer. The sensitive scholar, who can empathize with the people being observed, can sometimes identify aspects of a situation quite beyond those that seem relevant on the surface. But such empathy is only a beginning.

Patterns of behavior at various seasons of the year and at different times of day can be extremely important. Thus, the quality of description may be directly related to the frequency, the extensiveness, and the intensiveness of the time invested. An excellent description of what happens at a particular hour of the day in a family or a community might be quite misleading if it is assumed that the same types of activity continue at other hours of the day. Similarly, typical behavior patterns during the monsoon season in a rural village might be quite different from those during the dry season in that same village.

Further, the values, norms, and aspirations of the individuals being described typically represent subcultural modalities that differ markedly from the values, norms, and aspirations of the person doing the describing, and sensitivity to these differences is critical. For example, well-meaning professional agriculturalists in Nepal have been selecting new varieties of maize on the basis of the quantity of grain produced by each plant. The value placed on the grain can be related directly to the international training of those professional agriculturalists and to the network of other people those agriculturalists interact with in their own ministries of agriculture, in the international agriculture research community, and in the schools in which they did advanced study. All of these people tend to be concerned with the grain production of maize plants, which reflects the large-scale, capital-intensive, monocrop, labor-scarce agriculture of the Western world. However, the farmers in Nepal, who feed large numbers of ruminant livestock every day on small, mixed, labor-intensive, low-capital farms, are also highly concerned about the green parts of the maize plant.

The maize plants that produce the largest quantities of cereal grain have tended to be relatively short-stemmed plants, which produce less green material. But the green parts of the plant provide fodder for animals. It is not surprising that a group of professional agriculturalists, who have different values, norms, and aspirations, might not have inherently appreciated the value of the green parts of the maize plant to mixed-farming families in a place like Nepal. What is disappointing is that the description of the problems associated with producing maize in that country was not adequate to reveal this phenomenon (APROSC 1979, Ministry of Food, Agriculture, and Irrigation 1979).

Description Needs Depth

Of course, what is described will be based on the conceptualizations, the theories, and the hypotheses that concern the people making the description. It is impossible to describe everything about a small farm family. But if one has social impact analysis in mind, can empathize with the people being described, and show similar empathy for those who will attempt to understand the analytic material, then the description can be informed by both groups.

For example, we may take the case of Sundar Bazaar, a small remote rural village in the central part of Nepal. Located in Lamjung District, Sundar Bazaar has no motorable roads leading to it. In fact, in 1977, this village could not be reached even by motorcycle or bicycle. Pony trains regularly go through Sundar Bazaar carrying some freight; everything else is carried in or out by human beings. If you want to go there, you must walk, and walking time from the nearest motorable road is more than eight hours for people not accustomed to walking, less for others. It is at least five hours to the nearest grass airstrip, if you are wealthy enough to fly.

Most of the rural people who live in the Sundar Bazaar area have very small-sized farms by international standards. Four farms are distinguished from the rest because they are so large, encompassing, on the average, just over four hectares of land. The farms of the other sixty-six families studied are all much smaller than that, with an average size of just over half a hectare.

With regard to the density of the human population on the land, the average figures for Lamjung District, or even for the Sundar Bazaar area, tend to be quite misleading. For example, at the time of our study, Sundar Bazaar averaged 7.5 persons per hectare. However, density ranged from 24 persons per hectare on the smallest group of farms to only about 2 per hectare on the four "large" farms. For those people who cannot easily envision a hectare or an acre, on the smallest farms, each individual person has about 1.5 tennis courts on which to produce his or her living, compared to about 20 tennis courts per person on the biggest farms.

When these descriptive data were considered, it was conjectured that the lack of equity in landholdings might be overstated. However, observation had taught that some of the land, higher up on the hills, was usable only for grazing animals whereas the best land, lower down in the valleys and closer to the rivers, could be irrigated. An analysis of the percentage of irrigated land per farm by size of farm showed that the larger the size of the farm, the larger the proportion of high-quality irrigated land on the farm. In other words, the people with the most wealth had both the highest quantity and the highest quality of land.

The farmers with the smallest landholdings also tend to till the soil most intensively. The three smallest groups of farms seemed to be using around 180 percent of the land, which means that many of the fields are cultivated twice each year and some even three times. By contrast, on the very largest farms, even though these farmers have the best quality land, they seem to be using just over half (57.9 percent) of the land available to them. There are large numbers of animals on all of these farms, but as with the human population, the total livestock population per hectare is greatest on the smallest farms and significantly lower on the larger farms.

Description could go much further. The point here is that some depth of description provides insight into the nature of the life of the people being described. This insight, in turn, can provide a basis for social impact analysis.

Analysis via Energy Transformation

Beyond description, of course, analysis of what is going on in a particular situation, and how conditions change over time, is crucial in social impact analysis. If there is no change over time, one could assume that efforts to intervene in the system have had no impact. If things do change, then issues arise as to whether the new situation is "better than" or "worse than" the prior situation. Such assessments reflect normative and evaluative judgments of what is more desirable and what is less desirable.

Prior to such an assessment, and assuming that continuity and change are normal phenomena for any human group, there is the question of what should be measured. The highly differentiated, specialized money economies of North America and Western Europe lead scholars to make their measurements in terms of cash flow. The example below suggests that materials flow and energy transformation can also be used as indicators of continuity and change.[2] Energy flow can be used as a proxy for various kinds of change, just as cash flow is used (usually by economists) as a proxy for many kinds of change. Since concepts of poverty tend to be as culture bound as other indicators of what some individuals have termed "the quality of life," the rationale for the search for other indicators is associated with an attempt to "escape" the cultural norms associated with so many other indicators of change.

Drawing on data gathered in Nepal, we have attempted to estimate materials flow and energy transformation in farm family ecosystems. The analysis builds on the concepts of functional differentiation in rural social systems. With the family ecosystem as the basic unit, it considers shifts in social differentiation and energy transformation to be the central variables in a cycle of continuity and change (G. Axinn 1977, Axinn and Axinn 1979, 1980).

The majority of people in Asia, Africa, and Latin America live on small pieces of land and subsist by consuming what they produce and producing whatever they consume. Further, current census data indicate that in Asia, the total number and relative proportion of such families are increasing. These family farms differ from the large-scale, commercial, capital-intensive farming systems of North America and Europe, which are specialized in the production function. These small-scale, noncommercial, land- and labor-intensive units perform supply and marketing functions as well as production, and they are also heavily involved in personal maintenance, health care delivery, governance, and learning. Since they are less differentiated, these farming systems also tend to produce a great variety of outputs: cereal grain, livestock, and fruits and vegetables. From an agricultural economic perspective, they are integrated both vertically and horizontally. Their production is much less specialized than that of the large-scale farming systems.

Whereas cash flow may be an adequate indicator of the total flow of materials through the large-scale commercial farming system, it is less useful as a proxy for such activity in the small, mixed-farming systems. In a unit that sells its outputs for cash and purchases its inputs with the same currency, the flow of cash tends to correlate with the total volume of other activity and with relative wealth, and it may serve as descriptive proxy for the entire system. In the subsistence unit, which tends to recycle more materials than it exchanges with other systems, the flow of cash sometimes accounts for such a small proportion of the materials flow that it is misleading. For example, a small, mixed, subsistence farming system will be declared in "relative" or "absolute poverty" by international agencies if its annual cash income is below a certain mark. However, the same system may have a large kitchen garden, may provide its human members with more than adequate quantities of fresh milk and dairy products as well as some meat and eggs, and it may actually be so wealthy that the family which owns and operates it does little physical work. Since the "shadow production" consumed within the system tends not to be reflected in cash flow measures, the higher the proportion of internal materials flow, the less adequate a proxy such as cash income.

Energy transformation is an alternative proxy that can indicate change over time, both for the large-scale commercial farming systems and for the small-scale subsistence farming system, as well as transitional units in various stages in between. Just as a monetary value can be assigned to any sort of item, so can an energy value, and the two types of valuations can be compared. There is no special magic about energy values that makes them better than money values, but as descriptors of materials flow and other activity in a farming system, the use of energy values as a proxy offers some advantages.

One advantage of an energy measure like kilocalories (KCals) or British thermal units (BTUs), in comparison with such money measures as rupees or dollars, is that the relative values are defined and generally accepted as unchanging. The ratio of U.S. dollars to Indian rupees changes from day to day, but one KCal equals 3.968 BTUs by international convention, and the ratio tends not to change.

A second advantage is that while the cash price of one kilogram of rice, for example, varies from one place to another on any given day, and the world price of rice varies from day to day and year to year, the number of KCals in one kilogram of rice is relatively standard. Even with variation in the type of rice, its moisture content, and the way in which energy value is to be transformed (burned, eaten by humans, eaten by ruminants), the energy values are relatively more standardized than the money values.

And third, in systems that utilize cash for a relatively low proportion of all transactions, the assignment of cash values may be less valid than the assignment of energy values. However, such proxies assigned to a variety of materials should be considered as only approximations of a relative value, not precise measures of reality. Thus, the large calorie (KCal) is used here as a way of estimating relationships and nothing more.

Just as social phenomena described by money values are subject to certain economic "laws," the energy descriptor is conditioned by "the laws of thermodynamics" (Georgescu-Roegen 1975). Thus, engineering concepts related to energy flow can be as helpful to social analysis as economic concepts, and combining both may strengthen the analysis.

As will be demonstrated with data describing small farm family ecosystems in Nepal, it is possible and feasible to estimate the flow of materials and transformation of energy in such systems. Out of rudimentary efforts, there has emerged a conceptualization of the farming system; this rethinking has provided a base for sociological analysis of continuity and change and for demonstrating a relationship between social differentiation and energy transformation.

Within farm family ecosystems, the three major components are plants, animals, and humans. Although the model used here shares analytical techniques with similar models, it differs in that it permits an analysis of a basic subsistence ecosystem in which most materials and energy are recycled within the system, rather than exchanged with the outside world.[3] Major flows from the surrounding environment to the farm family ecosystem include solar energy, water, firewood, grazing and grass cutting, and small supplements to health and diet (such as salt and spices). There is a significant exchange of both human labor and animal draft power among the farm families in such a rural social system.

Major inputs to the human component of such a system are cereal grains, fruits and vegetables, milk and dairy products, meat, firewood, and water. The principle outputs of human energy take the form of labor. Learning and controlling (deciding and allocating) reflect small energy transformations and serve as triggering mechanisms as described by Adams (1974).

The animal component of the farm family ecosystem may include such livestock as cattle, buffaloes, goats, swine, and poultry. Major outputs from the animal component include draft power, manure, milk and dairy products, meat, and eggs. Inputs to the animal component are straw and fodder, cereal grain or grain by-products, human labor, tools and facilities (including stables and barns), and grazing facilities.

The plant component is the major energy transformer for the small subsistence farm family ecosystem. This component can be likened to the system's powerhouse as it converts solar energy into nutrients, which can be transformed by both the humans and the animals and which supply the bulk of their calorie requirements. In addition to solar energy, other inputs to this component include draft power, manure (or other fertilizer), human labor, tools, seed, and water, along with such other potential inputs as insecticides, fungicides, and herbicides. However, the magnitude of the solar energy available on each hectare of land is so much larger than all the other energy sources combined that the entire system can be viewed as one that takes a small fraction (estimated at 1 to 3 percent) of the available solar energy and uses this as a resource for all other activities.

An analysis of the flow of materials into and out of each of the major components of such a system permits a comparison between farm family ecosystems on different-sized pieces of land and facilitates the development of a perspective on the relationship among farms of various sizes in a rural social system. Such a model also offers a useful conceptualization to people who study the whole farming system. It permits an evaluation of the costs and benefits of production of any particular plant or animal commodity in relationship to all inputs and outputs as they flow through the system. One variety of cereal grain can be compared to another on the basis of not only the grain harvest but also the production of straw and other by-products, as well as costs in terms of seed, human labor, manure, and draft power. This conceptualization is also useful in addressing such questions as the potential substitution of small-scale garden tractors for animal draft power, since it permits the inclusion of several variables that may be overlooked by conventional studies (Axinn and Axinn 1979, 1980).

Relationship of Materials and Energy Flows to Social Differentiation

Estimates of materials flow and energy transformation in farm family ecosystems serve as indicators of functional differentiation. The supply, production, and marketing functions, in particular, can be compared among different farming systems. Farming systems that specialize in production will tend to have greater proportions of materials and energy flows from the outside (input supply) and greater proportions of such flows to the outside (output marketing). Less-differentiated farming systems tend to have a higher proportion of total flows within the farm ecosystem.

Social differentiation may thus be used as an indicator of change. Most strategies for rural development have been designed to increase functional differentiation in farming systems, and one reason that international attempts in rural development have not been more successful is that the designers of projects have tended to use economic indicators such as cash flow rather than assessments of social phenomena such as functional differentiation. Structural and functional analysis of rural social systems can provide a base for assessing change and for designing development strategies. Such phenomena as status, role, boundary maintenance, migration patterns, and value orientations may be much more significant indicators of change in rural social systems than annual cash income.

Similarly, farming systems that are less differentiated in function tend to carry on more different types of operations. A family that supplies its own inputs and consumes its own outputs will not specialize in one crop. Rather, it will tend to produce cereal crops, livestock, and fruits and vegetables. Conversely, the highly differentiated, large-scale dairy farm of mid-America, although it may produce milk from 300 cows daily, will probably sell 100 percent of that milk to a commercial firm. If the farm household requires a quart of milk, it usually purchases it from an outside supplier.

Neither of these "pure" types of farming systems actually exists among the rural social systems of the world. Even the most remote and undifferentiated farm family ecosystems tend to exchange some materials and energy with outside systems, and even the most commercially specialized farm family ecosystems tend to generate internally some of their necessary materials and energy and to produce some outputs that are consumed within the system.

An analysis of social differentiation in rural social systems indicates that the quantities of energy transformed also vary over time. The evidence presented below suggests that functional differentiation and energy transformation vary together. The more highly differentiated the farming system, the greater the quantity of energy it will tend to transform. Further, the more differentiated the farming system, the larger the farm itself is likely to be. The larger the farm, the greater the probable total flow of materials and energy per person. This wealth tends to be accompanied by social and political power.

The Recycling Ratio

The extent of functional differentiation in a farming system is indicated in this study by a recycling ratio. The higher the proportion of materials and energy flows that occur within the farm family ecosystem and its near environment, the higher the recycling ratio. The higher the recycling ratio, the less the farm family exchanges materials and energy with outside systems. Farms with a high recycling ratio are usually called subsistence farms. Farms with a low recycling ratio are referred to as commercial or market-oriented farms.

In terms of social differentiation, the recycling ratio deals directly with three functions: production, supply, and marketing. Farm family ecosystems with a high ratio tend to distribute resources among these three functions more evenly than those with a low ratio, which tend to specialize in the production function.

From the perspective of dependence and independence, farming systems that recycle larger proportions of materials and energy within the system are, by definition, more independent of other outside systems. Conversely, farming systems that recycle a smaller proportion, receive greater quantities of materials and energy from outside, and market greater proportions of their production are more dependent upon people and organizations outside the family ecosystem.

The recycling ratio can be useful as an indicator of change in a rural social system, but the normative issues of good and bad will depend upon what the society values in terms of its life-style. Thus, the community in which each farm family has a high recycling ratio may not benefit at all by the introduction of technologies that would reduce this ratio. On the other hand, if that community wants more of the goods available from the outside, then its goal may be a reduction of the recycling ratio, and technologies that will lead to that reduction may, in fact, be appropriate. Thus, the recycling ratio can become an indicator of change in rural social systems, but not the goal for rural development, which is normative. Assuming that each family and each society may determine its own goals, the recycling ratio can measure where they are and how they progressed in the direction chosen.

Development goals can be stated in terms of the optimal levels of materials flow and energy transformation. Similarly, the recycling of human labor, plant production, animal production, or other production can be separated from each other. Thus, a recycling ratio of human labor will demonstrate differences between families who must not only meet their own needs but also work as laborers (or servants) for others in order to sustain themselves and other families who have sufficient power to hire outside labor. This type of indicator allows a human group to set its developmental goals in a way that is less likely to be skewed by "outsiders' criteria" and the typical indicators of cash income.

By observing activities in farm family ecosystems, one can estimate the recycling ratio. This ratio, in turn, permits comparison between individual families and between rural groups that are of different cultures, are engaged in different types of agriculture, or are of different religions. It also permits the separation of subsistence agriculture—where the recycling ratio is very high—from market agriculture—where the recycling ratio tends to be much lower. From the perspective both of insiders who might systematically organize for their own development and of outsiders determined to assist with development, the strategies appropriate for farming systems with high recycling ratios are likely to be different from those best suited to farming systems with low ratios. Thus, programs of agricultural research, technological development, extension education, or market infrastructure would be quite different for the farming system with a high ratio than for the system with a low one.

To illustrate, attempts have been made to supply chemical fertilizer in areas in which the farms have a high recycling ratio. Since farmers in those areas tend not to buy and sell on the market, they tend not to perceive a need for such expensive outside inputs. Thus, the chemical fertilizer programs have tended to fail in that type of situation. Conversely, farms with a low recycling ratio and a high potential market output may need outside inputs to prevent depletion of soil fertility.

The recycling ratio for any group of farms indicates which farming systems are more "open" than others, and those with a high recycling ratio are characterized as relatively more closed. These farmers tend not to look to society to provide inputs of information via extension services, for instance, or material/energy inputs such as seeds and fertilizer.

Ultimately, the farmers with the highest recycling ratios make the fewest demands for support services or material/energy inputs and are the least likely to use those that are offered. Those with a lower recycling ratio are likely to be more open to new information provided by outside systems. It could be speculated that those with a low recycling ratio reflects a labor-energy surplus would be responsive to information about alternative employment opportunities, training for different occupations, or intensive agriculture options. Those farmers whose low recycling ratio reflects surplus production available to the market might be open to information on credit and marketing as well as alternative energy sources, such as mechanization and fertilizer, which would reduce their dependence on others in labor-surplus situations. Additionally, this group of farmers tends to be more specialized and, hence, looks to the bureaucracy to provide organizational management to expedite exchanges among specialized producers.

The recycling ratio, taken alone, may be considered to be neutral. It is merely a measure, like hectares or kilograms or calories. But the extent of functional differentiation, the quantities of energy transformed, and the degree of independence tend to relate to various other social, economic, and cultural indicators that are sometimes used to assess the quality of life. From these conceptions of function and differentiation come propositions that relate social differentiation to energy conservation and to dependence.

Because of the social dimensions of this approach in regard to rural development, it provides an alternative set of variables for assessing the social and cultural impact of change, and it makes possible new strategies for the social organization and administration of development. The major proposition that flows from this rationale is that there is a positive correlation between energy transformation and functional differentiation in farm family ecosystems. In addition, each of these characteristics of farm family ecosystems is related to size: There is a positive correlation between size of farm and quantity of energy transformed. Also, there is a positive correlation between size of farm and functional differentiation.

And, by definition, the extent of social differentiation in individual farm family ecosystems varies inversely with the size of the recycling ratio. The recycling ratio is thus a measuring device for identifying the position of a particular farming system on the continuum from subsistence agriculture to commercial market agriculture.

In some communities in Nepal, we were able to assemble data on materials and energy flows of the ecosystem. By combining the flows among the human, plant, and animal components on farms of a given size, we made a gross approximation of the total materials and energy flows in farm family ecosystems and their near environment by size of landholdings. The total materials and energy flows per farm family illustrate the relationship between wealth and average size of landholdings. The families that control the most land also have the greatest energy flow per farm family.

In Lamjung District, the very smallest farming systems, which send out both labor and draft power and bring in cereal grain, have a slightly lower recycling ratio than the three groups of larger systems, but all four major groups in this district (sixty-six of the seventy farms studied) recycle more than 90 percent of their total materials and energy flows. As might be expected, the four "large farms, which don't seem to fit with the rest of the Lamjung group, have a significantly lower recycling ratio of 77.09 percent. The second-smallest group of farms in the Lamjung area, averaging 0.39 hectare per farm, have the highest recycling ratio (96.37 percent), approaching what might be labeled complete subsistence. From there, as the farm size grows, the recycling ratio diminishes.

Discussion in Relation to Other Rural Social Systems

The positive correlation between quantities of energy transformed and functional differentiation is reflected in information available about other types of farm family ecosystems in other parts of the world. For the highly commercialized, large-scale, monocrop agriculture of Michigan, for example, indications are that farm family ecosystems may have recycling ratios as low as 2 to 5 percent. Almost all inputs are purchased on a commercial market, and close to 100 percent of the energy value of farm production is sold to specialized marketing firms. Wheat producers purchase bread from outside, and dairy-farm families tend to buy homogenized milk. They have not only differentiated (specialized in) the production function, largely eliminating the supply and marketing functions, but they tend to have further specialized to fewer and fewer different farm products. In quest of economies of scale, they have thus further differentiated the production function (Tummala and Connor 1973).

In the opposite direction, pastoralists in the Rift Valley of Kenya tend to have even higher recycling ratios than the small mixed farm in Nepal. The pastoralist family ecosystems must move with the rains, continually seeking water and grazing for their cattle, sheep, goats, and donkeys. As they move from one location to another, they take their families, livestock, homes (tents, etc.), and all other worldly goods with them. Such groups live on the milk (and blood) of their cattle and the meat of their sheep and goats. Only small and supplementary inputs like salt are purchased from outside. In times of drought, some grain or other foodstuffs might have to be purchased, and on those occasions, livestock must be sold or bartered. Normally, however, if there is any surplus, livestock numbers are increased. They represent savings or family wealth, and with no traveling banks or other investment possibilities, even surpluses are recycled internally. And with no traveling schools or health centers, most of these functions must also be performed by the relatively unspecialized, undifferentiated nomadic farm family. Therefore, recycling ratios may tend to be in the high eighties or over 90 percent (Dyson-Hudson and Dyson-Hudson 1970, Pratt and Gwynne 1977, and Campbell and Axinn 1980).

By definition, the higher the recycling ratio, the less the social differentiation. The data presented above, as well as the international comparative experience, tend to confirm that the less the social differentiation, the less the total quantities of energy transformation for each farm family ecosystem.

The Recycling Ratio in Social Impact Analysis

The conception of continuity and change in rural social systems being cyclical phenomena, based on the farm family ecosystem approach, can be useful for several different types of agricultural and developmental strategies.

From Agriculture to Farming Systems Research

Historically, the development of agriculture research systems has faced issues of social control, rewards and sanctions, reference groups, and which topics to study. One of the issues, beginning with the early organized efforts in Germany and Scotland and continuing with the establishment of state experiment stations in the United States, was whether to service the expressed needs of farmers or to let the growing scientific community decide which agricultural problems were appropriate for research. The formal research institutions have had not only to mediate between farmers' concerns and scientists' concerns but also to contend with the authority of the public political-economic forces that provide their sustenance. The latter tend to reflect the changing nature and values of the larger social system (especially urban forces) and particularly its power structure.

Thus, as European and North American societies became increasingly differentiated and industrialized, and as the scientific community also became increasingly specialized, agricultural research reflected these trends. Although this type of research was perhaps appropriate in countries like the United States, where highly specialized, large-scale, capital-intensive agriculture "fits" the larger social trends, it produced a style, a mind-set, and a level of differentiation that made it quite "unfit" for the small-scale, undifferentiated, labor-intensive farming systems in places like Nepal.

In the past three decades of agricultural research, the scientific community has had difficulty recognizing the fundamental differences between the types of farming systems found in much of Asia, Africa, and Latin America and those found in North America and Europe. During the past century, North American and European farmers have shifted from relatively high recycling ratios to relatively low recycling ratios—so low that studies of energy flow in Michigan in 1979, for example, did not even take into account such factors as human labor and animal manure, since the energy values of "inputs" such as chemical fertilizer, diesel fuel, electricity, and gasoline are so high that the other figures become insignificant by comparison.

The large-scale, commercial, specialized, and highly differentiated monocrop agriculture of the industrial countries has its own problems. In response, their agricultural research communities applied science to those problems and developed technologies that were appropriate. However, the attempt to transfer some of those technologies to the small-scale, mixed-crop and livestock, labor-intensive, and capital-short agriculture of the so-called developing countries was a dysfunctional exercise, and usually, the attempts failed. When the technology transfer did succeed, the problems that were caused sometimes tended to defeat the long-run development goals.

Perhaps the recycling ratio can inform agricultural researchers about the nature of the problems that would be appropriate to study for any particular type of agriculture. The aspiration is that science applied to the type of agriculture in which most materials and energy are recycled internally would result in technologies that would be less dominated by goals of increasing production and more concerned with reducing storage losses, increasing consumption, and increasing equity among various members of the rural social systems.

The assumption of a cycle of change, rather than the linear "progress" model, may encourage more historical analysis in agricultural research, which could reveal much from the past which might be useful in the future. Similarly, the conception of a farm family ecosystem, with change in any component affecting and constrained by the condition of all other components, may be useful to agricultural researchers who are turning toward farming-systems approaches. A farming-systems perspective should enhance the capacity of the highly specialized scientific community to relate to relatively undifferentiated types of agriculture by adjusting the research agency with different approaches to problem definition.

For example, the issue of the advantages and disadvantages of small garden tractors as substitutes for animal draft power is a subject for agricultural research. However, when only cash flow data are used, the analysis may lead to a different evaluation than when all materials and energy flows are taken into account. Such matters as the use of straw and other fodder by draft animals, allocation of child labor to livestock care, manure values, exchanges between the farm family ecosystem and its near environment should also be entered into the evaluative equation.

Further, agricultural researchers are less likely to declare that a new cereal grain selection is "improved" if they consider more than the grain yield. If the recycling ratios of the farming system are taken into account, some varieties will be rejected even when their grain yield is high, because their fodder yield may be insufficient or their requirement for innovation in procurement of outside inputs may make them less than feasible.

Agricultural Extension Education

Agricultural extension education perspectives might also be expanded by a farm family ecosystem approach. For example, in areas in which small farming systems have a very high recycling ratio, credit for purchase of inputs tends to be rejected or ignored by farmers because they usually supply their own inputs, consume their own products, and do not require large amounts of credit for operation. However, increased use of production credit by farmers is often at the core of rural development and agricultural extension programs.

If the outsiders planning the agricultural extension programs first analyzed phenomena revealed by the recycling ratio, alternative programs might be proposed. Technological improvements in the storage of home-grown seed and farmyard manure are more promising than production credit to farmers with high recycling ratios. Similarly, there are many agricultural extension programs in South Asia that make the assumption that farm families keep dairy cattle primarily for milk. Based on that assumption, the programs are designed to help farmers increase the milk production of those cattle, but the farm family ecosystem analysis reveals that in some parts of Nepal, as an example, the primary reason for keeping a cow is usually for the production of a male calf, which might someday supply draft power. The second reason is usually for the production of farmyard manure, which serves either as fertilizer or as fuel. For many families, milk production from their cows may be a third or even fourth (following certain religious functions) reason for keeping the cow. Such poorly planned extension education programs usually fail, because farmers wish to avoid any serious damage to the farm family ecosystem. However, it is normal to blame the farmer, as an "ignorant peasant," for not following the program's recommendations rather than to discover the weakness of the initial assumption.

Farm families with high recycling ratios can use many information inputs from agricultural extension education. Improved storage technology, for example, can stretch the harvested grain to more adequately meet the nutritional needs of the family through the whole year. New information on weather and resource variables can contribute to planting and rotation decisions that will expand production to provide food, feed, and seed for the farming system.

Symbiotic relationships among plants that are traditionally intercropped, as well as between plants and animals, can be recognized by agricultural research and supported by research and extension professionals. This support can expand the development of the skills and abilities (human capital) of the small farm family.

International Development Assistance

International development assistance can also be informed by the cyclical perspective and by the farm family ecosystem approach. The extent of functional differentiation, as well as the extent of energy transformation and the nature of materials and energy flows, all offer clues to outsiders as to what types of interventions are likely to be seen as "development" by insiders. These concepts may also provide strategic help in determining what is likely to succeed and what is more likely to fail. Examples of the failure to use this approach are much more plentiful than examples of its use.

The normal international development assistance assumption, whether by host country nationals, by donor country staff members, or by international organizations, has been that since development and modernization vary together along the straight line of advancing technology, whatever comes from the "more advanced" countries is obviously better for the so-called less developed countries. The fallacy is that in most cases, a technology invented in one system to solve some of its problems is not likely to "fit" very well in another, very different system. If introduced—like an animal organ transplant that is not appropriate for the new system—it is likely to be rejected, and it may cause damage to the rest of the system. Typical examples are petroleum powered tractors' being introduced to small mixed farming systems of Asia and Africa. These technological "improvements" in large-scale, monocrop, capital-intensive farming systems tend to be rejected after introduction to small-scale, multiple crop and livestock, labor-intensive farming systems.

Beyond the mechanization example, which is so obvious in retrospect, there are many less-obvious current examples. These include the promotion of increased cereal grain yields by extension systems controlled from central governments. It is often in the interest of government to increase grain production, since it is assumed that doing so will increase food supplies and perhaps reduce pressure on international exchange. However, it is often not in the interest of farm family ecosystems to do so, sometimes because the cost of such yield increases exceeds the net gain to the system. This result often occurs in areas where the only feasible way of achieving increased yields is to increase chemical fertilizer inputs. With the high costs of such fertilizer, the small mixed-farming system is often better off when its yields are lower.

This type of intervention is sometimes encouraged by international technical assistance, in association with international agricultural research units. Since the rewards to the professional staff members within host countries are much larger from the international research network than they tend to be from the local bureaucracy, evaluations of foreign materials with foreign criteria result in local recommendations that may not be in the interest of the local farmers. And just as international reward systems and values overwhelm national ones, both bureaucracies tend to overwhelm any influence small farmers might have on the nature of what is researched, what is extended, or what is the essence of international assistance programs.

Further Research Opportunities

There is some direct utility in assessing the impact of outside interventions on social systems and their cultures. Although progress is being made in this field, social and behavioral scientists have tended to be vague and general in their findings, particularly when compared with biologists and economists. This situation has encouraged international banks, development agencies, and governments to focus their attention on economic data and agronomic information. Merely knowing that certain customary practices may be in jeopardy because of the introduction of some new technology has not seemed to influence the people supporting the projects as much as "hard" data about expected increases in income or agricultural yields. Demographers have been more convincing, but their data tend to be at the macrolevel and less helpful for microlevel impact analysis.

Criteria besides cash flow and population figures are likely to be useful if social scientists are to make a contribution in assessing the impact of development interventions. There is so little documentation about phenomena such as the social organization and the administration of change agencies in the rural social systems of the world that the opportunity for rural sociologists seems particularly bright.

The very concept of a cycle suggests the need for more research on patterns and trends in technological change, not only in connection with recent innovations, but historically. Going back to ancient times, further documentation of change from the highly undifferentiated to the more differentiated is needed. Analysis of how social change accompanied shifts toward less-intensive exploitations of available energy resources and the social dynamics of the technological changes involved would have immediate utility in contemporary North America and Europe.

Researchers in the field of urban-rural and rural-urban migrations also could exploit the cyclical conceptualization by relating continuity and change in different parts of the world at different points in time to each other. Also, long-range migration and short-range migration patterns might well be analyzed from the perspective of social differentiation and energy transformation measures and related to continuity and change in types of farming systems. Here the opportunity includes the assembly of studies by ethnologists, archaeologists, historians, and others and making analyses from a rural social systems perspective (see, for example, Boulding 1976). With respect to phenomena like the recycling ratio, more detailed field research would contribute significantly. The descriptive base needs much additional work.

Studies of the decision-making process in the farm family ecosystem might reveal continuity and change in values and the value relationships associated with functional differentiation. The independence of a high recycling ratio versus the dependence associated with a low recycling ratio varies as a social goal from place to place and time to time. How and why this variation occurs needs further study.

Local basic human needs criteria may be associated more with the total quantity of materials and energy transformation than with the proportion that is recycled. More analyses in more parts of the world would add significantly to understanding of this phenomenon. Perhaps studies that identify opportunities for raising recycling ratios in farming systems in the United States, through such strategies as reducing energy inputs and diversifying functions, should be explored.

Beyond the use of social differentiation and energy transformation analysis within individual farming systems, there is great opportunity for scholars at the next level of analysis of social systems. At the village level, the Nepal study revealed that the collection of forage for livestock from the near environment, often from common pastures and forest lands, has a social significance. The collection of forage results in inputs of manure for plant production and soil fertility that are obtained away from the individual family ecosystem. The relationships between individual family needs and values and those of the larger community can be explored much further with this type of analysis. The larger questions of energy transformation and the flow of materials at the community level and linkages with the larger social system of which the community is a part are already being studied, and this conceptual framework may have utility for such investigators.

The various agroclimatic zones, ethnic groups, and types of farming systems offer research opportunities almost everywhere in the world. Among the objectives of such further research could be the refinement and improvement of the methodologies described here, expanding the understanding of farm family ecosystems as systems, comparative studies of farm family ecosystems in different cultural and geographic locations, and providing a better base for international scientific and technical exchanges.

Limitations of the Approach

The type of analysis reported in this chapter should be considered primitive. The opportunities for further work far outweigh the achievements to date. Within individual farm family ecosystems, time-use studies, such as those we made in Nigeria (Axinn and Axinn 1969), and a detailed quantification of materials flow among the plant, human, and animal components are needed. Further, the data from Nepal were collected at each location at one point in time. Trend data over the months of a typical year, or a period of several years, would strengthen the perspective. And comparisons of different types of family farming ecosystems using this sort of analysis would also be useful.

However, our analysis has shown that it is possible to measure materials flow and energy transformation within small family farms and to use these measurements to compare such farms in a rural social system. Such assessments may be more valid as indicators of quality of life than assessments of the annual cash income, which are so widely used at present.

Notes

The opportunity to participate in the research described here resulted in a very treasured era in the authors' lives. Our appreciation for this opportunity must be expressed to many: our home institution, Michigan State University, and our professional colleagues there who contributed encourgement and criticism; our host institution, the Institute of Agriculture and Animal Science (IAAS) of Tribhuvan University, and the administration, especially Dean Netra Bahadur Basnyat; the staff of IAAS, the IAAS students, and our field research assistants who participated in the data collection; the graduate assistants at Michigan State University who contributed to the analysis of the data; several individuals in the U.S. Agency for International Development who contributed ideas; and the support staff who typed the manuscript. We have attempted to integrate the help of many, but any errors that remain are our own personal responsibility. We are also grateful for the direct and indirect financial support we have received from Michigan State University and the U.S. Agency for International Development, including the support of the Title XII Famine Prevention and Freedom from Hunger provisions. Whatever insights result from this effort are dedicated to the rural families of the world, and especially to those of the Chitwan and Lamjung Districts of Nepal who generously shared their lives to provide the data.

1. These thoughts are consistent with the conceptualizations of the relationship between energy transformation and social and economic change of Cottrell (1955), Adams (1975), Georgescu-Roegen (1975), Odum and Odum (1976), Thomas (1976), and Rambo (1979). This approach to development attempts to transcend the focuses on modernization (Johnston 1977, Mellor 1976, Wortman and Cummings 1978) and dependency (Cockcroft, Frank, and Johnson 1972, Chirot 1977, Erb and Kallab 1975, Goldthorpe 1975, Oxaal, Barnett, and Booth 1975), and it flows from a human ecology approach (McKenzie 1926, Hawley 1968, Paolucci 1980), an ecosystem perspective (Paolucci, Hall, and Axinn 1977, Thomas 1976, N. Axinn 1977, Riddell 1981), and concerns for women in development (Tinker 1980, Boserup 1970, Boulding 1976, Chip and Green 1980, Dauber and Cain 1980).

2. Energy transformation refers to the change in the form of energy, as when calories in grass and straw are converted by cattle into calories in milk and

manure, or when calories in human energy are "transformed" into calories in firewood. For an explanation of such use of energy transformation as a "marker" of flow instead of the traditional money-value transformation or cash flow used by economists, see Adams (1975, 1979), Georgescu-Roegen (1975), Odum and Odum (1976), Thomas (1976), Tinker (1980), and Tummala and Connor (1973).

3. This conceptual framework is similar to that of Koenig and Tummala (1972) and one developed by Tummala and Connor (1973), both of which provide a technique for calculating the mass and energy flows into and out of similar agricultural systems. The model used here is also similar to that used in the work of Thomas (1974, 1976).

References

Adams, Richard Newbold
    1974   "The Implications of Energy Flow Studies on Human Populations for the Social Sciences." In *Energy Flow in Human Communities, Proceedings of a Workshop in New York, New York*, pp. 21-31. University Park, Pa.: U.S. International Biological Program and Social Science Research Council.
    1975   *Energy and Structure, A Theory of Social Power.* Austin and London: University of Texas Press.
    1979   "Observations on the Use of Energy in Social Structure Analysis." Working Paper. Center for Energy Studies, University of Texas at Austin.

Agricultural Projects Services Centre (APROSAC)
    1979   *Impact Study of Small Farmers Development Project (Nuwakot and Dhanusha Districts).* Katmandu, Nepal: APROSAC, February 1979.

Axinn, George H.
    1977   "The Development Cycle: New Strategies from an Ancient Concept." *International Development Review* 4: 9-15.

Axinn, George H., and Nancy W. Axinn
    1969   "An African Village in Transition: Research into Behavior Patterns." *Journal of Modern African Studies* 7(3): 527-534.
    1979   "Materials Flow and Energy Transformation on Small Farms of Nepal: A New Approach to Comparative Analysis of Rural Family Ecosystems." Staff Paper no. 79-23. Department of Agricultural Economies, Michigan State University, East Lansing.

Axinn, Nancy W.
    1977   "Rural Development and Education: A Family Ecosystem Approach." In *Proceedings of the International Conference on Rural Development Technology: An Integrated Approach*, pp. 535-544. Bangkok, Thailand: Asian Institute of Technology.

Axinn, Nancy W., and George H. Axinn
    1980   "The Recycling Ratio: An Energy Approach to Planning Rural Development." Contributed paper for the Fifth World Congress for Rural Sociology, Mexico City.

Boserup, Ester
    1970   *Women's Role in Economic Development.* London: George Allen and
            Unwin.

Boulding, Elise
    1976   *The Underside of History—A View of Women Through Time.* Boulder,
            Colo.: Westview Press.

Campbell, David, and George H. Axinn
    1980   *Pastoralism in Kenya.* American Universities Field Staff Report
            DJC-1-'80, no. 30.

Chip, Sylvia A., and J. J. Green, eds.
    1980   *Asian Women in Transition.* University Park, Pa.: Pennsylvania State
            University Press.

Chirot, Daniel
    1977   *Social Change in the Twentieth Century.* New York: Harcourt Brace
            Jovanovich.

Cockcroft, James D., Andre Gunder Frank, and Dale I. Johnson, eds.
    1972   *Dependence and Underdevelopment.* Garden City, N.Y.: Doubleday
            and Company.

Cottrell, Fred
    1955   *Energy and Society: The Relation Between Energy, Social Change,
            and Economic Development.* New York: McGraw-Hill Book Com-
            pany. Reprinted Westport, Conn.: Greenwood Press, 1970, 1974.

Dauber, Roslyn, and M. Cain, eds.
    1980   *Women and Technological Change in Developing Countries.* Boulder,
            Colo.: Westview Press.

Dyson-Hudson, R., and N. Dyson-Hudson
    1970   "The Food Production System of a Semi-Nomadic Society." In
            African Food Production Systems, edited by P. McLoughlin, pp. 91–
            123. Baltimore: Johns Hopkins University Press.

Erb, Guy R., and Vaeriana Kallab
    1975   *Beyond Dependency: The Developing World Speaks Out.* New York:
            Praeger Publishers.

Georgescu-Roegen, Nicholas
    1975   "Energy and Economic Myths." *Southern Economic Journal* 41
            (January): 347–381.

Goldthorpe, J. E.
    1975   *The Sociology of the Third World: Disparity and Involvement.* Cam-
            bridge: Cambridge University Press.

Hawley, Amos H.
    1968   *Roderick D. McKenzie on Human Ecology.* Chicago and London:
            University of Chicago Press.

Johnston, Bruce F.
1977   "Food, Health, and Population in Development." *Journal of Economic Literature* 15(3): 879–907.

Koenig, Herman E., and R. L. Tummala
1972   "Principles of Ecosystem Design and Management." *IEEE Transactions on Systems, Man, and Cybernetics* SMC-2; 449–459.

McKenzie, Roderick D.
1926   The Scope of Human Ecology. *American Journal of Sociology* 32(1): pt. 2.

Mellor, John, ed.
1976   *The New Economics of Growth.* Ithaca, N.Y.: Cornell University Press.

Ministry of Food, Agriculture, and Irrigation
1979   *A Preliminary Report 1977–1979: The Short Term Cropping Systems Potential of Five Sites of Nepal and Its Relevance to Similar Environments.* Katmandu, Nepal: His Majesty's Government, Ministry of Food, Agriculture, and Irrigation, Department of Agriculture, Integrated Cereals Project, Agronomy Division, Cropping Systems Staff. May.

Odum, Howard T., and Elizabeth C. Odum
1976   *Energy Basis for Man and Nature.* New York: McGraw-Hill Book Company.

Oxaal, Ivar, Tony Barnett, and David Booth, eds.
1975   *Beyond the Sociology of Development.* London: Routledge and Kegan Paul.

Paolucci, Beatrice.
1980   "Evolution of Human Ecology." *Human Ecology Forum* 10(3): 17–21.

Paolucci, Beatrice, Olive A. Hall, and Nancy W. Axinn
1977   *Family Decision Making: An Ecosystem Approach.* New York: John Wiley and Sons.

Pratt, D. J., and M. D. Gwynne
1977   *Rangeland Management and Ecology in East Africa.* London: Hodder and Stoughton.

Rambo, A. Terry
1979   *Development of a Conceptual Framework for Human Ecology.* Working Paper no. 4. Kuala Lumpur, Malaysia: Universiti Malaya.

Riddell, Robert
1981   *Ecodevelopment: Economics, Ecology, and Development—An Alternative to Growth Imperative Models.* New York: St. Martin's Press.

Thomas, R. Brooke
    1974   "Human Adaptation to Energy Flow in the High Andes: Some
              Conceptual and Methodological Considerations." In *Energy Flow
              in Human Communities Proceedings of a Workshop in New York.*
              University Park, Pa.: U.S. International Biological Program and
              Social Science Research Council.
    1976   "Energy Flow at High Altitude." In *Man in the Andes,* edited by
              P. T. Baker and M. A. Little, chap. 19. Stroudsburg, Pa.: Dowden,
              Hutchinson and Ross.

Tinker, Irene
    1980   "Women and Energy Program Implications." Washington, D.C.:
              WID/USAID. Mimeograph.

Tummala, Ramamohan, and Larry J. Connor
    1973   "Mass-Energy Based Economic Models." *IEEE Transactions on
              Systems, Man, and Cybernetics* SMC-3(6) (November): 548-555.

Wortman, Sterling, and R. Cummings, Jr.
    1978   *To Feed This World: The Challenge and the Strategy.* Baltimore:
              Johns Hopkins University Press.

7
The Mackenzie Valley Pipeline Inquiry in Retrospect

Ray Funk

The North is a frontier but it is a homeland, too, the homeland of the Dene, Inuit and Metis, as it is also the home of the White people who live there. And it is a heritage, a unique environment, that we are called upon to preserve for all Canadians.

What happens in the North will be of great importance to the future of our country. It will tell us what kind of people we are.
— Thomas Berger
Northern Frontier, Northern Homeland, Vol. 1

It has been several years now since Justice Thomas Berger released his landmark report, *Northern Frontier, Northern Homeland*, recommending a ten-year moratorium on the building of a pipeline in the Mackenzie Valley area of northern Canada. The release of the report on May 9, 1977, prompted a level of public response unprecedented for such an event. The initial press run of the report, a lavishly illustrated and lucidly written document selling for five dollars, sold out in a few days. CBC radio ran a two-hour special report on it, CBC television presented a one-hour special, and the story made banner headlines from coast to coast. In Toronto, the multinational oil companies and their allies lurched into a counterattack, but elsewhere in the country the response by many Canadians bordered on jubilation. In the North, and among native peoples throughout Canada, the report was hailed as a virtual declaration of independence (Sanders 1977, 4).

The intensity of the response to the report was hardly surprising considering the buildup that had preceded its release. Ever since the appointment of Justice Thomas Berger to head the inquiry that led to the report in March 1974, expectations had been rising, and the inquiry had combined elements of high drama, deep soul-searching, and traveling road show with the presentation of mountains of data. Citizens across the country were drawn to the inquiry by the vast magnitude of the project, the intense political debate that surrounded it, strenuous organizing and education efforts by many groups, and most of all, by the powerful images on television of northerners in their own communities eloquently expressing their love for their land and their hopes for the future to an endlessly patient justice.

The process of the inquiry and its report seemed to meet all the criteria that could be asked, other than those of the oil industry multinationals. Political scientists said it "represents the most comprehensive and thorough contribution to a public decision ever achieved in Canada" (Gray and Gray 1977, 515). The National Energy Board and the Canadian government expressed general support for Berger's findings and recommended an alternate pipeline route, which would satisfy many of the issues raised. The concerns and agenda of the northern native peoples had been lucidly expressed and seemed on the way to resolution in the context of broadly based sympathy from most segments of Canadian society.

Yet four years later, in 1981, the bright skies of 1977 seemed to have clouded over. The only portion of the alternate pipeline assured of completion would siphon southern Canada's gas into U.S. markets, and a new proposal to build an oil pipeline from Norman Wells (halfway up the Mackenzie Valley route) south to Alberta seemed destined for approval. Massive exploration and development projects in the Mackenzie Valley area were under way without any resolution of the crucial land claims of the natives or their self-determination issues.

Much of this activity was precipitated by the federal government itself through Bill C-48, which was intended to promote an aggressive exploitation of northern petroleum resources by the publicly owned oil corporation (Petrocan) and others. The objections of native organizations, territorial governments, and their allies were being overrun by a process so heavy-handed that the assertion by one analyst that "Bill C-48 slams the door in Northern faces" (Dirks 1981, 6) expressed a widespread consensus.

The president of Imperial Oil (Canada's Exxon subsidiary) proclaimed, "The Canadian Oil industry should be moving into our most promising Atlantic and Arctic properties like an army of occupation" (*Toronto Globe and Mail*, May 12, 1981). Justice Berger himself pointed out that the criteria of appropriate cold climate technology and rational development had not been met, that the industry's program amounted to a new "manifest destiny of Western man, and that even the language of the debate had become eccentric with conservationists considered radical and interventionists calling themselves conservatives" (Berger 1981).

However, by 1983 the pendulum seemed to have begun a return. The process of land claim settlement and the addition of native self-determination to the negotiating agenda had received a significant boost with the inclusion of aboriginal rights in the 1982 repatriation of the Canadian Constitution, and the proposed Norman Wells pipeline was on hold pending participation agreements with native groups (Plafiel 1983). Northern natives were also increasingly active in their participation in territorial governments, including widespread election to public office.

It appeared likely that the ten-year moratorium on construction of the actual pipeline would hold, and although Bill C-48 clearly breached the spirit of Berger's recommendations, the slump in the world's hydrocarbon demand and price still allowed for the development of arrangements that would be less colonial in nature than had seemed possible in the past. Even such subsequent events as the election of a federal Conservative government in 1984 and several setbacks in the negotiating process failed to alter the basic course established by the inquiry.

An interesting footnote in the unfolding saga of the inquiry's aftermath is that Berger resigned his seat on the British Columbia Supreme Court in 1983 in response to a furor in legal circles over his "unbecoming" advocacy of the entrenchment of aboriginal rights in the new Constitution of Canada. He was then retained by Alaskan native organizations to analyze and suggest solutions to the many problems arising from their earlier claims settlement.

In this context, it seems appropriate to take a second look at the Berger Inquiry for several reasons: first, to examine the inquiry itself and its adequacy as an effort at social impact analysis; second, to take a closer look at the consequences and aftermath of the inquiry; and third, to determine what generalizations about the social impact analysis process, and the contexts in which it occurs, can be drawn from this example.

The Project and Its Background

The most obvious aspect of the pipeline project was the fact that its primary intent was to move northern gas to southern markets. Benefits to the population in the North were clearly a secondary consideration, although they figured prominently in the rationalizations of many of the supporters of the scheme. Thus, from the start, the question of social concerns was not so much one of analysis and strategy but a question of getting social concerns on the agenda at all.

This problem was compounded by the fact that the normal regulatory process focused on the National Energy Board, which is competent to consider only technical and economic factors. Furthermore, although there exists a nominal degree of self-government through territorial councils, the Canadian North is in effect governed by the Department of Indian Affairs and Northern Development (DIAND) from Ottawa. This department has evolved into a schizophrenic bureaucracy, which acts as the constitutional trustee of the native peoples on the one hand and promotes a highly industrialized, resource exploitive, wage-based strategy of northern development on the other. The conflict of interest inherent in this situation is regularly resolved in favor of high technology development (Keith et al. 1976, 65).

The project itself actually consisted of two competing proposals. Canadian Arctic Gas Pipeline Limited, a Toronto-based consortium of multinational oil companies led by Imperial Oil, intended to build a line

2,400 miles from Prudhoe Bay in Alaska to the U.S. border, delivering both Canadian and Alaskan gas to markets in the south. A rival proposal by the Foothills Pipelines Company, a breakaway faction of Arctic Gas made up of private western Canadian interests, sought finally to build an 800-mile pipeline from the Mackenzie Delta to existing pipelines in Alberta (Keith et al. 1976).

Most of the attention focused on the Arctic Gas proposal, which was described as the largest project ever undertaken by private enterprise (Sanders 1977, 4). It was estimated it would cost up to $10 billion to complete and require 7,200 people in its construction (Berger 1977, 1:ix). The construction phase was expected to last four years with the actual laying of pipe occurring over two winters. It was projected that about 800 permanent employees would be required to operate and maintain the pipeline over its thirty-year life. The application alone cost $60 million to prepare and weighed three tons (Bregha 1979, 51).

The pipeline was to be a complicated series of buried and raised segments crossing first the caribou and seal habitats of the northern Yukon, then the ecologically fragile Mackenzie Delta. From there it was to proceed down the Mackenzie Valley, which is a favored hunting and fishing area as well as an area of erratic permafrost patterns. In all, over 600 river crossings would have to be made (Berger 1977, 1:16).

In the path of this juggernaut were thirty-five northern communities ranging in size from small villages of a hundred people to substantial towns of several thousand. This population was made up of approximately 12,500 Indians (the Dene) and Metis, 2,500 Inuit, and 15,000 white people (Berger 1977, 1:17). Most of the white population was engaged in either government activities of infinite variety, resource exploration, or the service sector. What the native population did became the basis for considerable debate before the inquiry, with pipeline supporters arguing that they were largely part of a wage and welfare economy and natives and others maintaining that they were reluctant participants in a mixed economy, the most positive aspect of which was the renewable resource-based activities of hunting, trapping, and fishing (Gray and Gray 1977, 512).

Three major elements made up the larger context of the project. The first of these was the dependency relationship between Canada and the United States, which has plagued Canadian decision making for generations. Not only were the major participants in the Arctic Gas consortium from the United States, but much of the impetus for the project came from the need for gas in that country. The U.S. government was keenly interested in gaining access to Prudhoe Bay gas and was debating whether to endorse an El Paso Gas proposal to build an Alaskan gas pipeline and transport liquified natural gas south by ship or via an overland route through Canada (Bregha 1979, 39). The Canadian government was a willing accomplice to the pipelines scheme, since it saw it as a way to attract foreign capital and, at the same time, balance the country's trade deficit with the United States (Watkins 1977).

The second factor was the growing awareness of an energy crisis, which had somewhat contradictory effects on the project. The initial scare in 1967, coupled with the discovery of the Prudhoe Bay reserves, had spurred increasingly productive exploration of Canada's north, and at the same time, the rising prices made the exploitation of the newly found resources increasingly feasible. However, after the 1973 crisis, there was an increasing concern that Canada itself might run short of gas for domestic use, the corollary of which was a growing feeling, reflected by the regulatory agencies and the government, that exporting major amounts of Canada's gas might not be prudent (Bregha 1979, 43).

The third factor was the Canadian political situation as the election in 1972 had left Pierre Trudeau's Liberals in a precarious minority position and dependent on the New Democratic party (NDP) support for survival. The NDP, which has a democratic-socialist orientation, demanded greater public planning of resource use, Canadian control, and sensitivity to native claims and environmental impacts as the price for its support for the Liberal energy policy.

The Inquiry

In 1974, the federal government was caught in a dilemma as its active support and planning with respect to northern gas had resulted in a proposal that its regulatory mechanism was unable to credibly cope with. The oil corporations, the U.S. government, and the pressure of energy developments were pulling it one way; the NDP, which reflected widespread support for a new approach to decision making, was pulling it another. Therefore in March 1974, the government mandated an ad hoc inquiry to examine the mass of documentation that was piling up as a result of its own internal studies and those of the pipelines proponents and to hold hearings in order to determine the terms and conditions under which a pipeline was to be built.

In a surprise move, designed to allay widespread skepticism about its motives, the government named Justice Thomas Berger to head the inquiry. Berger had previously been an NDP Member of Parliament and its provincial leader in British Columbia. His legal career prior to his appointment to the British Columbia Supreme Court had been distinguished by the fact that he was "the lawyer who almost alone developed the legal concept of aboriginal rights in Canadian law by means of a number of cases culminating in the historic Nishga case in 1972 where the Supreme Court of Canada recognized aboriginal rights for the first time" (Waddell 1983).

Justice Berger wasted no time in expanding the scope of the inquiry to include an assessment of the overall effect of industrial development of the North and its effect on the northern people and their environment. In fact, one observer noted that it was "much more than an inquiry into a gas pipeline, it became an inquiry into the future of the North, and, finally an inquiry into the future itself" (Bregha 1979, 115). Berger reserved the right to subpoena documents, the bulk of which the companies and the government had kept secret (Keith 1976, 158), and proclaimed that he intended to conduct an "Inquiry without walls" (Berger 1976, 9).

The inquiry without walls concept was unprecedented in that an attempt was made to involve all possible interested parties. There were of course formal hearings at which proponents, intervening antagonists, and experts had their day. In addition, Berger moved staff, media, and experts into all thirty-five northern communities that would be affected, many of them isolated, so that native peoples could participate on their own terms and on their own turf. He also persuaded the CBC to set up a special network to broadcast the highlights of each day's deliberations across the North in six languages. Following the formal and local hearings in the North, he added fuel to the nationwide interest these hearings had generated by taking the inquiry to ten cities in southern Canada. In all, he heard testimony from over 1,000 witnesses in six languages, and the transcripts filled 40,791 pages. Commission staff members, many of whom had been active in studies preceding the inquiry itself, examined a bibliography in excess of 350 entries. The eventual cost of the inquiry ran to $5.3 million (Berger 1977, 2:225).

A key factor in the attempt to ensure that all voices were heard was the federal government's funding of intervening groups. These included the Committee for Original People's Entitlement (COPE), the Indian Brotherhood of the North-West Territories, the Metis, the Canadian Arctic Resources Committee (CARC), the North-West Territories Chamber of Commerce, the North-West Territories Association of Municipalities, environmental groups in southern Canada, and others. Funding for these groups totaled $1.8 million and was given with no strings attached (other than accountability) to enable them to mobilize sufficient resources to give them an independent voice, analyze the mountain of often-technical data, and conduct their own studies (Berger 1977, 2:225).

The evidence presented ranged from highly technical discussions of the immensely complex technology the project would employ to angry threats of blowing up the pipeline if the voices of native people were again ignored. Particular attention was focused on social and cultural concerns, with the history of native contact with white society, the relationship of the Dene and Inuit to the land, and the prospects for an indigenous economy getting a sympathic hearing.

Evidence and Findings

In the end, Berger rejected both gas company proposals and ruled that for environmental reasons, pipelines should never be built across the ecologically delicate northern Yukon and Mackenzie Delta areas. He assumed that northern oil and gas would eventually be tapped (as did the native groups), but he recommended that a ten-year moratorium be placed on the Mackenzie Valley portion of the line. These ten years were to be used to work out critical technical details, to provide an opportunity to settle native land claims, and to launch an integrated, rational development program with native participation. There were over a hundred specific recommendations for further study and action. The complete evidence supporting these findings and their details is beyond the scope of this chapter, but a review of the evidence involving social impact analysis is in order.

Culture

The report does not indicate exactly how many or which of the ethnographic studies done among the Inuit and northern Indians over the last century the inquiry considered, and since the report is not footnoted, it is necessary to infer references unless specific names are mentioned in the text. Much of the evidence came from the native peoples themselves, although the report states that the observations of anthropologists support the persistence of native values (Berger 1977, 1:96). Anthropologists who are referred to by name include June Helm on traditional leadership, Peter Gardiner on respect for individual freedoms, and Joel Saviskinsky on the sharing ethic.

The report generalizes that "the attitude of many white people towards the North and native northerners is a thinly veiled evolutionary determinism" (Berger 1977, 189). A considerable proportion of the cultural evidence consisted of a historical recounting of the evolution of native-white contact in the area, and the effect of the schools received particularly negative comment (Fumoleau 1976, T'Seleie 1976, Berger 1977, Usher 1975, Page 1973). A great deal of what is broadly defined as culture was also covered under other headings.

Social Impact

In spite of the dozens of studies commissioned by the government, the applicants, and others, Berger and other observers (Keith et al. 1976, Gray and Gray 1977) noted that social impact issues had not been as adequately handled as environmental questions. If the government's own publication *Monitering Socio-Economic Change* (Palmer 1974) is indicative of the level of many of these studies, this comment is not surprising, since that work relies entirely on standard indicators that have little relationship to northern life-styles.

Much of the social impact analysis presented by the applicants and the government is included in a document entitled *Mackenzie Valley Pipeline Assessment,* a compilation done by twenty-six bureaucrats, two scholars, and two consultants (including three sociologists but no anthropologists). Its conclusions were based on the assumption that the pipeline would only speed a well-established process of evolution from a traditional to a modern way of life among native peoples and that gains in employment, training, and social amenities would offset the unavoidable social consequences. Although it regretted the fact that natives would become a declining minority in the North, it said this was an irreversible trend. There were, however, fifty-six items on which the group called for further study, including nine major gaps in social impact information (Pipeline Assessment Group 1974).

Opposing this point of view were several social-work and health professionals, a number of social scientists who dealt with the question in the context of economics, and most convincingly, the native peoples themselves. Much of the evidence consisted of graphic descriptions of current problems the native people's were having in dealing with the invasion of their territory and their fears about the future (T'Seleie 1976). There was also argument by analogy to the recent Alaskan experience, a situation Berger had assessed firsthand. Economist Peter Usher empasized that any job strategy should aim at long-term gains (Berger 1977).

The justice's approach to the question is exemplified by the following quote from his report: "I do not want anyone to think that I regard the evidence of these social scientists as decisive in itself. If we are to truly try and understand what the native people want and what kind of a life they seek, we must let them speak for themselves" (Berger 1977, 2:11). In the end, the report came to the unambiguous conclusion that "the social impact that I foresee in the Mackenzie Valley and the Western Arctic, if we build the pipeline now, will be devastating—I use the word advisedly—and quite beyond our capacity to ameliorate in any way" (Berger 1977, 1:143).

Economic Impact

Economic impact proved to be the major battleground of the hearings with both sides interpreting the question of economics in a broad sense. This emphasis on economics is hardly surprising given the financial magnitude of the project and its long-term implications for sources of livelihood in the North.

The argument of the proponents of the pipelines were put forward most forcefully by the Gemini North group, the research arm of the Arctic Gas consortium, whose findings were presented directly to the inquiry members as well as being incorporated in the assessment group's report. These arguments were explicit in assuming that incoporation into the wage economy was in the best interests of the native peoples and that the pipeline was the best thing that could happen to the wage economy. In fact, it was asserted that every native who wanted a job could get one, and that natives would give up their other pursuits in large numbers to do so (Pipeline Assessment Group 1974). One representative of Gemini North, sociologist Charles Hobart, cited research he had done that indicated that wage employment was the prime objective of a vast majority of the native peoples (Hobart and Kuffer 1978, 64).

Even more contentious was the related Gemini finding that trapping and hunting were pursued seriously by only 100 natives in the area and that income from trapping was worth a mere $188,000 annually with an additional $197,000 worth of food obtained through hunting (Berger 1977, 1:108). This assertion prompted a full-scale counterattack by the native groups; with both major groups, the Dene and the Inuit, launching major baseline studies. Their studies were designed both to demonstrate the persistance and vitality of their indigenous economies and to lay the basis for land claims based on use and occupancy.

The Inuit study, coordinated by Peter Usher on their behalf, drew on Usher's previous five years of research in the North, including a two-year in-depth study of the Bankslanders on Sach's Island (Usher 1970). Within a basic metropolitan-hinterland framework, it reviewed the history of northern development from the standpoint of the Inuit and their values. Drawing on Inuit information, it concluded that in sharp contrast to the Gemini North estimates, there was an annual production of $800,000 worth of fur and $1.6 million worth of food. These resources came from an area covering 1.5 million square miles, which the Inuit laid claim to (Usher et al.).

If anything, the Dene sponsored and conducted even more extensive research. The cornerstone of their efforts was a baseline land use and occupancy study, which they controlled and largely conducted themselves with training and technical assistance from experts hired by them. The reasoning behind this study was expressed by Phoebe Nahanni:

> We know that anthropologists and white researchers had previously attempted to integrate a study of our land-based activities in their theses. But our community leaders and community people expressed their dislike for the invasion of their privacy by outsiders who did not speak their language. We know from past experience that government research by white researchers has never improved our lives. Usually white researchers spy on us, the things we do, how we do them, where we do them and so on. After all these things are written in their jargon, they go away and neither they nor their reports are ever seen again. We have observed this, and the brotherhood resolved to try its best to see that, in future, research involves the Dene from beginning to end. [Nahanni 1977, 23]

This study, which directly involved more than two dozen people over two years, found that trapping and hunting were central to the lives of 1,075 families and that their activities were spread out over a 450,000-square-mile area (Nahanni 1977, 26). This picture of an integrated indigenous economy was supported by another Dene-sponsored study at Fort Franklin by Scott Rushford (anthropologist) who found that 50 percent of the residents were engaged in significant renewable resource-based activities worth from $3,200 to $3,900 per family in 1974. He felt that in spite of a pattern of increasing dependence, this level of activity coupled with the persisting values of the people could serve as the basis for a modern, locally based, and locally controlled economy (Rushford 1977, 32-45). A study by Michael Asch at Fort Simpson came to similar conclusions (Asch 1977), as did a study done for DIAND at Old Crow by geographer J. K. Stager (Stager 1974).

Further work on behalf of the Dene by Watkins, Jelliss, and Merriwell was done on the macroeconomic level of analysis. They concluded that the project was essentially colonialist in nature and that very little, if any, of the $4.4 billion in economic rents that would accrue over the life of the project would benefit northerners unless their claims were settled in a way that guaranteed self-determination (Watkins 1977, Merriwell 1977, Jelliss 1977).

Justice Berger's response was that while the project's proponents had presented evidence that a pure wage economy was in the best interests of the people, the testimony of 1,000 people had indicated otherwise (Berger 1977, 1:109). On the local level, he concluded that an integrated, not a dual, economy existed and that the renewable resource segment should be actively supported. Recognizing that pipeline development would eventually come, he stressed the need for both a settlement of claims and the development of native institutions to arrive at an equitable distribution of rents, and to develop mechanisms that could integrate that kind of development into native life-styles. With regard to the economic presuppositions of the pipeline supporters he said, "It is paradoxical to suggest that a large-scale frontier project designed to supply energy, the modern staple, to the metropolis will result in regional self-sufficiency" (Berger 1977, 1:120).

Other Impacts and Alternatives

A great deal of scrutiny centered around the technological details of plans for the pipeline and the effect on the environment the pipeline would have. The project was criticized both for its absolute environmental effects (northern Yukon and Mackenzie Delta) and its effect on renewable resources that are essential to the development of an indigenous economy. Berger also found that many technical assumptions involving cold-weather construction, such as the effects of permafrost, methods of river crossing, and provisions for logistic support, were based on inadequate research data. The impact on treaty claims of premature development was judged to be negative, as was the related concern about the development of local institutions (Berger 1977, 2:196).

The inquiry members rejected both pipeline proposals on the assumption that there would be no negative local effects if the pipeline did not proceed (although Arctic Gas waved good-bye to $150 million). In addition to renewable resource development and the settlement of claims, Berger felt that the moratorium period should include the development of appropriate training programs, the development of community action plans to contain the pathologies of growth and provide for integrated community-based planning, and the public planning of an infrastructure system.

The inquiry looked favorably on the suggestion of a rail corridor rather than a pipeline, but this alternative was not actively pursued by either the applicants or the government. Justice Berger also hypothesized that a pipeline from Prudhoe Bay along the Alaska Highway—a proposal rushed forward by the Foothills group that would bypass Mackenzie gas—would present less critical problems (Berger 1977, 1:xiv).

The Aftermath

The fact that the National Energy Board and the government accepted the Berger Report's rejection of the Mackenzie Valley pipeline was partly due, no doubt, to the existence of the less problematic alternative route along the Alaska Highway, which they approved with some haste. The Liberal government also moved in the direction of greater control of the oil industry, with the ironic result that much of the controversial present activity in the area is on behalf of the publicly owned energy corporation, Petrocan. The call for more study seems to have been partially heeded as a 1978 publication lists 218 studies in progress in the North, 9 of which dealt directly with the inquiry and a number of others with concerns raised by it (Rosenberg 1978).

The governmental response to the linking of a moratorium to the settlement of claims has been ambiguous. Government support for the Imperial Oil pipeline from Norman Wells seems as much precipitated by the desire to put pressure on the sluggish negotiations as by the need for the oil. As well the question of the good faith of the Liberal government, later retrenched with a solid majority, was a matter of some doubt since the Liberals did not accept an agreement that they themselves initiated with the Inuit. More recently, the Conservative government elected in 1984 has shown itself to be more sympathetic to the agenda of the oil transnationals than previous governments had been.

On the other hand, the inclusion of aboriginal rights in the Canadian Constitution has already spawned a major constitutional conference involving the federal and provincial governments as well as Indian, Metis, and Inuit representatives. This conference gave de facto recognition to the concept of "first nations" and committed the participants to an ongoing process of negotiations. Although this process has proved somewhat frustrating, its continuation is an indicator of the momentum generated by the inquiry since Canada is generally experiencing an era of political conservatism.

The most notable effect of the inquiry has been on the evolution of the native community. Even during the inquiry period there was a determination never again to make a James Bay type of land-for-money trade-off, and the Dene adopted a ringing declaration of self-determination to support that position. This concept has spread, with the result that land claims have proliferated across Canada. The preparation of land claim cases and the development of constitutional positions have meant that the ability of native organizations to sponsor and conduct research has become increasingly sophisticated. Coupled with this capability has come an enhanced exploitation of the opportunities presented by the considerable array of available media and political forums, which is essential for developing support for social and political change in contemporary society. This combination of research and political sophistication was dramatically highlighted by the televising of the March 1983 constitutional conference, which provided a broad stage for native groups to showcase their confident ability to shape their own future.

The Berger Inquiry has become a legend, at least in Canada, and the initial evidence suggests that this designation is justified both at the level of methodology and at the level of myth. Subsequent inquiries in Canada have included methods developed by the Berger Inquiry, such as preliminary rulings, funding of a broad range of intervenors, community hearings, and freedom of information. The principals involved in the inquiry still enjoy folk-hero status.

Adequacy of the Inquiry

Questions of the adequacy of the inquiry include the quality of baseline information, the level of participation, the level of analysis, and the practical worth of its findings. Although perfection is unlikely in an imperfect world, all of these criteria were largely met.

Baseline Data

The question of baseline data is one that hinges as much on utility as on quantity. The largest volume of data received by the inquiry dealt with technical feasibility and environmental effects, as would be anticipated by the nature of the project and the massive expenditures by proponents and the government on research in this area. Overall, it appears that these data were comprehensive enough to permit decisionmaking.

A key question raised by the inquiry is why many observers, including Justice Berger and the native community, were clearly uncomfortable with the adequacy of the sociocultural data that were available in spite of the massive and expensive effort to provide the data. Certainly the volume of data available, which included a compendium of studies compiled by DIAND that required seven volumes, does not indicate a lack of resources brought to bear on the question. Also, although individual studies could be criticized from various perspectives, there is no indication that the individual experts were either incompetent or unprofessional in the conduct of their studies.

What does emerge is the impression that the studies lacked a comprehensive methodological model that would permit generalizations on the level the inquiry required. Indeed, Berger's criticism was that the studies were too narrow and specialized, and he concluded that "this limitation, which distorts rather than enlightens, represents the worst aspect of conventional impact analysis. It also suggests the necessity for developing a methodology that is sufficiently comprehensive to encompass the wide range of variables, a variety of conflicting interests, and a realistic span of time" (Berger 1977, 2:229).

In an attempt to compensate for this perceived inadequacy, and lacking the time to commission and conduct comprehensive studies itself, the inquiry ordered that all relevant material be made available to all interested parties, an order backed by the power of subpoena and by funding to undertake an analysis of the competing materials. Funding for studies targeted by interested groups, particularly native groups, enabled them to attempt to fill data gaps that they perceived to be critical. Also, the weight the inquiry placed on community testimony, which was given with a dramatic sense of occasion and importance, focused many of the sociocultural issues in a way that influenced the political context to an extent rarely achieved by scholarly endeavor.

A tentative conclusion suggested by this scenerio is that although the experts' role would certainly have been enhanced by a more comprehensive methodology, it is doubtful that any single methodology could have yielded baseline data more "useful" than the pluralistic analysis of available data, research targeted by affected groups, and direct participation did in this instance. Certainly, the public inquiry model incorporating elements includes a number of self-corrective mechanisms, which a single "comprehensive" study probably could not duplicate.

In the view of northern natives, the most critical gap in data was in the area of land use and occupancy, information they felt was essential both in the analysis of their present and future way of life and as a basis for their claims. Probably the most successful aspect of the inquiry was that it precipitated, and then took seriously, the massive participatory research program that was launched by the native groups to supply this information.

Participation

The second question of adequacy, that of participation, has already been alluded to. Ian Waddell, presently an NDP Member of Parliament who was Special Council to the Inquiry, has stated that "we were very conscious of the fact that we were ploughing new ground with the process itself" (Waddell 1983). Indeed, it is hard to conceive of ways in which the participation base could have been broadened when one considers the funding of the research and personnel of independent groups, the multilingual community hearings, the radio hookup, the southern tour, the attractiveness of the report itself, and the intangible but real factor of Thomas Berger's deportment and personal attitude toward the participants.

Analysis

A key requirement of any social impact assessment is the level of analysis to which the evidence is subjected. Although there have been accusations by leftists (Sanders 1977, 4), that the analysis was essentially liberal, this view is hard to justify unless the criteria by which these things are judged are totally linguistic. By any other standards, the report is a masterful example of the linking of environmental, sociocultural, and microeconomic and macroeconomic factors into a coherent picture that can serve scholars, community participants, and governments equally well. That the report is not more theoretically explicit in its micro-macro linkages is more the result of the fact that models for such an analysis of modern capitalistic societies, and particularly mixed economies (such as Canada's), are inadequate than it is a reflection on the scope of Justice Berger's thought.

Spread Effects

The fourth criterion of adequacy is that of spread effects and the practical use of the findings. As has been noted, the impact on the consciousness of both the participants and the public was beyond expectations, in fact, the inquiry itself became a major political event in the largest sense (Jackson 1977, 6). That its recommendations have not been fully operationalized is much less a result of their applicability than it is a factor of power relationships and institutional structures.

The question then becomes one of whose power was enhanced and whose was constrained as a result of the inquiry. Although a fuller analysis of this question is warranted, the evidence would initially support the hypothesis that it was the power of the northern and native groups, and the champions of controlled and socially sensitive development in southern Canada, that was strengthened. It is too much to ask that one inquiry deliver a final coup de grace to the power elites in Canada, both public and private, but their reactions indicate that they did feel some pain. They certainly lost both face and money.

Generalizations About the Analysis Process

If the Berger Inquiry is judged as a successful example of social impact analysis, it then becomes pertinent to ask what generalizations about social impact analysis this example suggests and to what extent the process is replicable. The latter question is relevant because of the scale of the project, the resources available to the inquiry members, the domestic politics of Canada, and the fact that the inquiry was not conducted by expatriates.

As suggested by Derman and Whiteford, Jackson, and others, the question of the participation of the people affected by a project is a key variable. The Mackenzie Valley experience strongly supports such an assertion, since such participation not only helped to provide otherwise unavailable data, it also served as the basis for ongoing institutional changes in the relationship between northern natives and southern populations, and between supporters of exploitive development and balanced development in all of Canada. This change occurred at a consciousness level as well as through organizational forms that developed out of that consciousness.

In addition to highlighting the necessity and effectiveness of participation, the Berger Inquiry provided some useful examples of how barriers to participation can be overcome. Although it can be argued that ideology and resources may make the possibility of this model unique to Canada or contexts like it, it would seem that the process of participation is essential to enough elements of social impact analysis to make it indispensable. This point suggests that anyone engaging in analysis without the possibility of open participation in a locally relevant form is engaging in the perpetration of a farce.

Several other issues flow from the emphasis on participation, the most important of which is the ownership of knowledge. Derman and Whiteford have indicated that the transfer of knowledge begins with the analysis process and that this transfer is one of its basic goals (Derman and Whiteford 1981). Jackson provides a similar analysis using the concept of Paulo Freire that the empowering process is essentially one of oppressed peoples' finding their own voice (Jackson 1977, 6). It is only through participation that people can discover their own history and culture and reflect on the cricumstances of their own lives, especially if these circumstances involve dependence and colonial-type domination.

The issue of ownership of knowledge can also be analyzed in Marxist terms if social impact analysis is viewed as a technology, which Whiteford's definition (technology includes materials, knowledge, and skills that when exercised, can do a particular kind of work) indicates it is (Derman and Whiteford 1981). If it is a technology, it also becomes one of the means of production, and anyone engaging in the social analysis of a people without transferring that ability is in fact withholding one of the means of production, which the presence of the analyst indicates is essential in a particular situation. The words of Phoebe Nahanni earlier in this chapter eloquently assess this relationship.

A second issue arising from participation is that full participation helps set the agenda and the scope of the debate. In the Berger Inquiry, it was obvious that what planners and experts deemed important was not in fact what was on the minds of the people. For this reason, if for no other, assessors should value participation since it is impossible for any assessor, particularly a cultural outsider, which Justice Berger was, or an expatriate, which most foreign aid assessors are, to anticipate either the range and complexity of local concerns or the local perceptions of linkages. Thus, participation can considerably reduce the number of what are euphemistically termed "unforseen results."

The second major issue is that of linkages, an issue that also has received considerable attention. The Berger Report indicates that the question of linkages both between various local phenomena and between the local community and larger systems cannot be ignored, and may well be central to the analysis. It is also obvious from Berger's analysis that Schwartz's concerns about intermediary linkages and the findings of Corbett and Whiteford (quoted in Schwartz) about the penetration of local communities by central planners are useful conceptual tools (Schwartz 1981). Furthermore, the Berger Inquiry indicates that the inquiry process itself can become a potent factor in establishing various kinds of formal and informal linkages, and that it can become an element in the larger political debate in a society.

The issue of linkages raises the likelihood that these will vary considerably in various political and economic environments, which means that the assessment process will play a substantially different role depending on the context. In a centrally planned economy, the assessment process might become an intermediary link as defined by Schwartz. In an ideal participatory democracy, this process would probably be diffused throughout all the stages of planning and implementing a project. In the mixed context of Canada, where both public and private elites operating in a pluralistic political environment were attempting to implement a project without meaningful local involvement, the inquiry served to crystalize the dialectic between outside forces and local people. The awareness emerging from the clarification of this dialectic serves as the basis for growing consciousness and the resultant realignment of institutional forces (Jackson 1977, 22).

The last major issue raised by Justice Berger's efforts is that of social theory and the philosophy of the assessor. It is clear that Berger's previous involvement with native rights issues and his human empathy for the people appearing before him, as well as his democratic-socialist political orientation, were significant factors in both the process of the inquiry and his analysis of the evidence. In crass terms, an unreformed monetarist who hated Indians would have produced a much different report. The unescapable conclusion is that not only the analysis but the whole assessment process, and even the evidence that comes to light, are directly dependent on the social philosophy of the people who are charged with the responsibility for the assessment. This point means that if the empowerment of people and meaningful social change are to occur as the result of a project, the social impact assessment must be done by people who are philosophically committed to those ends. Again, Thomas Berger has expressed this idea as well as anyone when he states in his conclusions that "in the end, no matter how many experts there may be, no matter how many pages of computer print-outs may have been assembled, there is the ineluctable necessity of bringing human judgement to bear on the main issues. Indeed when the main issue cuts across a range of questions, spanning the physical and social sciences, the only way to come to grips with it and resolve it is by the exercise of human judgement" (Berger 1977, 2:229).

References

Asch, Michael
1977   *The Dene Nation*, ed. Mel Watkins. Toronto: University of Toronto Press.

Berger, Thomas
    1976   "The Mackenzie Valley Pipeline Inquiry." *Queens Quarterly* 83:1
            (Spring).
    1977   *Northern Frontier, Northern Homeland.* 2 vols. Ottawa: Department
            of Supply and Services.
    1981   Untitled article. *Toronto Globe and Mail.* May 12.

Bregha, Francois
    1979   *Bob Blair's Pipeline.* Toronto: James Lorimer.

Dene Declaration
    1976   *Canadian Forum* (November).

Derman, Bill, and Whiteford, Scott
    1981   Lecture notes, IDC 838, Michigan State University.

Dirks, Gursten
    1981   "Serving Notice on the North." *Canadian Forum* (November).

Economic Staff Group, Northern Economic Development Branch, DIAND
    1974   *Regional Impact of a Northern Gas Pipeline.* 7 vols. Ottawa: In-
            formation Canada.

Forth, I. G.; Brown, I. R.; Feenen, M. M.; Parkins, J. P.
    1973   *Mackenzie Valley Report: Some Implications for Planners.* Ottawa:
            Information Canada.

Fumoleau, Rene
    1976   "The Treaties—A History of Exploitation." *Canadian Forum* (No-
            vember).

Gray, J. A., and Gray, P. J.
    1977   "The Berger Report: Its Impact on Northern Pipelines and Decision
            Making in Northern Development." *Canadian Public Policy* 3:4
            (Autumn).

Hobart, Charles, and Kuffer, George
    1978   "Impact of Oil Exploration Work on an Inuit Community." *Arctic
            Anthropology* 15:1.

Ittinuar, Peter
    1981   *Speech to House of Commons, May 15, 1981.* Ottawa: Hansard.

Jackson, Ted
    1977   *Dene Learning for Self-Determination and the Mackenzie Valley
            Inquiry.* Toronto: Participation Research Project.

Jelliss, Arvin
    1977   "The Loss of Economic Rents." In *The Dene Nation,* ed. Mel
            Watkins. Toronto: University of Toronto Press.

Keith, Robert F., et al.
    1976   *Northern Development and Technology Assessment Systems.* Ottawa:
            Information Canada.

McCullum, Hugh
    1975   *This Land Is Not for Sale.* Toronto: Anglican Books.

MacGregor, Ray
    1981   "This Land Is Whose Land." *Macleans*. June 1.

Manual, George
    1976   "An Appeal from the Fourth World." *Canadian Forum* (November).

Matter of Respect
    1976   *Canadian Forum* (November).

Merriwell, John
    1977   "The Distribution of Benefits from a Pipeline." In *The Dene Nation*,
            ed. Mel Watkins. Toronto: University of Toronto Press.

Millar, James, and Fedirchuk, Gloria
    1975   *Mackenzie River Archeological Survey*. Ottawa: Information Canada.

Nahanni, Phoebe
    1977   "The Mapping Project." In *The Dene Nation*, ed. Mel Watkins.
            Toronto: University of Toronto Press.

Northerners Meet Munro with Skepticism and Anger
    1981   *Toronto Globe and Mail*. May 18.

O'Malley, Martin
    1976   *The Past and Future Land*. Toronto: Peter Martin Associates.

Page, Robert
    1973   "The Image of the North." *Canadian Forum* (June).

Palmer, John
    1974   *Monitoring Socio-Economic Change*. Ottawa: Information Canada.

Peacock, Donald
    1977   *People, Peregrines, and Arctic Pipeline*. Vancouver: J. J. Douglas.

Pipeline Assessment Group
    1974   *Mackenzie Valley Pipeline Assessment*. Ottawa: DIAND.

Plafiel, Rudy
    1983   "Natives Raising Sovereignty Demands." *Toronto Globe and Mail*.
            March 9.

Richardson, Boyce
    1976   "James Bay and Mackenzie Valley." *Canadian Forum* (November).

Rosenberg, Gertrude
    1978   *North of 60: Current and Research and Studies Relating to Northern
            Social Concerns*. Ottawa: Department of Supply and Services.

Rushford, Scott
    1977   "Country Food." In *The Dene Nation*, ed. Mel Watkins. Toronto:
            University of Toronto Press.

Sanders, Larry
    1977   "The Berger Day." *Canadian Dimension* 12:3.

Schwartz, Norman
1981   International Development Projects, Communities and Social Impact. Paper presented to Social Impact Analysis and Development Conference, Michigan State University.

Souchotte, Sandra
1981   "Natives Likely to Get a Stake in Pipeline." *Toronto Globe and Mail.* May 2.

Stager, J. K.
1974   *Old Crow, Yukon Territory, and the Proposed Northern Gas Pipeline.* Ottawa: Information Canada.

T'Seleie, Frank
1976   "My People Are Waking Up." *Canadian Forum* (November).

Usher, Peter
1970   *The Bankslanders: Economy & Ecology of a Frontier Trapping Community.* Ottawa: DIAND.
1975   "Northerners and the Land." *Canadian Dimension* 2:3 (October).

Usher, Peter, et al.
1976   *Inuit Land Use and Occupancy Project.* 3 vols. Ottawa: Department of Supply and Services.

Waddell, Ian
1981   *Question in House of Commons, May 14, 1981.* Ottawa: Hansard.
1983   Private correspondence.

Watkins, Mel
1977   *The Dene Nation: The Colony Within.* Toronto: University of Toronto Press.

Part III

Social Impacts of Development Strategies

8
Poverty in Rural Costa Rica: A Conceptual Model

Peggy F. Barlett
Polly F. Harrison

The role of social scientists in international development has expanded in several ways over the past twenty-five years. At present, the primary roles are to design and implement social impact analyses, to troubleshoot as consultants on specific development projects, and to carry out follow-up evaluation studies. This chapter will report on an unusual team effort to provide an overall model and theoretical approach to help the U.S. Agency for International Development (AID) mission in Costa Rica in the formulation of a broad development strategy to ameliorate rural poverty in that country. The central question that faced the team was the following: Given that Costa Rica has experienced considerable economic growth and a rising standard of living in urban and rural areas over the last two decades, and given that it has relatively sophisticated redistributive and social-service mechanisms, why do there persist in rural areas of Costa Rica substantial pockets of poverty? The team was asked to define causes, correlates, and locations of poverty in Costa Rica.

Poverty, in particular, is a difficult and potentially ethnocentric concept. For AID programs to successfully attack "poverty," they must have a clear and accurate notion not only of who the poor people are and where they are located but also of the fundamental causes of that poverty. The Costa Rican team experience was successful in providing a theoretical framework, a working model, and case studies to test the model in a format that was useful to the mission.

Methodology

The team was made up of four North American anthropologists and a sociologist from the National University of Costa Rica.[1] All had carried out long-term field research in rural Central America, had also worked previously with AID in some capacity, and offered skills in general development theory, land reform and agrarian political structures, public

health and nutrition, agriculture, demography, economics, and psychological anthropology. The team carried out its collaborative task in one
month, and the final report was subsequently written by the team leader.

The work began with intense appraisal of various approaches to poverty
currently in use in Costa Rica. Discussion included several independent
researchers and representatives of the Costa Rican National Planning
Office and the National Nutrition Information System. Using the field
experience of the team members, the usefulness of each approach was
assessed, and a working model of the causes and processes of poverty
emerged. The model, which is discussed later in this chapter, included
the observable results of poverty as seen in the lack of fulfillment of
basic needs, economic insecurity, and a lack of control over personal and
familial destiny and well-being. A series of field trips to five major sites
and twenty-one villages allowed the team to test the model's utility in
clarifying these observable results of poverty and the forces that led to
them. The model was then revised, and the findings were presented to
the mission.

Aspects of this methodology were both traditional and innovative.
The goal was a loosely structured, in-depth exploration that could lead
to the formulation and testing of hypotheses about the causes and
configurations of Costa Rican poverty. The team did not seek to carry
out extensive data collection by administering a new survey. Instead, it
was seen as crucial to strive for a synthesis of work previously carried
out and a joining of diverse theoretical, methodological, and political
approaches to address a problem not previously addressed by any specific
team member. Since the topic was broad ranging and complex, interviews
with rural men and women were carried out in an informal, open-ended,
anthropological manner but were guided by an outline of specific questions
generated by the model. The one-month time period was sufficient only
because of each group member's in-depth experience with Costa Rica.
Not only were personal contacts in the different regions important, but
also researchers had had contact with areas over long periods and could
see the longitudinal processes of change and the way they affected the
poor. Finally, the team sought to maintain maximum interaction among
the team members and the different government and aid groups interested
in the outcome. This effort affected the reception of the final report and
also strengthened the deliberation of the team.

Poverty indicators usually deal with the results, not the causes, of
poverty. With its unusually good censuses, Costa Rica has a wealth of
detailed measurements on standard of living, distribution of resources,
and access to facilities (Gonzales 1980). The tendency of most studies is
to look at these indicators and work backward to suggest ultimate causes
(Seligson 1980a). Very detailed maps have been produced by the National
Planning Office (OFIPLAN 1979), and they indicate percentages on the
county level of certain indicators of poverty such as malnutrition, poor
housing, low education, and infant mortality. These maps use the basic

needs perspective and seek to measure the satisfaction of those needs within each geographical area.

There are several problems with beginning an inquiry into the causes of poverty by focusing on indicators. First, the classification of a region as showing high levels of these poverty indicators tends to hide the fact that within these areas, there is still a diversity of wealth and poverty. A "poor canton" is more accurately seen as one with a higher *percentage* of people living in these circumstances while other cantons have a lower percentage (Herrick and Hudson 1977). Team members who had lived for extended periods in rural areas that could not be labeled "extremely poor" on the poverty maps protested that there were nevertheless extremely poor people in the areas studied and that there were wealthy people in even the extremely poor cantons as well.

Another problem is that when poor cantons are identified, researchers are led to ask, What is special about them? Why do they show so many signs of poverty while other areas do not? Thus, attention focuses on the unique aspects of certain geographical areas and the fact that since all areas of Costa Rica have *some* percentage of poor people, some causal forces may be much the same in all areas is ignored. An adequate model of poverty must address the generative forces throughout the country as well as the more special forces that make poverty more prevalent in certain areas. In addition, poverty indicators suffer from all the problems of survey data. The questions may be inappropriate measures, the data may be uneven or outdated, and different indices may target different areas as "extremely poor" (Cespedes et al. 1977).

Approaches to Poverty in Costa Rica

The next step in developing the team's model of poverty was the consideration of the team's own theoretical approaches and those of other pertinent studies and government reports. Of the perspectives currently in use in Costa Rica, six can be separated: three academic approaches, which aim more toward the conceptualization of poverty, and three nonacademic approaches, which aim more toward policy and ameliorative action.

1. From the perspective of the *Parsonian structural functionalist approach*, poverty is seen as a manifestation of a breakdown in some aspect of the social system. This condition is seen as a pathology that is dysfunctional to the stability and maintenance of an otherwise healthy social system. Poverty is conceptualized as a set of rules that belong to certain actors who act and interact in ways that tend to dislocate, disenfranchise, or marginalize them. The main concern of this approach is, not to identify the cause of the pathology, but rather to label and understand its manifestations in individuals' lives (such as "the culture of poverty," alcoholism, or poor housing). By changing the roles played by individuals, it is possible to repair the pathology and to restore the equilibrium of the system.

The Parsonian approach has its greatest popularity in universities and in national and international scientific institutions in Costa Rica, but it is also shared in part with sectors of the general populace. The perspective has influenced several administrations of the National Liberation Party (PLN) and has served as a basis for a wide range of action programs to attack existing subsystems and manifestations of poverty (such as pensions for low income families, subsidies to improve poor housing, and rural health posts). The Parsonian perspective has been the most useful of the approaches that are common in Costa Rica because it enables one to connect a theoretical explanation of poverty to the wide range of data by which poverty is measured. At worst, the structural-functional approach may tend to "blame the victim," but the materials studied by the team did not reflect this bias.

2. The *systems approach* to poverty begins with a conception of the social system as a complex interaction among the diverse parts. Its methodology generally seeks to isolate a manageable subsystem and study all of the activities, inputs, and outputs of that unit. The subsystem is often a "black box" whose interior workings are unknown or imperfectly understood; its contents are knowable mainly through observation of what happens to inputs as they emerge as outputs. On the basis of that information, the researcher suggests what interventions will bring about the desired result in changing poverty.

The time frame of the systems approach is short, and it takes as "given" the larger socioeconomic environment of the poor. Long-term patterns in the interaction of the system have generally not been the focus of work using a systems approach. Although links are sometimes noted between the subsystem studied and the larger national or international system in which it operates, these linkages are not the focus of intervention, nor are historical links the subject of concern.

The systems approach has generally been used by academics or technicians concerned with specific applied problems: agricultural economists, agronomists, and engineers. The systems approach has produced a large number of intensive microstudies and has helped government ministries make better use of resources and identify possible solutions to specific problems. The farming systems approach, for example, can be used to provide useful guidance to plant breeders, but its recommendations may ignore international market constraints or the differential distribution of technology.

Some analysts describe systems theory as a modified structural-functional approach, but in Costa Rica, they form two separate perspectives, which are generally used by different people for different purposes. Both approaches are somewhat bounded in their capacity to explore causality; to understand interrelationships among components, be they strata or subsystems; or to deal with longitudinal and historical dynamics.

3. The *dialectical approach* to poverty sees a close relationship between poverty and wealth. Groups of people who can be defined as poor are seen to have concrete relationships with other groups, and these rela-

tionships determine that some will be impoverished while wealth will be accumulated by others. The focus of research interest here is less on the groups of "poor" than on the historical process by which there emerges the current economic and social relationships between the various groups. Poverty indicators are thus seen as an outward manifestation of this evolving interaction, in which one sector of the population struggles to deprive another sector of the wealth it has produced. The implications of the approach are that poverty can only be remedied by a restructuring of the relationships among the groups of people within the social and economic system and that efforts to redress specific characteristics of poverty are unlikely to be successful if the forces that generate those characteristics remain intact.

The dialectical approach has generated a growing body of literature with a fairly wide readership in both academic and popular circles, but it has had the least effect of the three academic perspectives on political decisions in Costa Rica. One problem is that the unit of study tends to be large, such as all of Central America, and thus implications are less easily translated into recommendations for direct action on specific problems. The dialectical approach is the only one to include any notion of social conflict, and while it has been used in the organization of the rural poor and in the formation of labor unions, this use has been more the exception than the rule.

4. Of the three nonacademic perspectives toward poverty, the *fascist approach* sees the poor as an illegitimate threat to the wealth of the rich and favors the repression of any actions the poor might take to redress their grievances. Such repression may be carried out by the public security organs or by paramilitary groups, but their goal is, in either case, the armed control of the poor.

5. The *democratic approach* stresses "popular participation" in the political arena as a means to ending poverty. The underlying belief is that the poor are poor because they are marginal to the political process and do not have access to the sources of power. Through incorporation into the democratic political process, they will have the means to resolve their problems. Proponents of this perspective aim primarily at motivating the poor to work on the community level but also to take a greater role in national politics as well.

6. The *revolutionary approach* attempts to end poverty through a fundamental change in the economic and social relations that are judged to be its cause. Supporters of this approach see the political arena as the appropriate sector in which to take power from other social classes and to restructure the economy. Adherents of this perspective aim at organizing the poor to change the system, not just to participate in it.

A Model of Poverty

The model of poverty developed, tested, and refined by the team attempts to unite the statistics of poverty indicators—and the reality of

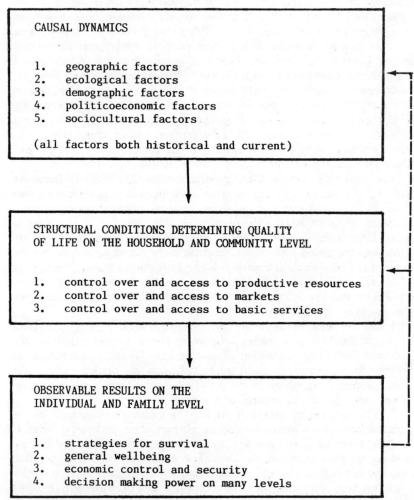

Figure 8.1 A causal model of poverty

daily life they reflect—with the larger forces that generate those conditions. The statistical indicators of poverty, including such variables as the ability to satisfy basic needs, access to health and educational resources, and security of income, can be measured on the individual or family level, the bottom level of the model (see Figure 8.1). The observable results of poverty can be seen in the level of economic control and security, the level of general well-being, the sense of having options and decision-making power on many levels (personal, familial, community, national), and specific strategies for family or personal survival. The notion of poverty in this model is expanded beyond simple malnutrition or relative deprivation to a more complex interaction of material and other conditions of life, which are observable to the researcher.

The individual's or family's experience of poverty is the result of complex causal dynamics, involving geographic, ecological, demographic, political, economic, and sociocultural forces, acting both· in the present and in the past. These larger forces are the top level of the model and may be seen in a regional, national, or international context. This interaction of generative forces provides on the community or household level (the middle level of the model) specific conditions of (1) control over and access to productive resources, (2) control over and access to markets, and (3) control over and access to basic services.

As Figure 8.1 shows, this conceptualization of poverty in Costa Rica begins with national- and international-level dynamics, which structure access to the determinants of the quality of life on the household and community level and which, in turn, cause manifestations in the individual and the family that might be labeled "poverty." The model shows feedback arrows from bottom to top in order to recognize the linkages that feed back and feed forward cybernetically. The model draws from the ex-periential specificity of the Parsonian approach and incorporates the historical and causal analysis of the dialectical approach with the inter-relations of levels of reality characterized by the systems approach.

The goal of the feedback loops in the model is not to suggest that "everything causes everything" but to allow flexibility. Specific variables will be more important than others in determining local-level conditions of comfort or poverty in any given case. Only in studying one location at one time can the primacy of some causal variables be determined. The model urges the researcher to take into consideration a wide range of factors and the consequences of their interactions.

This model avoids several unproductive approaches to poverty. First, it avoids classification of the poor into taxonomies of life-style based on descriptive characteristics. Poor people are located in the model as real human beings in historical circumstances of time and space, not as statistical or logical abstracts. The integral connection between poverty and wealth is recognized, and the long-term processes of social change are incorporated into the explanation of one of the outcomes of that change—poverty. Nor is poverty attributed solely to geographic isolation or a degraded resource base. When such facts emerge, they are embedded in a political, economic, and sociocultural analysis of why resources were channeled elsewhere or why a resource base was degraded. The importance of linking poverty and wealth to groups of interrelated people made it possible for the team to avoid categorizing tribal Indians as automatically poor. Although their material conditions of life are simple, such Indians can enjoy considerable economic security and control over their life decisions, and no one is enriched by their labor. The model requires more analysis than simply a measure of material possessions and life-styles. (A visit to the northern Indian reserve, however, showed a rapid movement toward poverty since both Nicaraguans and Costa Rican whites are encroaching upon this territory.)

A brief example of the interactions of this model can be seen in the Atlantic Coast banana regions of Costa Rica, an area identified by some nutritional measures as having a relatively high percentage of poverty. The development of the banana industry in that area cannot be understood without reference to such macrolevel factors as the market for bananas in the United States; the political decision to build a railroad to the Atlantic Coast (based on the international market for coffee); the ecological situation, which was suited to the monocrop production of bananas; and the availability of labor in other areas of Costa Rica and the Caribbean to migrate to the banana plantations. Geography and climate conspired to make transportation difficult and forced isolated communities to be dependent on the railroad for communication and transportation. These historical forces affected the household and community structures, so that small, independent banana farmers had problematic marketing relations with the railroad and the United Fruit Company and schools and medical facilities came to be provided by the banana plantations rather than by the national government.

Access to land for family farms was also constrained by the plantations, making expensive food purchases and economic dependence on plantation jobs necessary. An analysis of poverty in the region today finds, on the lowest level of the model, that the lack of security in plantation work affects not only the family's economic and nutritional well-being but also their attitudes toward their jobs, their willingness to join unions, and their desire to own farmland. The relatively high wages of banana plantation workers must be set off against the high costs of food, clothing, shelter, and transportation to understand the levels of malnutrition in the area. The model generates awareness of a wide range of contributing factors to these malnutrition indices and suggests that simple interventions, such as a school lunch program, are likely to have limited effects.

This illustration of the model also shows how individual-level results feed back into the other two levels. Participation in union activity can affect the community-level access to such resources as roads, schools, and clinics. Banana-zone strikes can also affect national and international relations and may contribute to the decline or rise of political groups in the capital city. Rising wages and improved infrastructure may attract in-migration to the banana areas, increasing competition for land and jobs (restructuring national demographic patterns) and contributing to increased soil depletion and erosion (affecting, in turn, the ecological conditions of the region and the country).

The model is useful for social impact analysis to trace the links and effects of specific government programs. It provides a middle-level framework (see Chapter 5) in order to see the strategies of specific families and the context in which those strategies evolved. In light of Morgan's comments about the "magnitudes of misery ahead" (see Chapter 1), it is imperative that social scientists provide a framework that can link population dynamics, degraded resources, and economic/political trends to the more or less secure adaptations of individuals to those conditions.

Nicoya—Causal Dynamics and Historical Trends

The western Guanacaste peninsula of Costa Rica was one of the five regions visited by the team; and in the canton of Nicoya at its southern tip, the utility of the model and the generative forces of poverty became abundantly clear. In the detailed look at this one region that follows, the contrasting conditions in three communities will be combined with the cases of two families to illustrate the realities of poverty in the region and the kinds of recommendations generated by the model.

Nicoya's Indian chiefdoms were conquered in the earlier phases of the Spanish colonial period, and isolated, mixed white, African, and Indian agriculturalists subsisted for several hundred years with limited ties to the highlands of Costa Rica (Waibel 1929). In the latter half of the nineteenth century, migrants from the central valley were pushed into new regions by the expansion of coffee haciendas and by the growing population density (Hall 1976, Nunley 1960, Seligson 1980b). Carving out farmland and pasture from the abundant forests of the Nicoya region, these migrants settled among the small and medium farmers and the few cattle haciendas in the area. These new settlers increased the population density of Nicoya and intensified the traditional land uses, leading to a somewhat greater emphasis on livestock production. Government programs were initiated in the 1930s to introduce improved breeds of cattle and pasture grasses, and the success of these activities increased the profitability of cattle production, which led to further deforestation. The Nicoya region still remained geographically and culturally isolated from the capital city and the rest of Costa Rica because of its poor road and river transportation facilities (Biesanz and Biesanz 1944, Wagner 1958).

Cattle ranching increased rapidly in the 1950s as bridges and all-weather roads were completed throughout the peninsula, connecting it with the mainland. High livestock prices and favorable world market conditions further encouraged large landholders to increase cattle production. Over the next twenty years, from 1955 to 1973, the amount of land in pasture jumped from 48 percent to 75 percent of the region (IFAM/AITEC 1976). Forest lands declined, fallow periods were eliminated, and the growing population of the area saw a declining soil fertility of many fields. Rice, the most important crop of the zone, came to be replaced by pasture and corn in these weaker soils, and diseases and declining yields hurt the small agriculturalists most severely. Cropland declined from 29 percent of the land surveyed in 1955 to only 11 percent in 1973. This process of transition from mixed crops and livestock to cattle ranching brought about a severe decline in employment possibilities for landless laborers.

The 1960s saw a reversal of the trends of previous decades as population began to flow out of Nicoya. The economic and ecological changes in the region pushed landless and small farmers to look for work on the banana plantations and in urban areas. Out-migrants were disproportionately men, seeking employment, which left behind communities with skewed female-male ratios. The population growth rate declined as a result of separations, abandonments, and high percentages of single women (Thien 1975).

The 1970s saw the widespread collapse of smallholder agriculture. A brief government program to support basic grains production only fostered increased mechanization and created worsening terms of trade for the small producers (Thurber 1980). High national rice production by the end of the decade resulted in stagnant prices, and credit for small farmers was scarce or nonexistent. In addition, the shift to pasture created ecological disruptions. Many residents and some scientific observers say that the annual rainfall has declined and that the dry season now is longer. The vast deforestation of the peninsula has combined with erosion problems to lower the carrying capacity of some pastures to one-fourth of their previous levels. With fertilizer prices soaring, small farmers cannot overcome the degraded resource base with input purchases. Thus, the ecological and geographic characteristics of Nicoya have been modified by economics, politics, and demographic forces and have, in turn, cybernetically interacted with them to transform the region.

Dynamics of Poverty at the Household and Community Levels

Three communities in the Nicoya area will illustrate the different outcomes of these processes on the middle level of the model. The historical forces just outlined created different conditions for each of the three communities (called here Alpha, Beta, and Gamma) in their control over and access to productive resources, markets, and basic services.

Located on the eastern shore of the Nicoya peninsula, Alpha was a "boom village" in the 1960s when it was the docking point for the launch to the mainland. Families in Alpha supported themselves partly by commerce and services to travelers and partly by fishing and farming along the coast. Although the simple wooden boats of most Alpha fishermen reached only nearby coastal waters, fishing traditionally sufficed to bring a good cash income to supplement farming. Access to markets was no problem given the good road and constant traffic passing through the village.

The well-being of many Alpha families has been hurt by two major changes in recent years. First, the launch was replaced by a ferry with a new docking point to the north, which made Alpha a commercial ghost town. Income derived from the flow of people and goods dried up, and markets for fish and other products were more problematic as well. Second, just as Alphans were becoming more dependent on fishing, fish and shellfish populations in the coastal estuaries declined. Chemical effluents from mechanized rice production to the north, particularly drift from aerial spraying on large tracts, damaged marine life. Further, these small-scale fishing people now suffered from competition with larger, commercial boats from the mainland. Such high-powered craft not only fished a wider area but also reached markets faster, which meant better prices. Thus, both ecological degradation and technological competition affected the community. Families in Alpha faced a severe reduction in their subsistence options, and diet information gathered by the team reflected this situation. Much of the diet was purchased, leaving the families vulnerable to Costa Rica's rapid inflation, and most of the fish catch was sold for needed cash rather than consumed at home. In Alpha, many households were made up of women and children. Some received remittances, but others were struggling to survive by the sale of eggs, chickens, ice cream and by taking in laundry. These strategies for survival were seen by the Alphans themselves as tenuous and relatively unproductive.

Beta provides a sharp contrast to Alpha. Until the mid-1960s, Beta was a quiet farming village with many independent farming families and a few larger estates that employed hired labor. Roughly one-third of the households in the community were landless (though most were able to rent land to supplement their wages), and the majority of the land was owned by a small number of large or absentee landholders. The majority of the people of the village, however, were small or medium-sized farmers who were active in school and civic groups and energetic in making community improvements such as building a church, a graveled road, and a community center.

Government programs and incentives in rice production led to increased mechanization and labor displacement in Beta, and the forces noted above pushed many landholders more toward cattle ranching as well. One nearby farm, with over 4,000 acres, moved from providing work for eighty resident families to hiring just four full-time hands. As laborers were displaced and migrated to join the poor in other regions of Costa Rica, small and medium farmers who needed occasional hired help suffered as well. The loss of workers to supplement family labor combined with soil depletion, input cost increases, credit shortages, and low commodity support prices to drive small and medium farmers out of agriculture.

By 1980, Beta had become a suburb of the town of Nicoya. With the new ferry slip came a new highway through the village. The road attracted some middle-class professionals and real estate speculators who bought lots and built fancy homes. Facing soaring land prices, young couples could no longer afford to buy farmland, and with the fragmentation of already small family plots, the land was often sold to outsiders. The constant traffic of trucks, buses, and cars turned the attention of people in Beta outward, and the level of community activity diminished.

The decline in employment opportunities in agriculture limited survival options for landless families who wished to remain in Beta. The most secure option was a steady job on a large farm, but such jobs were rare, and many workers found they were fired just before they had completed ninety days of work so that the landowner could avoid social security taxes and other legal obligations. Opportunities for temporary wage labor were also scarce because of the advent of mechanization. Land to rent for agriculture was seldom available, but when it was, rents were required in advance, and few poor families had access to extra cash before planting time.

Salaried white-collar or public-sector jobs provided an important option for some landless families. Although most adults did not have sufficient education for such jobs, high percentages of their children did attend high school. Some adults even commuted to town on the evening bus for the nocturnal high school. With diploma in hand, many people obtained jobs in distant cities while others found work with such employers as the National Park Service or in skilled trades. These salaried employees were often the mainstay of whole family networks of otherwise marginal people in Beta.

Thus, Beta changed from a diverse farming and ranching community to a predominantly cattle-ranching area characterized by large estates and a few landless laborers. Families that remained in the village were often sustained by remittances from out-migrants, and with the change in transportation modes, the village began to lose its independent character and was in the process of becoming a suburb of the canton capital. The poverty of Betan families must be seen in the context of this economic, ecological, and social transformation.

Conditions in the third community, Gamma, reflect a transition from farming to tourism. Located on the western side of the peninsula and more isolated than either Alpha or Beta, Gamma, until the 1970s was less attractive both to migrants and to mechanized farmers. The same forces that led to a decline in farming throughout the region hurt farmers in Gamma, but farming had not yet collapsed when the study was done. Close to beautiful beaches, the area began to attract tourists and investors once an adequate road had been built by the government. Services such as a health post, a school lunch program, electrification, and piped water were provided. Regular bus service was slow, but it provided adequate access to local markets and urban health and educational facilities. Access to basic services was inadequate only for the hamlets further into the interior of the peninsula from Gamma, which were cut off seasonally by rising rivers and streams. This geographic barrier interrupted schooling and hampered access to health care and may be an important factor in the high infant mortality statistics of this area.

Several familiar patterns were observed in Gamma: low prices for agricultural products and high input and transportation costs had weakened the farming economy. Ecological changes—both weather and soil depletion—contributed to this decline. Livestock production became dominant, employment opportunities declined, and many young men left to seek work elsewhere. The remaining rice producers protested government policies that favored other regions, and credit for production was generally unavailable. Inflation hurt farmers, ranchers, and laborers alike, and so far, the beaches have brought only higher land prices and little increased employment, though a few landless families have moved closer to the coast in search of seasonal jobs.

Organized efforts to change the conditions in the area were few. In a community near Gamma, a group of landless families invaded a large absentee-owned farm and began to cultivate it. Such land invasions have occurred in several areas of Costa Rica and represent the most active response to a general alienation from large landholders, from the national government, and from "capital." On the one hand, the team heard many Alpha, Beta, and Gamma residents describe Costa Rica as a place of freedom of speech where kidnappings and torture are not problems as they are in nearby countries. On the other hand, many families felt the government works against the poor and is bought off by the rich landowners. Personal security with regard to crime was high; crime was seen to be an urban problem and not yet an issue in rural Nicoya. But throughout these conversations, there was revealed a sense of *limits*, of the finiteness of the land, jobs, oil, food, and places to migrate, and a growing anger and frustration because of the monopoly of resources by a few.

Two Families: In Contrast

The complex dimensions of poverty can be illustrated by two Nicoyan families interviewed during the team's visit. The first lived beside a large farm in Alpha, and the father was a peon, or hired hand. The members of the second family were independent farmers in Gamma. The peon family was at home on Sunday afternoon—relaxing, watching television, and talking together. There were three young children, all of whom were well dressed in T-shirts and shorts or pants. The husband wore a stylish cotton-print shirt, leather shoes, and store-bought trousers. The wife had on a fashionable cotton dress. Their house was three years old, dating from the time when the husband began to work for this landowner. They had previously lived on the other side of town but had moved to live on the *patron's* land. The house was made in the modern style, with a varnished wood porch out front, a corrugated metal roof, glass windows, and stuffed vinyl furniture. With the television set and the purchased clothing, it would not be possible to label this family "poor." Talking with the father, however, revealed an essential insecurity in his life, a sense of having no control over his employment. He had lost work several times before and once had lost his social security medical coverage. That loss had been particularly traumatic because one of his children was asthmatic and had had several bad episodes when the family could not afford to take him to the doctor.

In sharp contrast was the farming family in Gamma. Their house was a typical Guanacaste *rancho*, of which few can be seen nowadays. The walls were rough hand-hewn boards, and the light came in freely through the holes in the walls. It had a thatched roof, and the furnishings were rough, handmade benches and a table. There were a few plastic buckets and cooking implements, but many of the kitchen items were made from gourds and other natural materials. The father wore no shoes, and his clothing was homemade. The mother and daughter wore plastic sandals and homemade dresses. Clearly, in terms of material possessions, this family was very poor. Yet, in contrast to the peon family, which did not offer the team hospitality, this family offered a snack of rice, beans, tortillas, fried eggs, homemade sour cream, and coffee. A large corn cake sat on the table. When discussing their diet, they admitted that the rice shortages in the past year had affected them, too, but when asked what they ate when there was no rice, they replied: "Oh, there are always eggs. And beans. We're happy eating beans without rice." The family had three to four *manzanas* (five to seven acres) of land and rented a bit more. They had cows, pigs, and chickens and grew all their own corn and beans. "I hardly buy anything at the store," boasted the father. Only salt, lard, and coffee were major weekly purchases.

These two cases illustrate the observable results of poverty on the individual and family level. The strategies for survival of the peon family involve efforts to keep good relations with the landowner to preserve the steady income. General well-being at the moment can be said to be high, but security is low, and past experience shows that this family's well-being is fragile. They are at the mercy of the landholder, who may decide to sell the farm or fire his worker, and replacement jobs are hard to find. In contrast, the members of the independent farming family have a secure diet and are grateful to escape the ravages of inflation that have hurt their sons, who must purchase food. Their standard of living in terms of consumer goods is far below what most Costa Ricans would consider acceptable. They have great security with simple consumption patterns. Neither family feels it has much power over the larger forces that are eroding agriculture in the region, but the daily lives of the farmers are free from the control of an employer. The sons of the farmer have left the area to work on the banana plantations in the central valley. The father says they do not live better there, but they have been able to find work, and there was no land or work available in Gamma. The children of the peon are still young, but his own siblings and his wife's have migrated elsewhere. For both families, this loss of nearby relatives cuts down on the number of people they can count on for emergency help—lowering their security and leaving their survival strategies even more fragile.

Recommendations

When the model was presented to the AID mission, the structural determinants of poverty were emphasized. In the area of markets, for instance, the decision made by the National Production Council to shift credit for most agricultural production out of Nicoya and to support mechanized rice production in another area of Costa Rica had had massive effects on the well-being of farmers in Nicoya. Alternative income sources have not been created, and out-migration has been the main alternative for displaced farmers. That malnutrition rates should be high in a region in which traditional agriculture has collapsed and female-headed households are common (and jobs for women scarce) should come as no surprise. Likewise, the government's support of cattle production and the credit policies that favor larger ranching units have acted to generate the conditions of poverty as well. School feeding programs, rural health posts, and mobile medical teams can make an impact on the services the poor receive, but they cannot touch the generative causes of poverty. As the region is further degraded ecologically, cattle ranches consolidate ever-larger holdings, and inflation takes its toll on the families that struggle to purchase food, such ameliorative programs will face an even more difficult task.

In the end, the model helped the AID mission clarify the kinds of interventions that may tend to address the situation of the poor. Since credit for cattle production has long been a part of AID's activities in Costa Rica, revealing the consequences of such programs makes possible a reconsideration. Important decisions have to be made, not only by the donors of aid funds, but by the government itself. Will landless and small farmers benefit at the expense of the large mechanized rice farmers, the cattle ranchers, or the absentee landowners? Is the commitment to a nationwide participation in a rising standard of living sufficient to offset the loss of income because of reduced cattle exports, the costs of reforestation, or lowered rice production if chemical spraying is curtailed to protect fisheries? Will international lending agencies allow such a policy, given that it will hurt short-run debt repayment, even though it may be crucial for long-run economic prosperity and political democracy?

Access to productive resources, to markets, and to basic services must be combined together to reverse the decline in the standard of living of the rural poor. The subsistance farmer just described is a remnant of a dying way of life, and his children have already moved on, landless and illiterate, to try to find work on the banana plantations. This analysis of the Nicoya canton shows that within the historical context of one place, it is no mystery why, in the context of economic growth and relatively high per capita income and functioning redistributive and social service mechanisms, there persist in Costa Rica substantial pockets of rural poverty. The same forces that have generated the wealth and rising national incomes, and the tax revenues by which redistributive and social service mechanisms are supported, have generated as well the conditions of poverty in Costa Rica.

The Impact on AID

The AID mission in Costa Rica responded positively to the team's analysis and recommendations. There was agreement that, for the most part, rural poverty was heterogeneous and woven throughout the fabric of social and economic life. Emphasis was shifted away from a focus on "pockets of poverty" toward a structural view, in which poverty was linked to national policy and economic dynamics, social class, job security, and access to the factors of production. Given this view, the mission staff concluded that there would have to be fundamental alterations in national development and trade policies. Like any structural change, these alterations were viewed as potentially challenging, and in the Costa Rican case, as a test of the durability of the social consensus and the collective will of a population accustomed to improvement and not to sacrifice. Program prescriptions turned to increased availability of agricultural credit, land, and technical assistance and, for instance, the development of agroindustrial enterprises in cattle-producing zones. There was talk of forthcoming austerity, the need for exchange rate and currency and adjustments as well as budgetary and trade policy reform, and the development of nontraditional exports.

Recommendations to address rural poverty in the 1980s were rapidly overcome by the economic crisis in Costa Rica. The period just prior to the team's efforts had been marked by some disturbing trends, some of which have been noted above in the lives of people interviewed: a decline in real economic growth and per capita income, which began in 1977; inflation over 25 percent from 1977 to 1979; rising unemployment; declining agricultural productivity; and a 50 percent currency devaluation. An economic analysis by the Academia de Costa Rica, sponsored by and concurred with by AID, attributed these trends to declining terms of trade, increases in world oil prices, decreases in coffee prices, exhaustion of hitherto successful import-substitution and land-extensive industrial and agricultural strategies, a public sector grown too large and inefficient, and a constriction in private capital flows. The predictions were for these trends to continue and get worse, in the absence of a serious stabilization effort. The poor were expected to suffer most and to need increasingly the very social welfare programs that had contributed to the fiscal problems.

The year after the team's report, 1981, these same macroeconomic trends intensified: Imports contracted sharply, triple-digit inflation followed by persistent devaluations wrecked the budget and public confidence, the public-sector deficit soared, unemployment increased, and foreign exchange reserves and foreign lending to Costa Rica further declined. Cutbacks in social services, especially in health and welfare, added increasingly to the burdens on the poor. Observers attributed these patterns to the results of long-term trends and expected such second-generation effects as increased childhood malnutrition, infant mortality, crime, and acts of terrorism. Solutions were seen as correspondingly long-term and potentially stressful for the traditional Costa Rican social compact, particularly if there were a popular perception that the government was not addressing the basic problems appropriately.

The development approach that was adopted was based on a dynamic private sector (in keeping with the policies of the new Reagan administration) and a "growth with equity" model. Economic stabilization, employment generation, and the development of nontraditional exports were the general goals, and specific efforts were indicated in the areas of balance of payments support, financial recuperation (particularly in the private sector), and food aid to redress shortages. Technical assistance was indicated for the public sector (especially in health-related areas) to enhance efficiency and lower recurrent costs, for agriculture to improve access to the factors of production, and for family planning, housing energy, and technology. Thus, the focus of efforts turned away from the rural poor specifically and toward more general efforts to address the national crisis.

By 1983, programs and policies to ameliorate the economic situation could be seen as tending to worsen some of the same structural conditions identified by the team report as contributing to rural poverty. In late 1983, the government of Costa Rica, published a document entitled *Economic Policy: Strategy and Actions, 1984–86* under the joint authorship of a special commission of high-level representatives from the Central Bank and the Ministries of Planning, Finance, and Exports and Investment. The document expressed commitment to the consolidation of the stabilization program begun in mid-1982. In an agreement with the International Monetary Fund, this stabilization program had brought inflation back to a 10 percent annual level, restructured the public-sector external debt, and unified currency exchange rates. The persistent problems remaining to be addressed were identified as public sector finances, high unemployment, a continued drop in exports, only minimal recovery in domestic production, and disheartening forecasts for the market prices of traditional exports over the next few years. These trends were further complicated by the context of regional economic depression and political instability.

The corresponding strategy opted for by the Costa Rican government, and to all appearances supported by the international donor community, was a maximum possible increase in traditional exports, such as beef, bananas, and coffee; the provision of stimuli for investments in new export-oriented activities; and the penetration of new markets by Costa Rican products. The cornerstones of a proposed consolidation of economic stability were reduction of the fiscal deficit and a reorientation of the monetary strategy, to be carried out by policies favoring employment generation, social equity, and a greater role for the private sector. The corresponding AID strategy centered on support for structural reform (thus maintaining some commitment to the steps needed to address rural poverty) but was tied also to parallel support for export-led economic growth. Much of this growth was to come from agriculture, aided by better planning, adjustments in interest rates and commodity pricing policies, increased production and diversification efforts, national foodgrain self-sufficiency, improved agricultural credit, and efforts to increase land ownership. Attention to equity issues was implicit in programs aimed at employment generation, improvement of low income housing, vocational training, and access to family planning—all through the private sector.

What appears to have happened is that the sharpening economic crisis, which began to be felt in 1978, together with a trend on the part of the U.S. government toward the philosophies undergirding the Kissinger Commission Report, have made it harder to focus on the poor as a target group, both practically and philosophically. AID portfolios for the years since the team report reflect very little that is new in the history of AID development activities in Costa Rica. What has changed is emphasis, priority, rhetoric, and ideology. In the arena of national policy and debate, the poor have not disappeared from concern as that would be antithetical to the Costa Rican tradition. Instead, the social programs fashioned in years of plenty are reeling under the blows of the years of lean. It is ironic that the anthropological response to the persistence of poverty identified the very macroeconomic political forces that overwhelmed both the country and the AID mission's original charge to the team. The poor and the team's recommendations have been overtaken by events.

Notes

1. The team consisted of Polly Harrison, AID regional social science adviser and team leader; Francisco Escobar, University of Costa Rica; Stephen Sellers, Harvard University School of Public Health; Jefferson Boyer, University of North Carolina; and Peggy Barlett, Emory University. The team also benefited from the input of Mitchell Seligson, Miriam Wouters, and Mario Tristan. This summary of the team's experience draws heavily from the final report, written by Harrison, and from the survey of theories of poverty contributed by Escobar, but all five team members cooperated to produce the ideas and data presented here.

The authors would like to express their appreciation to all the above contributors to this project and especially to the members of the AID mission in Costa Rica.

References

Biesanz, John, and Mavis Biesanz
    1944   *Costa Rican Life.* New York: Columbia University Press.

Cespedes, V. H., et al.
    1977   Poverty in Costa Rica: Methodological Problems in the Determination of Some of Its Characteristics. San Jose: Academia de Centro America. Mimeograph.

Gonzales, Vega, and Claudio Gonzales
1980 Costa Rica: Problemas Economicos Para la Decada de los 80. San Jose: Academia de Centro America. Mimeograph.

Hall, Carolyn
1976 *El Cafe y el Desarollo Historico-Geografico de Costa Rica.* San Jose: Editorial Universidad de Costa Rica y Universidad Nacional.

Herrick, G., and B. Hudson
1977 *The Nature of Poverty in Costa Rica.* San Jose.

Hirschman, Albert O.
1967 *Development Projects Observed.* Washington, D.C.: Brookings Institution.

IFAM/AITEC
1976 *Resumen Cantonal: Nicoya.* San Jose.

Nunley, Robert E.
1960 *The Distribution of Population in Costa Rica.* Washington, D.C.: National Academy of Sciences, National Research Council.

OFIPLAN (Oficina Nacional de Planificacion de Costa Rica)
1979 *Mapeo de La Pobreza.* San Jose.

Seligson, Mitchell
1980a *Notes on the Etiology of Poverty in Costa Rica: Memorandum to CDSS Working Group and Anthropologists.* San Jose: USAID.
1980b *Peasants of Costa Rica and the Development of Agrarian Capitalism.* Madison: University of Wisconsin Press.

Shyrock, Henry, and Jacob S. Siegel
1976 *The Methods and Materials of Demography.* New York: Academic Press.

Thien, Tin Myaing
1975 Contraception in Costa Rica: A Sociocultural Study of Three Communities. Unpublished dissertation, Department of Anthropology, Columbia University. Ann Arbor, Mich.: University Microfilms #75-25, 734.

Thurber, C. E.
1980 Politicians, Bureaucrats, and Peasants: The Case of the Costa Rican National Program of Basic Grains. *Practicing Anthropology* 2:5-6.

Wagner, Philip L.
1958 Nicoya: A Cultural Geography. *University of California, Publications in Geography* 12(3):195-250.

Waibel, Leo
1929 White Settlements in Costa Rica. *Geographical Review* 29(4):529-560.

9
Nutrition, Social Impact, and Development: A Mexican Case

Kathryn G. Dewey

Introduction

Although the need for social impact analysis of development projects has become increasingly apparent in recent years, the methodological approach for such evaluations and the specific measures that should be used are not quite as clear-cut. The purpose of this chapter is to advocate the inclusion of indicators of nutritional status in social impact analysis. I will begin by discussing *why* nutrition should be an important component of evaluating changes brought about by development, then I will discuss *how* nutritional indices can be used in social impact analysis and the *kinds* of changes in nutrition that often accompany development. Finally, I will describe the results of a case study in southern Mexico in which the impact of agricultural development on diet and nutrition was examined.

Nutritional Factors in Social Impact Analysis

The difficulty of defining and measuring development has been a subject of debate for many years, and it is not my intention to reiterate the arguments here. However, it is worthwhile to repeat what has been pointed out by many people: that the traditional measures of development used by economists, such as the rate of growth in gross national product and per capita income, do not adequately reflect changes in the quality of life in different segments of a population. Numerous examples exist of countries and areas that have experienced substantial economic growth but little or no improvement in food consumption or nutritional status for the lower income groups (e.g., Chile: Hakim and Solimano 1978; Mexico: Hernandez et al. 1974; India: Thimmayamma et al. 1976). Even in the newly rich oil-producing nations such as Libya, malnutrition continues in the face of widespread increases in wealth (Mamarbachi et al. 1980). It is critical, then, that social impact analyses of development include indicators that reflect quality of life better than the standard economic indices do. If carefully designed, nutrition studies have the potential for being extremely useful in this regard, as measures of nutritional status are both relatively quantifiable and clearly related to living conditions. It is important to note, however, that studies that incorporate nutritional indicators should assess not only the *average* nutritional status, but also the *distribution* of malnutrition. A great deal of information is often obscured by the use of the "meaningless mean."

Nutritional Indices in Social Impact Analysis

Although there have been attempts to include nutritional indices in assessing development, discussions focusing on this topic often become mired in the difficulties of how to define and measure malnutrition. This situation occurs because there is no one definition of malnutrition, rather, there are several categories of measurements that can be made, all of which reflect nutritional status. There are five broad categories of nutritional indices, which can be labeled conveniently from A to E as follows:

A. *Anthropometric.* Anthropometric measurements of nutritional status include all measures of the physical dimensions of the human body. Because growth and fatness are usually closely related to the adequacy of a person's nutritional intake, anthropometric measurements such as weight; stature (length or height); circumferences of the head, arm, or leg; and skinfold thickness are considered good overall indicators of nutritional status, especially for children who are still growing. Such measures have the advantages of being relatively easy to make and of being widely understood by most people. To assess malnutrition by measuring growth, however, necessitates an understanding of the distinction between current, acute malnutrition and past, chronic malnutrition. If a child is low in weight for his or her age, for example, it may be due to inadequate growth in the past, or excessive thinness at present, or to a combination of both. One needs measures of *both* weight and height in order to differentiate between these possibilities: Information on height can indicate long-term malnutrition, and information on a child's relative weight-for-height can indicate current malnutrition (fatness).

Another consideration in the use of anthropometric measurements is the choice of the growth reference data, or "standards," to be used. Should one use data gathered from a population in which growth is assumed to be optimal but which may be of a different ethnic background, or should one use data from a population of the same background for which growth may not be optimal? There is currently an ongoing debate about which of these alternatives is preferable (see Neumann 1979, for example); the choice depends greatly on the availability of adequate reference data in each situation.

B. *Biochemical.* Biochemical measures of nutritional status include measurements of nutrient levels (or precursors or metabolites of nutrients) in the blood or urine, such as hemoglobin and hematocrit, which reflect anemia, serum levels of vitamin A or ascorbic acid, and urinary thiamin and riboflavin. Although biochemical measures are probably the most accurate indicators of nutritional status for particular nutrients, they require laboratory assistance and can be quite expensive. Their use depends on the kinds of malnutrition prevalent in a population (e.g., vitamin A deficiency, iron-deficiency anemia) and the extent to which investigators wish to determine the levels of "subclinical" nutrient deficiencies.

C. *Clinical.* The third category of measures of nutritional status is the assessment of clinical signs of malnutrition, such as the classic symptoms of scurvy, rickets, goiter, pellagra, and other nutrient deficiencies. In some cases, such symptoms are relatively easy to detect and require little expertise to recognize, but in others, there is a great deal of subjectivity in their assessment. For this reason, there may be considerable interobserver variability in detecting clinical signs of malnutrition. Furthermore, many clinical symptoms do not appear until the nutrient deficiency has become extreme, and thus, many cases of less severe malnutrition may go unnoticed. Nonetheless, clinical assessment is an important tool in many situations.

D. *Dietary.* Measurement of dietary intake is an important, though often laborious, component of nutritional assessment. Techniques for estimating dietary intake include group or household inventories and individual measures of dietary intake such as food records, dietary recalls, and food frequency lists (see Marr 1971). Calculations of amounts consumed are usually compared with recommended allowances or standards in order to estimate the magnitude of any nutrient deficiencies that might exist. The major drawback to dietary intake assessment is that there are numerous sources of error owing to intentional or unintentional bias in reporting intake, the inability of respondents to remember everything they have eaten, differences between different interviewers, inaccuracies in estimation of amounts, variation in nutrient content of foods, and incomplete food consumption tables, in addition to the normal daily variation in food consumption of individuals. For this reason, studies that have as an objective the assessment of nutritional status should always include other measures in addition to dietary intake information. Despite the problems associated with dietary assessment, it is a necessary part of nutritional assessment if the investigators wish to determine which nutrients are most likely to be insufficient in any given population. It has been through dietary studies in the past two decades, for example, that investigators have recognized that inadequate protein intake is much less common than previously assumed and that the prevalence of protein-calorie malnutrition is more a result of inadequate energy intake than of inadequate protein intake.

E. *Ecological.* The final category of nutritional assessment includes general measures within a community that reflect nutritional status. These include a variety of health and social statistics, but the most useful for gauging malnutrition are data concerning infant and child mortality. These mortality rates are strongly influenced by nutrition, either directly, if malnutrition is extreme, or indirectly via increased susceptibility to infections. Statistics on morbidity and mortality rates for specific illnesses such as gastrointestinal infections can also reflect general nutritional status. Depending on the agricultural system, data on food production and distribution can be useful if they are detailed enough to show more than just average figures. The advantage of ecological measures is that they can usually be obtained through existing data, and thus require little time or money. However, they do not directly measure nutritional status.

From the preceding categorization, it is quite obvious that there is a wide variety of nutritional indices that can be used in social impact analysis. The choice of which measures are most appropriate depends on the characteristics of the target group(s), the kind of study design that is feasible (e.g., longitudinal versus cross-sectional), and the level of approach that is desired (usually determined by how much time and money are available). Christakis (1973), for example, lists three levels of nutritional assessment: minimal, mid-level, and in-depth. The measures included in each of these levels vary with the age group as well: There are separate lists of measures recommended for infants and children (birth to twenty-four months, two to five years, six to twelve years), for adolescents, for pregnant and lactating women, for adults, and for the elderly. Each level includes anthropometric, biochemical, clinical, dietary, and "medical and socioeconomic" measures.

Many of the nutritional indices can be easily incorporated into social impact studies, even if the investigators are not experts in nutrition themselves. It takes relatively little training, for example, to measure the height and weight of children, to determine morbidity and mortality figures, or to ask a few simple questions relating to dietary intake. The kinds of quantitative information that can be collected by including nutritional indicators may provide more compelling evidence of changes in quality of life than other measures: Few people would argue that an increase or decrease in the number of malnourished children is not important, for example, whereas there might be an argument about whether certain changes in social structures are desirable or undesirable.

What Changes in Nutrition Are Likely?

Elsewhere (Dewey 1979), I have elaborated more extensively on how diet and nutrition may be affected by development, specifically agricultural development. Sadly, most of the examples one finds (from the few studies that have been done) show that for the majority of rural families in the Third World, agricultural development is more often associated with deleterious dietary changes than with improvements in nutrition. There are a number of effects of agricultural development that may have an impact on nutrition. First, agricultural development in many parts of the world has drastically changed land tenure relations and the distribution of land. Although in some cases this change results in a more equitable distribution of land, in most cases the result has been that small farmers have access to less land and the number of landless peasants increases. Since nutritional status has been shown to be directly related to land availability (Valverde et al. 1977, Rawson and Valverde 1976), changes that reduce the amount of land available to small farmers are likely to have negative nutritional consequences. Critics of the Green Revolution have pointed out that agricultural development is often accompanied by an increased stratification in wealth. Because nutritional status is usually closely related to economic status, this increased stratification leads to greater poverty and malnutrition among the poorer segments of a population. Agricultural development projects that foster a transformation from subsistence production (meaning that food produced is consumed in the home) to commercial production often result in a loss of control over production by peasant farmers as they come to rely more and more on credit and technological inputs. The increased risk associated with cash cropping may lead to a greater possibility of indebtedness and marginalization of peasant families. All of these changes can jeopardize the health and nutritional status of a family in the long run.

Even under conditions in which land tenure and economic status are not greatly affected, the shift from subsistence to commercial production can affect diet and nutrition in a number of ways. The most obvious result of a shift to cash cropping is that the family now has cash in place of food. In principle, if the cash obtained is at least equivalent to the amount needed to purchase the food that would have been produced, then the family should be able to have the same diet as before. However, the situation is vastly more complicated. For example, foods that are purchased may not be of equivalent nutritional value as those previously produced at home, especially if the most nutritious foods are prohibitively expensive (such as vegetables, fruits, meat, and milk). In addition, the family may need (or may choose) to use the cash for other purposes, such as taxes, clothing, prestige items, or alcohol. The quality of the diet may subsequently suffer, especially for the younger children.

Other effects of the shift from subsistence to commercial cultivation include changes in the types of crops grown, e.g., from a diverse polyculture to a monoculture cash crop. This change can have a dramatic effect on dietary quality, as is evidenced by the situation in several areas in Africa in which diverse crop mixtures of yams, maize, rice, beans, groundnuts, vegetables, and pineapples are being replaced by less labor-intensive crops, such as cassava, so that more time can be spent growing cash crops (see Idusogie 1969). Commercial production usually is accompanied by a reduction in the length of fallow periods, which results in a reduction in the availability of wild plants and wild game as the extent of secondary vegetation decreases.

Finally, it must be pointed out that the larger social impact of the shift to commercial production can also affect nutritional status. For example, with a decrease in subsistence production, the reciprocal exchange of food and other products may also decline as cash becomes the major means of exchange. Those families in a community who previously survived in part because of a social system that encourged the sharing of food may find themselves in jeopardy during times of scarcity. In addition, it has been noted that the staus of women in a community may be detrimentally affected by increased commercial production. Since women are generally the "gatekeepers" of food within a family, such a change can ultimately harm the nutritional status of family members, especially the younger children (see Stavrakis and Marshall 1978, for example).

In the remainder of this chapter, I describe a case study in an area of southern Mexico that has undergone considerable agricultural development in recent years. Many of the types of dietary change described above are illustrated by the results of the case study.

Impact of Agricultural Development on Diet and Nutrition in Tabasco, Mexico

The Study Area

The state of Tabasco, where the Plan Chontalpa has been implemented, has undergone considerable agricultural development in recent years, resulting in a rapid expansion of land devoted to commercial cash crops and pasture for cattle. It is a hot, humid tropical lowland area (rainfall 2,000–4,000 mm. per year) located on the Gulf Coast in southeastern Mexico. Much of the area was subject to periodic flooding for several months each year until an extensive drainage project was begun in the 1950s. The drainage project was the forerunner of the Plan Chontalpa, a large-scale project initiated by the Mexican government in the late 1960s in order to increase agricultural production in the area. Within the Plan Chontalpa, there are twenty-two adjacent collective *ejidos* (peasant communities cooperatively organized by the government), which were formed through the expropriation of existing ejidal and private lands and the mandatory relocalization of residents into the new collectives. Agriculture in each ejido is based on a combination of private and collective production: Each family has a two-hectare plot of land to farm as they wish in addition to the thirteen hectares per family that are devoted to the collective production of cash crops and cattle. Members of each ejido (*socios*) are paid wages for their work on the collective land. Approximately 200 families live in rows of government-constructed cement-block houses in a central village (*poblado*) within each ejido and are provided with basic services such as water, electricity, primary schools, and in seven of the twenty-two ejidos, a health clinic. Surrounding each family's house is a small *solar* (household garden area), which is generally used for fruit and shade trees and for raising domesticated animals. Although members of the plan make up the majority of the workers, there is a large number of *libre*, or nonmember, families who attempt to find work within the ejidos as well. Libre families generally live in thatched houses on the outskirts of each poblado, and they are usually relatives or children of socios or are families who were not able to become members of the plan when it was begun (primarily landless laborers).

Outside of the Plan Chontalpa, there are scattered villages in which both subsistence and commercial farming are practiced to varying degrees, usually in combination with wage labor. The village of Tecominoacan (abbreviated to "Teco" in this chapter), located on the southern border of the Plan Chontalpa, represents an area in which a mostly self-provisioning, subsistence agriculture is being increasingly replaced by cattle production. Teco was chosen for this study in order to investigate the impact of the expansion of cattle production in addition to serving as a comparison with the Plan Chontalpa. About half of the approximately 165 families of Teco have at least part of their land devoted to pasture for cattle.

The recent expansion of oil exploration and production in Tabasco has greatly affected the entire study area. Although there are increased job opportunities for skilled laborers, the primary effect for most families has been the inflation of food prices in the area. The high cost of food coupled with a reduced production of subsistence crops by many families has made it extremely difficult for many families to obtain an adequate diet.

The Study Design

In order to assess the impact of the Plan Chontalpa on diet and nutrition and to examine the influence of agricultural change in general, a nutrition survey of 149 preschool children was conducted both within and outside of the Plan Chontalpa. Nutritional status was evaluated for children aged two to four years because children of this age are very susceptible to malnutrition and indices of growth can be easily measured as a reflection of nutritional condition. The study was designed as a cross-sectional comparison of children from three groups: from families who are members of the ejidos of the plan (socios), nonmember families (libres), and families in the nearby village of Tecominoacan (Teco). In the Plan Chontalpa, five ejidos were randomly selected, and in each ejido, families were selected at random until there were fifteen socio families with children two to four years old. Libre families were selected at random from the three ejidos that had a large number of libres living in them, and all of the libre families were selected from the other two for a total of twenty-five libre families. In Teco, eighty-five families were randomly selected, of which forty-eight had children two to four years old.

All families in the study were interviewed in the home to collect information on family history and demography, income, employment, education, child-care practices, food consumption, and agricultural practices and yields. In addition, two twenty-four-hour dietary recalls were completed for each child in the study. All interviews were completed during the 1978 summer growing season (June–August).

The nutritional status of the children was assessed using measures of anthropometry, blood biochemical measures, and a clinical evaluation. In addition, stool samples for each child were analyzed to determine gastrointestinal parasite levels, as such infections can have an important influence on nutritional status. All children were measured and examined in one month (September 1978) with the help of local medical personnel. Table 9.1 lists the indices measured and their nutritional significance.

Impact on Child Nutrition

Tables 9.2 and 9.3 illustrate the results for the anthropometric and biochemical measures of nutritional status of children in the Plan Chontalpa and in Teco. Weight, height, head circumference, arm circumference, and triceps skinfold are all expressed in terms of the percentage of the fiftieth percentile in the appropriate age and sex category for each child. Reference data for well-nourished children in Mexico (Ramos Galvan 1975) were used as standards, interpolated to monthly age intervals, for weight, height, head circumference, and arm circumference. No Mexican reference data were available for triceps skinfold, so reference data from the U.S. Ten-State Nutrition Survey (Garn and Clark n.d.) were utilized. (As comparisons in this study are made only within the sample, the source of the reference data is of little consequence). Weight for height is expressed as the percentile of each child's weight in relation to height (to the nearest half-centimeter), also using Mexican reference data. The biochemical measures in Table 9.3 are expressed as the percentage of children with acceptable levels for each measure.

In order to determine whether the Plan Chontalpa has improved the nutritional status of children, children of socios (members) were compared with those of libres (nonmembers) and with children outside the plan in Teco. No significant differences were found in any of the measures of nutritional status in Table 9.2 between socios and libres (Student t-test, all P values > .10). In Table 9.3, the only significant difference between socios and libres is that there are more libre children with acceptable values of transferrin saturation. These results imply that if the Plan Chontalpa has been of nutritional benefit, that benefit is not dependent on a family's status as a member or nonmember.

When children of both socios and libres in the plan are compared with children in Teco, the only significant differences are in triceps skinfold and in levels of Vitamin A: Children in Teco have greater triceps skinfolds, and more children in the plan have acceptable values of vitamin A. Children of libres, but not of socios, are significantly

TABLE 9.1
Measures of nutritional status utilized

___

Anthropometric

Measure	Significance
Weight for age	Reflects growth: both stature and fatness
Height for age	Reflects growth: long-term measure of nutritional status
Weight for height	Reflects body composition and fatness
Head circumference	Reflects brain growth up to 3 years
Arm circumference	Reflects growth and fatness
Triceps skinfold	Reflects fatness

Biochemical

Measure	Significance	Acceptable level
Hemoglobin	Reflects anemia	$\geq$ 11.0 gm/100 ml
Hematocrit	Reflects anemia	$\geq$ 34% packed cell volume
Ascorbic acid	Reflects intake of ascorbic acid	$\geq$ 0.2 mg/100 ml
Vitamin A	Reflects vitamin A stores	$\geq$ 20 mcg/100 ml
Riboflavin (gluta-thione reductase-FAD effect)	Reflects riboflavin nutriture	< 1.35[a]
Transferrin saturation	Reflects iron deficiency	$\geq$ 16%
Ferritin	Reflects long-term iron stores	$\geq$ 10 ng/ml
Serum cholesterol	Low levels may reflect inadequate caloric intake	$\geq$ 95 mg/100 ml
Serum albumin	Reflects protein status	$\geq$ 3.5 gm/100 ml

[a] For automated analysis (Garry and Owen, 1976)

higher in weight for height than children in Teco. These results indicate that children of members of the Plan Chontalpa are not appreciably better off nutritionally than children in Teco.

The above conclusion is also supported by the data obtained from the dietary recalls. Table 9.4 lists the mean dietary intake of several nutrients in the plan and in Teco, calculated from average values from the two twenty-four-hour dietary recalls collected for each child. Dietary intake data must be interpreted with great caution as there are many sources of error. Nevertheless, Table 9.4 demonstrates that the mean dietary intake of all nutrients except niacin and vitamin A is probably *higher* for children in Teco than for children of socios. The only significant differences between socios and libres are in intake of protein and niacin.

TABLE 9.2
Nutritional status of children in the Plan Chontalpa and Tecominoacan

		PLAN CHONTALPA		TECOMINOACAN
		Socios	Libres	
WEIGHT (% of standard)	N=	85.4 (70)	85.3 (21)	82.3 (39)
HEIGHT (% of standard)	N=	92.1 (76)	91.6 (24)	90.9 (48)
WEIGHT FOR HEIGHT (percentile)	N=	39.5 (70)	49.3 (21)	31.6 [a] (39)
HEAD CIRCUMFERENCE (% of standard)	N=	96.5 (70)	96.2 (21)	95.9 (39)
ARM CIRCUMFERENCE (% of standard)	N=	98.2 (70)	97.3 (21)	98.3 (39)
TRICEPS SKINFOLD (% of standard)	N=	91.4 (70)	91.6 (21)	103.2 [b] (39)
HEMOGLOBIN (gm/100 ml)	N=	12.34 (66)	12.22 (21)	12.20 (38)
HEMATOCRIT (packed cell volume %)	N=	36.79 (58)	36.16 (16)	36.30 (36)

[a] t-test of difference between means significant for Libres & Teco (P < .05)

[b] t-test of difference between means significant for Plan Chontalpa & Teco (P < .01)

TABLE 9.3
Percent of children with acceptable levels of biochemical indices of nutritional status in the Plan Chontalpa and Tecominoacan.

		PLAN CHONTALPA		TECOMINOACAN
		Socios	Libres	
ASCORBIC ACID	N=	49.2 (61)	57.9 (19)	56.8 (37)
VITAMIN A	N=	69.8 (63)	75.0 (20)	48.6 [a] (37)
RIBOFLAVIN	N=	56.5 (62)	52.4 (21)	46.2 (39)
TRANSFERRIN SATURATION	N=	65.6 (61)	94.4 [b] (18)	66.7 (36)
FERRITIN	N=	95.2 (63)	100 (20)	97.3 (37)
SERUM CHOLESTEROL	N=	96.6 (58)	94.1 (17)	100 (34)
SERUM ALBUMIN	N=	100 (58)	100 (16)	100 (33)

[a] difference between Plan Chontalpa & Teco significant (chi-square, P < .05)

[b] difference between socios & libres significant (chi-square, P < .05)

TABLE 9.4
Dietary intake of children in the Plan Chontalpa and Tecominoacan

	PLAN CHONTALPA		TECOMINOACAN
	Socios	Libres	
DIETARY QUALITY [1]	69.6	62.0	82.6 [b]
ENERGY	77.4	70.5	92.9 [a]
PROTEIN	97.9	83.9 [c]	107.5
CALCIUM	56.0	51.9	81.2 [a]
IRON	60.9	52.2	72.0 [b]
THIAMINE	103.4	102.6	140.8 [a]
RIBOFLAVIN	65.3	56.3	67.1
NIACIN	55.8	45.4 [c]	53.6
ASCORBIC ACID	75.7	69.1	101.7
VITAMIN A	33.7	26.0	26.5 [d]
N =	(76)	(25)	(48)

All values are expressed as the percent of the Mexican Recommended
    Dietary Allowances for children (in the appropriate age category).
[a] difference between Plan & Teco significant (Mann-Whitney U test,
    P < .01)
[b] difference between Plan & Teco significant (Mann-Whitney U test,
    P < .05)
[c] difference between Socios & Libres significant (Mann-Whitney U
    test, P < .05)
[d] difference between Socios & Teco significant (Mann-Whitney U
    test, P < .05)
[1]- mean % of Recommended Dietary Allowance (Mexican) for energy,
    protein, calcium, iron, thiamine, riboflavin, niacin, ascorbic
    acid, and vitamin A.

To summarize, the nutritional status of children in the plan, as reflected by anthropometric, biochemical, and dietary measures, is not better than the nutritional status of children in Teco. This situation is true despite the fact that the average per capita income is somewhat higher for families in the plan (see Dewey 1980a, 1980b for a further explanation). Furthermore, families in Teco were actually detrimentally affected by the Plan Chontalpa because most of the most fertile land of the villages was expropriated in order to form one of the ejidos of the plan. One might expect, therefore, that children in Teco would be more at risk of malnutrition, but this does not appear to be the case.

Impact on Parasite Levels

Although few differences were found with respect to nutritional status, there is a considerable difference in levels of gastrointestinal parasites between children in the plan and children in Teco (Table 9.5). The

TABLE 9.5
Incidence rates of gastrointestinal parasites
(percent of children)

	PLAN CHONTALPA (Socios + Libres)	TECOMINOACAN
All species	86.5	51.4
Entamoeba histolytica	4.1	10.8
Giardia lamblia	4.1	0
Necator americanus	4.1	0
Ascaris lumbricoides & dicorticado	35.1	16.2
Trichuris trichiura	51.4	10.8
Strongyloides stercoralis	35.1	18.9
Hymenolepis nana	4.1	0
Hymenolepis diminuta	6.8	0
N =	(75)	(37)

overall rate of child parasitism (presence of at least one parasite species) in the plan is 86.5 percent, compared with 51.4 percent in Teco. Although the level of parasite infestation among children before the resettlement is unknown, it is possible that the greater concentration of houses, and consequently of children, in the centralized poblados of the Plan Chontalpa compared to the more scattered houses in Teco is responsible for this difference. The most common parasites found were nematode worms: *Trichuris, Strongyloides,* and *Ascaris,* which are usually transmitted through contact with contaminated soil. Although the houses in the plan have bathrooms with toilets, often the small children do not use the bathroom but defecate instead in the small area around the house, the same area in which they play. When a subsample of forty-four families was reinterviewed, 60 percent of the socio mothers said that their young children did not use the bathroom. Of these, 78 percent played in the same area in which they defecated. Although the sample sizes are too small for the difference to be significant, children in the plan who used the bathroom had an average of 0.83 parasites while children who defecated outside had an average of 1.47. Families in Teco have neither bathrooms nor latrines, but the children generally defecate away from the house in an area not used for play or other activities. Of the mothers reinterviewed in Teco, only 31 percent said that their children played in the same area in which they defecated. Thus, it is likely that the closely packed houses of the plan, coupled with the children's habits, have led to higher levels of nematode parasites in the soil, although no data are available to determine whether this is in fact the case. I have included these results as an example of the kind of health effects of development projects that may not be foreseen without careful prior impact analysis.

Impact of the Plan Chontalpa

Why has the Plan Chontalpa not been successful in improving the nutritional status of children when improvement in social and health services was one of its original objectives? In order to fully understand the impact of the Plan Chontalpa, it is necessary to examine first the political and economic structure of this large-scale project in agricultural development. An evaluation of the Plan Chontalpa conducted by the National Commission of Science and Technology in Mexico (CONACYT 1976) describes some of the major failings of the project. Many of the criticisms were echoed by the families we interviewed as well.

From the start, the local *campesinos* ("peasants") were not involved in planning the project, and they have not played a major role in decision making throughout its development. The plan was conceived primarily as a means to increase agricultural production in the Chontalpa area, and although the original goals included land redistribution and improvements in social services, the government has largely imposed the project on the people. An institutional form of paternalism has resulted in the campesinos' losing control over agricultural production, because most decisions are made either by government institutions or by the institutions that supply financial credit. This pattern of development was recognized by many of the campesinos from the beginning, and in fact, there was armed opposition in some areas, which was subsequently "quieted" by the Mexican army.

The structure of agricultural production in the plan has also not been favorable to the campesinos. In each ejido, the socios are paid as *jornaleros* ("day laborers") for work on the collective land, even though they are officially the "owners." Because the credit institutions largely dictate the crops that are to be grown, socios frequently make the comment that "somos nada mas jornaleros por el banco" (we are nothing more than day-laborers for the bank). The CONACYT study reflects the same sentiment: The socios are faced with a permanent contradiction: "on one hand, they are owners of the land and partners in a collective enterprise; but on the other hand they are salaried, dependent for their survival on the advance payments they receive for their daily work. . . . It is not surprising, therefore, that their response—like any proletariat in any part of the world—is to work as little as possible in order to collect their salary" (translation from the Spanish, CONACYT 1976, pp. XII 21–22).

Socios working the collective land are entitled to a share of the earnings for each crop, and on a few ejidos, this annual share may be as much as $1,800 (U.S.). However, on most ejidos, earnings are trivial or nonexistent—in fact, in many cases crops are losing money. It is difficult to determine exactly why this situation occurs so often, but the likely reasons include agricultural prices, mismanagement, climatic factors, lack or misuse of machinery, diseases or pests, and other variables related to large-scale monocultures. The criticism has been made that the Plan Chontalpa is yet another example of the use of an inappropriate technology that is more applicable to temperate zone agriculture than to tropical agriculture (Barkin 1978). Whatever happens to the crops, the ejido must pay the credit and interest to the financial institutions, and the socios receive little or no money. The average debt per socio is more than $2,600 (U.S.). For families earning an average of about $35 per week, this debt represents about one and a half years of work.

Although the initial plans for the Plan Chontalpa called for 37 percent of the land to be devoted to basic annual crops (corn, beans, rice, etc.), 42 percent to perennial crops (cocoa, banana, sugarcane), and 21 percent to cattle production, the proportions have changed drastically through the course of the plan's development. By 1978, 65 percent of the land was devoted to cattle production, 30 percent to perennials (primarily sugarcane), and only 5 percent to annual crops. This change came about partly because of pressures from financial institutions, which preferred to give credit for cattle and sugarcane, and partly because of national-level pressure for increased cattle and sugar production. The change in the focus of agricultural production has caused further problems for the campesinos. Cattle production requires notoriously little labor input per hectare, and thus has reduced the availability of work. Sugarcane production, on the other hand, requires huge amounts of labor but only at certain times of the year, resulting in highly pulsed opportunities for work. As a result, on some ejidos even the socios have no work for large parts of the year while during the sugarcane harvest, migrants from all over the republic come to work in the cane fields, worsening social tensions and creating a very unstable labor situation. In addition, both cattle and sugar production require a great deal of credit. This need has contributed to the indebtedness of the socios, limited their possibilities for accumulating capital, and made them even more dependent on the credit institutions. The CONACYT study states, "The possibility of an indigenous development of benefit exclusively to the ejidatarios is not possible, because it would imply the reduction of the rhythm of capital accumulation by the centers of economic power (translation from the Spanish, CONACYT 1976, p. XII 4).

The net result of the problems of indebtedness and lack of employment is that many families feel they are no better off economically than they were before the Plan Chontalpa. Although average per capita income is somewhat higher for socio families, the difference is not great enough to have much of an impact for most of them. However, it is important to point out that there is a greater *variance* in income among socios than in Teco (see Dewey 1980b). In other words, stratification in wealth is greater within the Plan Chontalpa.

In addition to the political and economic impact of the Plan, the changes in agriculture brought about by the project have influenced diet and nutrition significantly. The original proposal for the Plan Chontalpa called for each resettled family to be entitled to a ten-hectare parcel, which would be farmed individually but with the benefit of collective credit organizations and improved agricultural services. An additional six hectares per family would have been in cooperative cattle reserves, worked collectively. However, by the time resettlement and collectivization took place, the plans were changed to the present situation, in which only two hectares per family are allocated for individual use and thirteen hectares per family are for collective production. Under this system, all collective production is sold, and socios are paid wages for their work on collective land.

This new form of land use has had a profound effect on the production of subsistence crops by each family. Although two hectares per year are generally considered sufficient to feed a small family, they are not adequate to allow for a fallow period, a traditional farming practice in the area. If a family uses the two-hectare parcel every year (with two growing seasons per year), yields will inevitably drop because of a decline in fertility. This result has already become apparent to some of the socios we interviewed. In addition to this problem, many of the family parcels are located quite far from the poblado, requiring a walk of one to two hours just to get there. After working from 6:00 A.M. to 1:00 P.M. on the collective land, cutting sugarcane for example, it is often simply not worth the effort for a socio to try to work his family parcel in the afternoon, when the sun is at its hottest. This example points out the fundamental conflict that exists between individual and collective production in the plan: Because each socio must work the collective land to earn wages, the family parcel is given second priority and is sometimes totally neglected. Although there are sometimes weeks in which no collective work is available, such periods are not predictable far enough in advance to permit a socio to devote that time to the family parcel. The result is that, as one socio told us, "some socios don't even know where their family parcel is located." Thus, subsistence production has declined greatly in recent years.

The ability of families to procure their own food has also been reduced by the ecological changes brought about as a result of the Plan Chontalpa. Vast areas of forest were cut down to create cattle pasture and fields for sugarcane and other crops. As a result, the availability of wild game and wild plants to be used as food has declined drastically. The large-scale drainage project, while successful in ending the cyclic inundations, increased the flow of water in the area, caused the salinization of some soils because of the entrance of seawater, and reduced the fertility of the rich alluvial soils by preventing the deposition of sediments (Barkin 1978). Many residents of the area claim that the reduction in fish and turtles, once extremely important in the local diet, has been caused by these alterations. Although areas outside of the ejidos have also been affected by the deforestation and drainage, a significantly greater percentage of the families in Teco still hunt, fish, and collect wild plants for food as compared with socios in the plan (35.4 percent, 74.4 percent, and 58.3 percent versus 13.2 percent, 27.6 percent, and 28.9 percent, respectively).

Resettlement into the densely populated poblados of the plan has also created problems for subsistence production. In Tabasco, the solar is used to grow a wide variety of fruit trees and other crops and to raise domestic animals such as chickens, ducks, turkey, and pigs. Although each family in a poblado has a small solar for these purposes, many of them complain that they cannot raise animals because they are wiped out every year when animal diseases spread rapidly from household to household. In Teco, the houses are not as close together, and the families have larger solars. It may be for this reason that families in Teco have significantly more chickens and turkeys than socio families (mean of 12.2 versus 6.7 chickens and 5.3 versus 2.2 turkeys per household, respectively, Mann-Whitney U test, $P < .05$). This difference can have a substantial impact on the diet, given that the price of chicken in the area in 1978 was a dollar per pound. Because of the small size of the solars and the recent construction of the poblados, the diversity of crops grown in the solars of the socios is also significantly lower than in Teco (mean of 7.4 versus 10.4 species per household, Student t-test, $P < .001$). The fruit trees of the solar can contribute substantially to dietary quality, since other sources of vitamins A and C are scarce. Children of families who have six or more crops in their solar consume significantly more vitamin C than children of families with fewer crops (109 percent versus 60 percent of the RDA, respectively, Mann-Whitney U test, $P < .05$).

Thus, the changes in land structure and the ecological changes resulting from deforestation, drainage, and resettlement have reduced the ability of families to procure their own food. How does this change affect diet and nutrition? Results from the study, explained in detail elsewhere (Dewey 1981), demonstrate that dependence on purchased foods is strongly influenced by both the degree of subsistence production and the diversity of crops grown. In addition, lower crop diversity is related to lower dietary diversity for preschool children. Lower dietary diversity and an increased dependence on purchased foods are both related to lower dietary quality, which is, in turn, related to lower anthropometric measures of nutritional status. Therefore, in the area of the Plan Chontalpa, where wages are low and food prices are very high, a higher degree of self-sufficiency in food production seems to be an advantage for agricultural families.

The Plan Chontalpa has thus resulted in a transformation from a population of mostly self-provisioning peasant families to a population that is almost completely dependent on wage labor. Although this change is not *necessarily* undesirable, in Tabasco the situation has led to an undermining of the ability of families to feed themselves adequately.

Conclusion

The results of the case study in Tabasco are illustrative of the kinds of changes in nutrition that often accompany development. Although it cannot be denied that the basic cause of hunger and malnutrition in the world is poverty, and that efforts to reduce poverty through development are the only long-term solution, it is critical that development projects be designed so as not to worsen health and nutritional status, which, of course, depends on *how* development is defined and carried out. Social impact analysis, both prior to the initiation of development projects and after they have been implemented, is an essential element in the process of ensuring that such projects are more successful in the future than they have been in the past.

References

Barkin, D.
 1978   *Desarrollo Regional y Reorganizacion Campesina: La Chontalpa Como Reflejo Del Problema Agropecuario Mexicano.* Mexico City: Centro de Ecodesarrollo, Editorial Nueva Imagen.

Christakis, G., ed.
 1973   Nutritional Assessment in Health Programs. *Amer. J. Pub. Hlth.* 63 supplement.

CONACYT
 1976   *Evaluacion del Plan Chontalpa.* Mexico: Centro de Ecodesarrollo.

Dewey, Kathryn G.
 1979   Agricultural Development, Diet, and Nutrition. *Ecology of Food and Nutrition* 8:265–273.
 1980a   The Impact of Agricultural Development on Child Nutrition in Tabasco, Mexico. *Medical Anthropology* 4(1):21–54.
 1980b   *The Ecology of Agricultural Change and Child Nutrition: A Case Study in Southern Mexico.* Ph.D. dissertation, University of Michigan.
 1981   Nutritional Consequences of the Transformation from Subsistence to Commercial Agriculture in Tabasco, Mexico. *Human Ecology* 9:151–187.

Garn, S. M., and D. C. Clark
 n. d.   *Anthropometries from the Ten State Nutrition Survey (1968–1970).* Ann Arbor: Center for Human Growth and Development, University of Michigan.

Garry, P. J., and G. M. Owen
 1976   An Automated Flavin Adenine Dinucleotide-dependent Glutathione Reductase Assay for Assessing Riboflavin Nutriture. *Amer. J. Clin. Nutr.* 29:663–674.

Hakim, P., and G. Solimano
 1978   *Development, Reform, and Malnutrition in Chile.* International Nutrition Policy Series no. 4. Cambridge, Mass.: M.I.T. Press.

Hernandez, M., C. Perez II, J. Ramirez H., H. Madrigal, and A. Chavez
1974   Effect of Economic Growth on Nutrition in a Tropical Community. *Ecology of Food and Nutrition* 3:283–391.

Idusogie, E. O.
1969   A Critical Review of the Role of Cash Cropping on the Nutrition of Nigerian Peoples. Ph.D. dissertation, University of London.

Mamarbachi, D., P. L. Pellett, H. M. Basha, and F. Djani
1980   Observations on Nutritional Marasmus in a Newly Rich Nation. *Ecology of Food and Nutrition* 9:43–54.

Marr, J. W.
1971   Individual Dietary Surveys: Purposes and Methods. *World Review of Nutrition and Dietetics* 13:105–164.

Neumann, C. G.
1979   Reference Data. In D. B. Jelliffe and E.F.P. Jelliffe, eds., *Human Nutrition*, vol. 2, *Nutrition and Growth*. New York: Plenum Press.

Ramos Galvan, R., ed.
1975   Somatometria Pediatrica Estudio Semi-longitudinal en Ninos de la Ciudad de Mexico. *Archivos de Investigacion Medica* 6 supplement 1.

Rawson, I. G., and V. Valverde
1976   The Etiology of Malnutrition Among Preschool Children in Rural Costa Rica. *J. Trop. Ped. Env. Ch. Hlth.* 22:12–17.

Stavrakis, O., and M. L. Marshall
1978   Women, Agriculture, and Development in the Maya Lowlands: Profit or Progress. Paper presented at the conference on Women and Food, January 1978, Tucson, Arizona.

Thimmayamma, B.V.S., P. Rau, V. K. Desai, and B. N. Jayaprakesh
1976   A Study of Changes in Socioeconomic Conditions, Dietary Intake, and Nutritional Status of Indian Rural Families over a Decade. *Ecology of Food and Nutrition* 5:235–243.

Valverde, V., R. Martorell, V. Jejia-Pivarel, H. Delgado, A. Lechtig, C. Teller, and R. E. Klein
1977   Relationship Between Family Land Availability and Nutritional Status. *Ecology of Food and Nutrition* 6:1–7.

10
Expansion of Commercial Cattle Production and Its Effects on Stratification and Migration: A Costa Rican Case

Peter M. Meehan
Michael B. Whiteford

Introduction

Today, a gradual but persistent trend is occurring in many of the developing world's peasant communities. It consists of a process in which lands increasingly are being used for agricultural production that is destined to go outside the local community. Included within this range of export commodities are such items as carnations grown on the former food producing lands in Colombia (Lappe and Collins 1979:294–295) and sugarcane plantations now being carved out of lands previously cultivated exclusively by small-scale peasant farmers (Taussig 1978). The effects of these agrarian shifts are by no means uniform. Certainly, on the one hand, the results often generate needed foreign currencies that the agricultural workers and the governments can use for other development efforts. On the other hand, it has been argued (Taussig 1978, Fleuret and Fleuret 1980) that many of these policies and programs have had a negative social impact, exacerbating the impoverishment of the poorest sector of the rural population. Thus, far from benefiting from the introduction of new technologies or increased agricultural outputs, landless laborers or farmers with access to small parcels of land often find themselves excluded even further from achieving a satisfactory livelihood.

This chapter examines the rise of commercial cattle production between 1963 and 1983 in an area of west central Costa Rica. The theoretical model tested here comes from the field of development economics and essentially consists of a conversion of the existing staple theory of economic growth (Watkins 1963, Hirschman 1977) to a technoeconomic theory of culture change. Specifically, this chapter examines two hypotheses: (1) Increased production of a land-extensive, labor-extensive staple leads to

178

increased social stratification, and (2) increased production of a labor-extensive staple leads to relatively greater outmigration of landless people for purposes of employment compared with other socioeconomic groups.

Staple Theory

By definition, staple products are imposed on local ecosystems either directly or indirectly by foreign (i.e., colonial or neocolonial) interests. According to Hirschman, staple theorists try "to show how the growth experience of a country is concretely shaped by the specific primary products which it successively exports to new markets. It is an attempt to show in detail how 'one thing leads to another' through the requirements and influence of the staple" (1977:72). When staple theorists begin to designate "how one thing leads to another," they are hypothesizing relationships between a staple and economic changes induced by the staple. In short, they are deriving propositions that, taken as a group, form the staple theory of economic growth. With such a theory, economists can explain and, thereby predict, the appearance of new economic enterprises and government services emanating from staple production in a particular region.[1]

Furthermore, staples are resource-intensive export products that "form the leading sector of the economy and set the pace for economic growth" (Watkins 1963:143). Staples, in short, dominate the economic profile of an area. This predominance, Watkins says, occurs for two reasons: "The limited—at first possibly non-existent—domestic market, and the factor proportions—abundance of land relative to labor and capital—create a comparative advantage in resource-intensive exports or staples" (1963:143). Plantation crops of many colonial and independent countries—tea in northeastern India and central Sri Lanka, coffee in Brazil, sugarcane in Cuba and Indonesia—fit this description. However, staples may be cultivated on small farms as well as on plantations, and the economic linkages arising from these different forms of organization may vary considerably.

Regardless of the size of the agricultural enterprise, the staple theorists view economic development as "a process of diversification around an export base. The central concept of a staple theory, therefore, is the spread effect of the export sector; that is, of export activity on domestic economy and society" (Watkins 1963:143).

In the area discussed in this chapter, labor extensivity is a property of the staple, cattle, which assumes importance in Fresco's development process. For this reason, analysis of the social spread effects of cattle production (the dependent variable)—increased social stratification and outmigration—is conducted in terms of labor extensivity (the independent variable).[2] This chapter also goes beyond scientific analysis of spread effects on the local level and looks at the international linkages to the local ecosystem. The clearest case for such historical analysis comes from the dependency, rather than the staple, theorists:

We see underdevelopment as intimately and causally related to the patterns of evolution of developed, industrialized societies. In brief, we investigate interrelationships between different economic, geographical, and cultural systems on a global basis over historical time. We consciously follow the general rule of social theory that states that when seeking to explain (or change) a *part- of something, in this case underdevelopment, we must* refer systematically to the whole, in terms of which that whole can be understood (or changed). . . . It is only in this way, and with a great emphasis on historical research, the development of underdevelopment can be understood. [Cockcroft, Frank, and Johnson 1972:x]

The keystone of the dependency paradigm is that the development or underdevelopment of Third World economies is primarily a result of historical linkage or dependence of the world's peripheral satellites (Third World areas connected to international metropoles through, for example, staple exports) with international metropoles (political and financial centers such as New York, Washington, D.C., or London). Here, dependence is conceived of as a "conditioning situation" in which the growth process of a Third World village, region, or country fluctuates according to political and economic decisions made in capitals of industrialized countries. Development refers to a "structural transformation of the economy, society, politics, and culture of the satellite that permits the self-generating and self-perpetuating use and development of the people's potential" (Cockcroft, Frank, and Johnson 1972:xvi). Underdevelopment, in contrast, is the process by which foreign or domestic investment in satellite areas acts to "extract surplus and, in the process, to impoverish the people, destroy local industry, deplete the soil and subsoil, and corrupt the local elites" (Hirschman 1977:90).

To summarize, staple theory is presented as a technoeconomic theory capable of explaining cultural changes in local ecosystems undergoing staple development. The cultural theory is derived from the staple theory of economic growth and seeks to explain social, rather than strictly economic, linkages arising from staple production. At the same time, the cultural theory calls for historical analysis of the process by which the staple was established in the local ecosystem.

The Rise of Commercial Cattle Production in Fresco

Although historical studies of international linkages to local ecosystems are available (Geertz 1963, Guerra y Sanchez 1964), none of them explicitly discuss these linkages in terms of the staple theory. For this reason, the present historical analysis is conducted in three steps. First, Fresco is described briefly as an ecosystem. Second, Fresco's cattle are analyzed to determine whether or not they do, indeed, qualify as a staple according to Watkins's criteria (1963:143). Finally, the process by which cattle as a staple came to appear in the local ecosystem is described.

Data for the analysis came from five sources: interviews with Fresco ranchers, interviews with Costa Rican agricultural officials, Costa Rica

Ministry of Agriculture reports, livestock reports of the U.S. Department of Agriculture's Foreign Service, and relevant publications from scholarly journals. The aim is to draw from these diverse sources and construct, insofar as is possible, a picture of the local, national, and international forces that coalesced in Fresco. These forces led to the conversion of 88 percent of the land to pasture by 1977. Admittedly, data from all three analytical levels are fragmentary. However, when the available information is pieced together, a picture does emerge that indicates the range of forces facilitating cattle development in Fresco and in Costa Rica.

Fresco's ecosystem comprises a seventy-three-household community on the western slope of Costa Rica's *meseta central* ("central plateau"), and topography and climate are particularly important physical factors. The altitude ranges from 1,110 to 700 meters above sea level over an area of six square miles, and the climate is marked by two distinct seasons. A seven-month summer lasts from September through March and is characterized by high winds and relatively little precipitation. The five-month winter brings with it lower temperatures, less wind, and heavy afternoon rains. Corn and beans are grown through the winter and harvested in September; the annual coffee crop is harvested in December.

Fresco's cultural system is marked by two corresponding socioeconomic/ geographic sections—here called Main Road and Back Road Fresco. Main Road Fresco covers the area flanking the well-traveled gravel road connecting Fresco with the provincial capital, Santiago, on the east and with the town of San Pablo on the west. The road, built in the early 1960s, is a vital transportation link for marketing commercial crops. All but three of Fresco's "modern" houses lie along or near this road, and five of the six automobile owners live on the main road. Most commercial and social activities occur at the junction of the main and back roads, where there are four general stores, a post office, an elementary school, a large church, soccer field, community center, and two coffee collection points. Back Road Fresco refers to the more isolated houses along a hundred-year old path, which narrows to a footpath before coming to a dead end. Back Road residents generally live in poorer housing and have fewer modern appliances than Main Road people.

Agriculture is the key to economic life in Fresco as 89 percent of the households are engaged in farming and ranching. Of this total, 88 percent derive their income exclusively from agriculture while the remainder have other income sources, primarily from government or small businesses. Until 1950, the traditional crops of corn, beans, and sugarcane dominated Fresco's agricultural profile, but postwar developments resulted in a massive conversion of land to pasture, coffee, and, to a lesser extent, tobacco. Currently, Frescanos have 88 percent of their land in pasture, 5 percent in coffee, and 1 percent in sugarcane. A similar land conversion occurred in Paso, some seventy kilometers south of Fresco, although in 1972 Pasanos had three times as much tobacco and one-half as much pasture as Frescanos do today (Barlett 1977:287).

Watkins defines a staple according to three criteria. First, staples form "the leading sector of the economy and set the pace for economic growth" (1963:143). Coupling Fresco land use data with Barlett's profit figures from Paso (1977:289), there is little doubt that cattle form the leading sector of Fresco's economy.[3]

Products	Profit/Manzana ×	No. of Manzanas	= Total Profit
Corn and beans	1,242 colones	48.75	60,547 colones
Coffee	923 colones	57.00	52,611 colones
Cattle	264 colones	1,028.00	271,392 colones

Although distributed very unevenly through the community, the profit from cattle is roughly four to five times higher than that from the other crops.

Second, staples are export products, and third, they are land extensive rather than capital and labor intensive. Watkins explains these criteria by saying, "The limited—at first possibly non-existent—domestic market, and the factor proportions—abundance of land relative to labor and capital—create a comparative advantage in resource-intensive exports or staples" (1963:143). Fresco's ranchers say that the bulk of their cattle is produced for export. Barlett (n.d.:121) found this to be the case in Paso as well and explains the drive to export in terms of the significantly higher export prices for cattle compared with the domestic prices. USDA statistics support these findings on the national level. In 1957, less than 2 percent of total cattle production—21,324,000 kgs.—was exported (USDA 1973:11). As early as 1965, cattle had moved into fourth place as a foreign-exchange earner behind coffee, bananas, and cocoa (USDA 1965:9).

The land-extensive characteristic of cattle is described by Strickon (1965) for Argentina and is verified for Fresco by the fact that 88 percent of the land is in pasture. Coupled with the fact that "cattle as a land-use option is low in labor and capital costs" (Barlett n.d.:118), Fresco's cattle clearly fit the case of a staple requiring "an abundance of land relative to labor and capital."

On all three counts, then, cattle in Fresco fill Watkins's criteria for staple productioin. They are the leading sector of Fresco's growth, are produced mainly for export, and are land extensive rather than capital and labor intensive.

Prior to 1950, Costa Rica had four resources that made it an attractive locale in which to develop a cattle industry. First, it had a relatively small population and an abundant supply of land, though much of it was forested (Tosi 1975). Second, it had raised a *criollo* stock of cattle ever since Spanish colonists arrived in the sixteenth century (Barlett 1976:118), and third, as a result of the Spanish interest in livestock, rural Costa Ricans had acquired a sizable stock of knowledge about cattle

raising. Fourth, an aggressive African pasture, called *jaragua*, was introduced into the area in the 1920s (Parsons 1976:130). With these resources,
it is not surprising that the availability of an export market and large
amounts of capital would transform the forest into pasture. From 1960
to 1975, for example, Costa Rica doubled the size of its herd to 1.7
million (Parsons 1976:124), and between 1963 and 1973, land was converted
to pasture for the cattle industry at the rate of 30,000 hectares (or 5
percent) per year. By 1973, 50 percent of all farmland was allocated to
pasture for cattle production (Solera-Ruiz 1981:3).[4] According to local
ranchers, the rapid conversion of forest to pasture on the national level
was paralleled in Fresco over the same period. As an example, Fresco's
largest rancher and most astute businessman held only 22 manzanas in
pasture in 1960, but over the next fifteen years he increased that amount
to 245 manzanas.

What caused the shift to pasture? The seeds of change are to be
found in one of Costa Rica's northern neighbors—the United States.
The unprecedented rise in U.S. living standards after World War II
included a greater appetite and demand by consumers for beef. In particular,
fast-food chains proliferated throughout the country and the world, and
cuts of inexpensive, low-grade beef were needed to make these new
ventures viable. U.S. cattlemen raised high-quality beef and charged a
commensurate price, so buyers looked elsewhere for less expensive
products. Costa Rican cattlemen responded by exporting U.S. $51.3
million of beef in 1977 (Solera-Ruiz 1981:1).

Costa Rica's abundant supply of land, friendly government, cheap
labor, and closeness to the U.S. market made it a natural place to turn.
A USDA report says, "Before 1957, nearly all of the beef produced in
Central America [including Costa Rica] went into domestic consumption;
since that time, production gains have tended to move into export
channels to Puerto Rico and the USA" (USDA 1965:iii). With the promise
of such a lucrative market, international agencies extended large amounts
of credit to Costa Rica for livestock development.

Most of the funds available from international institutions over the last
few years [$20–30 million] have gone into infrastructure development on
ranches. Costa Rica has a well-developed extension service; and government
facilities for research, animal sanitation and cattle registration are reputed
to be the most advanced in Central America. [USDA 1973:17]

Infrastructure development also took the form of new and improved
roads from producing areas to auctions and processing plants. Parsons
says that "road building has enormously facilitated this rapid conversion
of forest to cropland and pasture" (1976:123). Fresco's wide, gravel main
road—built in 1960, just as the export drive gathered momentum—was
a result of this development. Other necessary transportation linkages
were an international shipping service to the United States (USDA
1969:14) and a long-distance trucking service. "Without the direct re-

frigerated trailer service initiated in 1960 linking Central America and the massive U.S. market, it is doubtful that this new trade in boneless beef would have developed so rapidly" (Parsons 1965:157).

USDA figures spell out the success of the beef-export drive. Beef production nearly tripled from 21,324,000 kgs. in 1957 to 58,320,000 kgs. in 1972. During the same period, net exports of beef soared from 434,000 kgs. to 39,833,000 kgs., and most of the beef went to the United States (USDA 1973:11). As already mentioned, beef had moved into fourth place as a foreign-exchange earner as early as 1965. At the same time that exports rose so dramatically, however, per capita consumption of beef within Costa Rica itself actually *fell* from 20.0 kgs. in 1957 to 10.3 kgs. in 1972. This apparent paradox is explained by the price differential between domestic and export beef after the U.S. market opened up. In 1969, for example, packers paid 15.5 to 16 cents per pound for export steers and only 13.5 to 14 cents per pound for domestic steers (USDA 1969:14). Not surprisingly, "the price advantage that . . . favored export growth over domestic growth . . . also caused a domestic beef shortage, which was especially severe in the summer of both 1964 and 1965" (USDA 1965:5).

Clearly, then, the new export market to the United States—rather than increased domestic consumption—was the primary demand stimulus for the rapid livestock development. Lappe and Collins note (1979:289–290) that the extent to which Costa Rican beef is exported undoubtedly has resulted in nutritional problems within the country. In 1975, the Costa Rican Ministry of Health noted that between 43.2 and 62.5 percent of the country's preschool children suffered from nutritional deficits (USAID 1975:14), and the country's government declared that "childhood malnutrition constitutes the country's most severe social problem" (USAID 1975:2).

A series of international connections link Fresco's local ecosystem to the outside, the most vital of which are the market linkage with the United States and the international lending institutions, particularly the World Bank. Another set of linkages appeared with the introduction of African grasses and breeding stock from India, the United States and Mexico. The "transportation linkage" is the international shipping service and refrigerated trailer service.

Given the extent and type of Fresco's international linkages, dependency theorists would view them as primary determinants of the area's ability to develop or underdevelop over time. In fact, Frank (1972:12) has formulated a hypothesis predicting that Fresco would be an underdeveloping community because its growth has depended upon strong international linkages over the past twenty years. He explains this situation by saying that surplus has been extracted from the community (in this case, in the form of exhausted soil resources, perhaps) by supracommunity interests culminating primarily in the United States. To repeat Hirschman, the result is *underdevelopment* in which foreign interests, through their international linkages, "extract surplus and, in the process, . . . impoverish the people, destroy local industry, deplete the soil and subsoil, and corrupt the local elites" (1977:90).

Of Hirschman's underdevelopment yardsticks, substantial evidence is available correlating increased cattle production with extensive soil erosion in all of Costa Rica (Tosi 1975) as well as in Fresco (Meehan 1978b). Another yardstick, "impoverishment of the people," is difficult to measure, but it may be approached with the Fresco data through two dependent variables, social stratification and outmigration of landless people for purposes of employment.

Social Effects of Cattle Production—
Social Stratification and Outmigration

The stage is now set to examine the two propositions from staple theory that correlate the labor-extensive property of cattle with an increased outmigration of landless people from Fresco. At a theoretical level, the propositions are (1) increased production of a land-extensive, labor-extensive staple leads to increased social stratification, and (2) increased production of a labor-extensive staple leads to increased outmigration of landless people for purposes of employment. The propositions are drawn from the staple theory and from Barlett's observations in Paso: "The effects of this change [from forest to pasture] in land use are keenly felt by the landless farmers and small land-owners. . . . Increased social stratification and a declining standard of living for the landless from the area" has resulted (1977:300).

Social rank in Fresco appears to derive from a combination of cultural and economic bases. Parsons emphasizes its cultural basis when he says: "Stock raising is an activity congenial to the Latin value system. Ganadero [cattleman, i.e., rancher] like caballero [horseman, i.e., a term for 'gentleman'] is a term of respect. It carries prestige and it implies an attractive way of life easily entered" (1976:126). Barlett, however, disputes this assessment and emphasizes the economic basis of social rank in Paso:

> While the "cattleman on his horse" is an important cultural status symbol in parts of Costa Rica, in the Puriscal areas [the province containing Paso and Fresco], this status is not the goal of large land holders who have shifted to pasture. . . . Their higher status derives more from their increased income than from any attempt to obtain more leisure or to avoid working the land directly. [Barlett 1977:121]

Cancian's economic conception of social rank in terms of "possession or control of resources" (1972:216) is used to operationalize the first theoretical proposition: Increased production of the land-extensive, labor-extensive staple, cattle, in Fresco leads to increased disparities in the control of resources among different socioeconomic groups. Here, "increased production of the land-extensive, labor-extensive staple, cattle" is measured by the extent of land in pasture. As indicated earlier, the extent of land in pasture in Fresco has increased substantially over the past twenty years. "Control of resources" is measured by landownership and six levels of categories of living among four socioeconomic groups.[5] All data were gathered in the course of interviews with household heads in their homes.

The interaction of the variables in the proposition can be explained in the following way. As Strickon (1965) makes clear, cattle production—compared with virtually any type of crop production—is a land- and labor-extensive (rather than intensive) activity. Cattle require rotation from field to field and vaccinations and spraying for pests, and pastureland must be periodically weeded. Yet, labor requirements are low. As more land is converted to pasture, larger landholders are able to achieve higher returns from their land with only a minimal diversion of their new income stream to laborers in the community. Further, land previously rented by landless laborers is converted from crops to pasture; thus, the squeeze on the lower-income groups is magnified. As a result, a small number of large landholders acquire control over the bulk of Fresco's most valuable resource, land; convert their new income into an array of more expensive items; and, in this way, raise their rank in the social hierarchy by economic means.

The basic criterion for distinguishing one socioeconomic group from another in Fresco is landownership because land is the key resource. Following Barlett's divisions in Paso, these groups can be divided into four categories: landless (0–.9 manzanas), small landholders (1–6.9 manzanas), medium holders (7–39.9 manzanas), and large holders (40 manzanas or more). A breakdown of Fresco farms according to the number of manzanas revealed clusterings of the farms into these four divisions.

Pasture ownership is directly related to landownership. Large landowners, for example, have over 90 percent of their land in pasture. Beyond land/pasture ownership, stratification (or differences in resource control among socioeconomic groups) is measured according to six levels of living criteria: house modernity, water source, radio ownership, television ownership, refrigerator ownership, and automobile ownership. House modernity provides an overall measure of level of living.

Table 10.1 presents data correlating land/pasture ownership with house modernity. Distinctions between traditional, modern, and ultramodern housing are clear, and the movement toward modernity involves progressively more expenditure and carries with it more prestige. Traditional houses are characterized by unpainted wood exteriors, a lack of windowpanes, and either dirt or unfinished wood floors. Modern houses are painted, contain windowpanes, and have floors of either unfinished wood, varnished wood, cement, or tile. Ultramodern houses have the same features as modern houses except that at least a proportion of the ultramodern house, usually the entrance and front living room, is made of cement.

TABLE 10.1
Land ownership and house modernity

	Traditional		Modern		Ultra-modern	
	WOI*	WAI**	WOI	WAI	WOI	WAI
Landless (0-.9 m) n=22	0	17	5	0	0	0
Small (1-6.9 m) n=21	1	10	1	9	0	0
Medium (7.0-39.9 m) n=19	0	9	3	7	0	0
Large (40.0 + m) n=11	0	2	2	5	2	0

* WOI, "with outside income," refers to households earning part or all of their income outside agriculture. This abbreviation holds throughout.

** WAI, "with agricultural income," refers to households earning all of their income in agriculture. This abbreviation holds throughout.

It is clear that landless people, particularly agricultural laborers living exclusively on an agricultural income, have the poorest housing. These are the farm wage laborers who often need to rent land in order to grow their own crops. In fact, all the traditional houses of landless people are owned by those whose sole source of livelihood is agriculture; only landless people with a nonagricultural income own modern houses. Thus, it appears that, within the landless class, there are actually two subcategories, and the nonagricultural subcategory achieves higher rank than the totally agricultural subunit.

The picture changes rapidly in the small-farm group composed of farmers with little, if any pasture. Here, the distinction between traditional and modern housing is more equal, and there is little disparity between agricultural and nonagricultural income earners. A similar distribution occurs at the medium-farm level; but in this category, the nonagricultural income earners appear only in the modern house category.

In terms of stratification, the large farm/ranch level, with 71 percent of the pasture, is particularly interesting. Only 18 percent of the eleven large holders own traditional houses whereas 77 percent of the landless,

TABLE 10.2
Land ownership and level of living

	Radio		Water		TV		Refrigerator		Car	
	WOI	WAI	WOI	WAI	WOI	WAI	WOI	WAI	WOI	WAI
Landless n=22	3	17	3	3	3	0	0	0	0	0
Small n=21	2	17	1	12	0	3	0	0	0	0
Medium n=19	3	16	3	10	2	3	2	2	0	1
Large n=11	5	6	5	6	4	2	3	2	3	2

people, 26 percent of medium farmers and 58 percent of large

52 percent of the small, and 47 percent of the medium farmers have traditional houses. The presence of any traditional housing at all on the large-farm level is explained best perhaps by the fact that both of these ranchers are over seventy years old and are less inclined than younger people to depart from traditional housing forms. The remaining large holders have a mean age of forty-eight, and no less than 64 percent have modern houses. However, the clearest evidence of increased stratification in Fresco is the emergence of a new type of more expensive and prestigious house—the ultramodern house—only at the large holder level. The appearance of this housing is critical because it provides concrete evidence of the increasing stratification resulting from the new source of income, cattle production. Thus, as people move up the economic ladder, they move into progressively more modern housing.

An analogous pattern emerges in the level of living scores (see Table 10.2). Radio ownership provides a baseline from which to compare the living standards of the four classes because 94 percent of Fresco's households own radios, and beyond this ownership, disparities in living standards are highly pronounced. Whereas 27 percent of landless people have indoor tap water, 62 percent of the small and 68 percent of the medium holders have it. A full 100 percent of the large holders have indoor water access. Television sets are a relatively scarce commodity; nevertheless, 14 percent of the small-farm holders, 26 percent of the medium farmers, and 54 percent of the large holders own televisions.

Similar to ultramodern housing in the previous table, evidence of increasing social stratification resulting from pasture conversion is clearest in refrigerator and automobile ownership. First, both are reserved exclusively for medium and large holders. Further, the two medium-farm refrigerator owners with agricultural income only are both recognized *ganaderos* ("cattle ranchers") in the community. One owns thirty manzanas of pasture and the other recently sold a large portion of pastureland. The one car owner on the medium-farm level is the same person who sold his land. Five of the eleven ganaderos own refrigerators. In terms of status, the automobile clearly resembles the ultramodern house variable as (with one exception in the medium group) it separates the large holders from the rest of the community. It creates a new step on the stratification ladder against which other steps (such as radio or television ownership) are thrown into relief, and it provides perhaps the clearest evidence of increasing stratification arising from Fresco's move to commercial cattle production.

In summary, data from Tables 10.1 and 10.2 tend to support the proposition that correlates increased pasture conversion and cattle production with increasing social stratification. In both tables, the increase is shown most clearly in the emergence of new steps—ultramodern houses and automobiles—on the stratification ladder, reached only by the largest cattle producers.

Migration is "a form of geographic or spatial mobility involving a change of usual residence between clearly-defined geographic units" (Shryock 1976:300). Outmigration here refers to movement of individuals from Fresco to another community. Thus, the operationalized proposition: Increased production of the labor-extensive staple, cattle, leads to increased movement of landless people from Fresco for purposes of employment. As "increased production of the labor-extensive staple, cattle," is measured by the extent of land in pasture, "movement of landless people from Fresco for purposes of employment" refers specifically to the number of offspring of household heads who have moved from the community in order to find a job. The mechanism by which the labor-extensive property of cattle is felt in the migration behavior of Frescanos is very similar to that described for social stratification—except in its result. Because landless people are *landless*, they must earn income by renting land or by working for a larger farmer or rancher. However, both of these income sources are reduced as more land is converted to pasture for cattle production. As stated earlier, cattle raising requires little labor. Thus, ganaderos are able to achieve higher returns from their land with only a minimal diversion of their new income stream to laborers in the community. Further, as land previously rented by landless laborers is converted to pasture, the squeeze on lower-income people is heightened (cf. Barlett 1977:30 for an analogous situation in nearby Paso). The hypothesis result is increased movement of landless people from the community in order to find employment.

A comparable situation has been described for other areas of Costa Rica where considerable outmigration is taking place (cf. Schmidt de Rojas 1976, Dierckxsens et al. 1976). For the province of Guanacaste,

TABLE 10.3
Land ownership and outmigration

| | OUTMIGRATION | | | | |
| | 1972–1977 | | 1967–1972 | | |
	For Marriage	For Work	For Marriage	For Work	TOTAL
Landless (0.–.9m) n=22	2	13	1	7	23
Small (1.0–6.9m) n=21	4	3	2	3	12
Medium (7.0–39.9m) n=18	15	9	4	1	29
Large (40.0 --) n=11	1	0	2	0	3

the area of greatest outmigration in the country, a 1976 study showed an alarming rate of consolidation of lands between the 1953 and 1973 censuses for the purposes of increasing pasturage for beef production. That region today is marked by (1) a significant reduction in the number of small agricultural plots and (2) high levels of un- and underemployment (IFAM/AITEC 1976:39). Interestingly, one of the results of this type of social change has been an apparent *increase* in childhood malnutrition during those twenty years—an exception to the basic trends occurring elsewhere in the country (cf. Whiteford 1981:72–74).

Outmigration data for Fresco were gathered through the use of interviews, and household heads were specifically asked names, destination, reason for leaving, and amount of time elapsed since departure of all household members who had left Fresco permanently.[6] Because the proposition associates the outmigration of landless people with the increased conversion of land to pasture, outmigration was measured over two time periods—from 1967 to 1972 and from 1972 to 1977.

Table 10.3 presents data correlating outmigration with land/pasture ownership over the two time periods. Of the twenty-three outmigrating landless people, no less than 87 percent left in order to seek employment. In short, the vast majority of the landless outmigrants left Fresco in search of employment, and their number nearly doubled in the later period. The figure for the landless people compares with 50 percent of the small, 34 percent of the medium, and no large holder outmigrants who left Fresco in search of employment. Thus, a clear trend emerges.

that associates the amount of land owned with the amount of outmigration for employment purposes. The large percentage of landless people migrating for employment reasons tends to support the proposition.

In the small- and large-farmer classes, comparatively few people left for marriage or employment reasons, and their numbers increased or decreased only slightly from one period to another. Thus, their migration behavior is roughly as might be expected.

Findings on the medium-farm level, however, are surprising as they show more outmigration than any other group. This situation may be explained by the fact that medium-farm families had almost four times the number (twelve) of women migrating for marriage purposes in 1972–1977 and twice the number of women (four) migrating for marriage purposes in 1967–1972 than any other group. This abundance of marriage-motivated women in the medium group explains that group's large amount of outmigration. Nevertheless, no fewer than nine of the twenty-four medium holders (six more than among small holders though still four less than among the landless) migrated for employment reasons between 1972 and 1977, and the available data suggest no further explanation for this large number.

As stated earlier, however, the landless group clearly has the largest proportion and absolute number of outmigrants for employment reasons compared with other groups. Thus, despite the large number of work-motivated outmigrants at the medium holder level, the evidence tends to support the outmigration hypothesis.

Clear trends appear in both data sets to support the stratification and outmigration proposition. In the case of stratification, the level of living measures show a clear break between the landless/small and medium/large holders, clearly suggesting that the appearance of new measures of social status in Fresco can be attributed to the increased income received from cattle production by only a very small percentage of the people. Although the large number of work-motivated, medium holder outmigrants is a bit confusing, a definite trend associating increased land/pasture ownership with decreasing percentages of work-motivated outmigration is shown. More important support of the proposition, however, lies in the fact that the largest proportion and number of work-motivated outmigrants appears in the landless class. For this reason, the proposition is supported, and it appears that the "land squeeze" on landless people arising from increased cattle production is a factor in their decision to migrate.

Conclusion

In this chapter, we have presented two propositions of a theory of culture change and tested their validity with data from a local Costa Rican ecosystem undergoing staple development. We began by explaining the basic concepts and conditions of the existing staple theory of economic growth, and then turned the focus to an analysis of economic and social variables as they fit into the local ecosystem framework. The theory and framework were then used to relate the social "spread effects" of cattle production in Fresco to the labor-extensive, land-extensive "properties" of the staple, cattle. Dependency theory from economics was invoked to substantiate the claim that a historical analysis of the international linkages helps to generate the fullest explanation of sociocultural change in local staple ecosystems.

With the existence of cattle as a staple established, the staple theory of culture change was used to derive and test the two hypotheses that increased production of land-extensive, labor-extensive staples leads to increased social stratification and that increased production of land-extensive, labor-extensive staples leads to increased outmigration of landless people for purposes of employment. Clear trends in the data supported both hypotheses, so it was concluded that cattle production in Fresco has been a significant cause of increased social stratification and employment-motivated outmigration of landless people. The social impact of the programs and policies that generated the pattern of production are clearly reflected in the changing patterns of stratification and migration.

Notes

The research on which this chapter is based was carried out by Meehan while participating in an ethnographic field school in Costa Rica directed by Whiteford during the summer of 1977. The authors appreciate the support of Iowa State University and especially the assistance of ISU's World Food Institute. The Wenner-Gren Foundation for Anthropological Research provided write-up support for this document, and this support is gratefully acknowledged. Peggy F. Barlett's gentle guidance and theoretical direction is also gratefully acknowledged. Much of the material here comes from Meehan (1978a) and was reworked by Whiteford. Fresco, the name of the community in this study, is a pseudonym.

1. For example, an outstanding example of economic linkage occurred in Sri Lanka with the appearance of an excellent railway system when the British built their tea-plantation industry after 1850. The railroad enabled tea to be carried efficiently to Colombo tea auctions.

2. "Land extensive" refers to the fact that pasture for cattle production requires a large amount of land for efficient production. "Labor extensive" refers to the low labor requirements of cattle.

3. One manzana equals 1.7 hectares. At the time of the study, one colon equaled U.S. $0.12. It should be noted that three manzanas of corn and beans and three manzanas of coffee represent large plots of these crops on Fresco farms.

4. As DeWalt points out, the remarkable growth of the cattle industry by no means was restricted only to Costa Rica: "In every [Central American] country, the number of cattle has increased rapidly, and the production of meat has skyrocketed. Compared with twenty years ago, Central America now has 80% more cattle and produces 170% more beef" (1982:3).

5. Using levels of living categories, based on the presence of certain "material" possessions, is another method of assessing economic well-being (cf. Whiteford 1981, DeWalt, Kelley, and Pelto 1980).

6. In this chapter, "outmigration" refers specifically to the *offspring* of household heads who had left the community permanently.

References

1976   Labor Efficiency and the Mechanism of Agricultural Evolution. *Journal of Anthropological Research* 32(2):124–140.

1977   The Structure of Decision Making in Paso. *American Ethnologist* 4(2):285–308.

Cancian, Frank
1972   *Change and Uncertainty in a Peasant Economy.* Stanford: Stanford University Press.

Cockcroft, J., A. G. Frank, and D. F. Johnson
1972   Introduction. In *Dependence and Underdevelopment,* ed. J. A. Cockcroft, A. G. Frank, and D. F. Johnson, pp. ix–xxix. New York: Doubleday.

DeWalt, Billie
1982   The Big Macro Connection: Population, Grain, and Cattle in Southern Honduras. *Culture and Agriculture,* no. 14:1–12.

De Walt, K., P. Kelley, and G. Pelto
1980   Nutritional Correlates of Economic Microdifferentiation in a Highland Mexican Community. In *Nutritional Anthropology: Contemporary Approaches to Diet and Cultures,* ed. N. Jerome et al., pp. 205–222. Pleasantville, N.Y.: Redgrave.

Dierckxsens, W., M. Fernandez, S. Quevedo, R. Vasquez
1976   *La Reproducion de la Fuerza de Trabajo.* San Jose: Instituto de Investigaciones Sociales, Universidad de Costa Rica.

Fleuret, Patrick, and Anne Fleuret
1980   Nutrition, Consumption, and Agricultural Change. *Human Organization* 39(3):250–260.

Frank, Andre Gunter
1972   The Development of Underdevelopment. In *Dependence and Underdevelopment,* ed. J. A. Cockcroft, A. G. Frank, and D. F. Johnson, pp. 3–18. New York: Doubleday.

Geertz, Clifford
1963   *Agricultural Involution.* Berkeley: University of California Press.

Guerra y Sanchez, Ramiro
1964   *Sugar and Society in the Caribbean.* New Haven: Yale University Press.

194   Peter M. Meehan and Michael B. Whiteford

Hirschman, Albert O.
1977   A Generalized Linkage Approach to Development, with Special
         Reference to Staples. *Economic Development and Culture Change*
         25 (Supplement):67–98.

IFAM/AITEC
1976   *Estudio de Servicios Basicos en 30 Cantones. Parte II: Perfiles Co-
         munales.* San Jose: Departmento de Planificacion, Seccion de In-
         vestigacion.

Lappe, France Moore, and Joseph Collins
1979   *Food First: Beyond the Myth of Scarcity.* 2d ed. New York: Ballantine.

Meehan, Peter M.
1978a   Staple Theory as a Techno-Economic Theory of Culture Change,
         with Special Reference to the Rise of Commercial Cattle Production
         in a Costa Rican Community. Unpublished MS Thesis, Iowa State
         University.
1978b   Cultural Ecology and the Internationalization of Small Scale Cattle
         Production in a Costa Rican Community. In *Through the Eyes of
         Others: Student Ethnography in Costa Rica,* ed. Michael B. Whiteford,
         pp. 24–52. Papers in Anthropology no. 2, Department of Sociology
         and Anthropology. Ames: Iowa State University.

Parsons, James J.
1965   Cotton and Cattle in the Pacific Lowlands of Central America.
         Journal of Inter-American Studies 7:149–159.
1976   Forest to Pasture: Development or Destruction? *Revista de Biologia
         Tropical* 24 (Supplement 1):121–138.

Schmidt de Rojas, A.
1976   Distribucion Espacial de la Poblacion y Migraciones Interiores. In
         La Poblacion de Costa Rica, ed. M. E. Fernandez et al., pp. 75–
         104. San Jose: Editorial Universidad de Costa Rica.

Solera-Ruiz, Carlos
1981   Assessment of the Goals and the Policies of the National Devel-
         opment Plan 1979–1982 for Beef Cattle in Costa Rica. Unpublished
         Ph.D. dissertation, Iowa State University.

Strickon, Arnold
1965   The Euro-American Cattle Complex. In *Man, Culture, and Animals,*
         ed. A. Leeds and A. Vayda, pp. 229–258. Washington, D.C.:
         American Association for the Advancement of Science.

Taussig, Michael
1978   Nutrition, Development, and Foreign Aid: A Case Study of U.S.-
         Directed Health Care in a Columbian Plantation Zone. *International
         Journal of Health Service* 8(1):101–120.

Tosi, Joseph A., Jr.
1975   *Los Recursos Forestales de Costa Rica.* San Jose: Centro Cientifico
         Tropical.

United States Agency for International Development (USAID)
   1975   Nutritional Assessment for Costa Rica. Washington, D.C.: USAID.
           Mimeograph.

United States Department of Agriculture (USDA)
   1965   *The Beef Export Trade of Central America.* Washington, D.C.:
           Foreign Agriculture Service Monograph.
   1969   *The Beef Cattle Industries of Central America and Panama.* Wash-
           ington, D.C.: Foreign Agriculture Service Monograph.
   1973   *The Beef Cattle Industries of Central America and Panama.* Wash-
           ington, D.C.: Foreign Agriculture Service.

Watkins, Melville H.
   1963   A Staple Theory of Economic Growth. *Canadian Journal of Eco-*
           nomics and Political Science 29:141–158.

Whiteford, Michael B.
   1981   *The Socio-Cultural Etiologies of Nutritional Status in Rural Costa*
           Rica. Papers in Anthropology no. 4, Department of Sociology and
           Anthropology. Ames: Iowa State University.

Part IV

Issues of Power,
Participation, and Advocacy

11
Development and Women: Critical Issues

Christine Obbo

Scholars have found that if they wish to extract funds from various organizations, current fashion dictates that they at least claim an interest in development somewhere in their research proposal. Better still, scholars who wish to have lucratively funded research must get themselves in the various Washington, D.C., consultancy registries—it appears that next to the government, consultancy is the second largest employer in that city. Governments and research funding organizations feel that foreign assistance must take into account regions or sections of the population that have been hitherto neglected. The catchall word, "development," has been in currency since the 1950s,[1] but it is only in the past decade that women have been "discovered" as an important component in the development process and regarded as worth focusing attention on in domestic and international discussions dealing with research and the allocation of funds.

The prevalence of famine, poverty, illiteracy, and disease in the developing countries has led to the recognition that the development decade of the 1960s was more or less a failure. The failure has been partly attributed to the neglect of women, who in most countries constitute over half the population and are the main subsistence producers, educators, and managers of family welfare. The subject of the role of women in development is now being pursued with a vengeance, some would say. Numerous microstudies have documented women's economic contribution[2] and how poorly they have benefited from development policies.[3] Current arguments and studies have revived an old idea proposed by Dumont (1966, 1969) that to integrate women in the development process, the development "kit" must include "adequate technologies," "basic needs technologies," or "appropriate technology."[4]

In short, development has become a booming industry for scholars, bureaucrats, and private as well a government agencies. It is within this scenario that the critical issues of women and development will be examined. This chapter briefly reviews the problems facing scholars, then deals with the internal and external factors that hinder or enhance the effectiveness of policies and technologies.

Scholarship

Women entered the North-South dialogue[5] at the Mexico World Conference, which was the climax of the United Nations International Woman's Year, in 1975. Although Western feminists insisted that inequalities between the sexes were critical to all women, Third World women felt that the fundamental issue was the economic underdevelopment of their countries by the capitalist Western nations. In addition, the missionary zeal of some Western feminists provoked a Nigerian journalist attending the Mexico conference to express boredom with the new "great white hopes" and to repudiate "intellectual imperialism" as exemplified by the "patronizing" expressed wishes to radicalize Third World women in their struggles against sexism.[6] This statement put into words the repugnance educated African women have always felt about certain Western attitudes.[7]

In 1976, the African women attending the Conference on Women and Development at Wellesley College pointed out that just as economic imperialism or neocolonialism meant that Third World countries continued to provide raw materials for Western industries and constituted a ready market for industrial consumer goods, intellectual neocolonialism also continued to exploit and underdevelop African scholarship.[8] Western scholars continue to go to Third World countries and obtain data that they take home to process into "theories" to be packaged as development models for Third World countries.

The central issue is the lack of input from Third World scholars during the important stages of data collection, processing, and packaging. The African women at the Wellesley conference felt that although they had been invited to attend, they found the conference organizers heavy handed and insensitive, as was shown by their use of "patronizing and insulting" language during dialogues with them.[9] Part of the statement they issued read as follows: "We recognize that the primary reality of our societies today is unquestionably that of neocolonialism which presents severe obstacles to us as African peoples as women and as researchers, and which is the major obstacle to development in the broadest sense."[10] Elsewhere it has been pointed out that even Western women, while waving the flag of sisterhood, are very protective and defensive as they carve out a niche for themselves as experts for research institutes and funding agencies.[11]

Not only have scholars been sensitized to regard women as a legitimate area of inquiry just recently, but social science theories and methods for studying women are generally inadequate. Scholarship on women is at a "muddling through" or teething stage. Concerned African women who want to contribute to the articulation and possible solutions of problems faced by women in Africa are experiencing a sense of exclusion and frustration at the manner in which these issues are discussed externally. These factors led to the formation of the Association of African Women for Research and Development (AAWORD), whose aim is to make African women researchers known and to share data collection and theory generation with foreign researchers. They expect their insider status will help correct the "ethnocentrism" and "faulty methodology" that is often employed in research on Africa by consultants and subcontractors employed by foreign agencies to distribute aid.

But while African women researchers see research and aid as tools of external domination, they have encountered another bind in the form of domestic sexism. This problem has been perspicuously stated this way: "Locally, they suffered from isolation as issues concerning women are not considered important enough to discuss."[12] African research institutes have not considered either the study of women or the recruitment of women researchers to be among their priorities.[13] Men at the research institutes will cover up their scientific ignorance by arguing against the appropriateness and relevance of studying women because they know all about women. At this point the issue is funding,[14] but even when this hurdle is overcome, individual committed scholars in many countries tend to remain in isolated positions in universities or in agencies, both national and international, that do not recognize the value of their work (Papanek 1981: 216). This is part of the problem in developing macrotheories on women.

Consequently, it is difficult to find research that encompasses a cross-cultural, international, and interdisciplinary approach to the specific problems of women and development and how they relate to policy. The research on women and development suffers from not being integrated into the broad frameworks used to analyze and predict economic, social, and political trends and issues in development generally.

Internal and External Constraints to Policies and Technologies

Sullerot has warned of the unwitting revenge of the women in the world today, who are indispensable to the solution of the world's great problems, particularly overpopulation, starvation, underdevelopment, and illiteracy. She pointed out that without the positive contribution of women, population control, economic development, and education policies cannot succeed—even when imposed by the most powerful leaders (1971: 248).

In Africa, the 1960s ushered in political independence and programs to "develop" and "modernize." Schools, hospitals, roads, and hotels were built, but within a short time it became clear that the colonial elites, the postindependence elites, and the expatriates were becoming entrenched in their exclusive use of the amenities. The basis of most countries remained peasant agriculture. Except in a few countries that had mines, agriculture contributed over 80 percent of the gross domestic product, provided employment for about 70 percent of the labor force, and produced over 60 percent of all exports.[15] Each year, the peasants were called upon to work even harder. There was visible material wealth that the peasant worked harder and harder to acquire even though bicycles, transistor radios, clothing, and other domestic industrial goods such as china and enamel cups, plates and bowls, aluminum saucepans, and blankets were being produced locally by subsidiaries of multinational companies.[16] At the same time, it was also becoming noticeable that the elites were driving big cars and shopping abroad. This was modernization!

As the volume of cash crop production increased, the land available for food production decreased. Since feeding the family is the woman's "duty" in Africa, as in most agrarian societies, many women found it necessary to engage in income-generating activities in order to feed their families, but these activities depended upon the traditional skills of brewing beer, making baskets, braiding hair and even digging.

The economic contributions of African women have always been recognized although not publicly rewarded. In colonial times, the officials knew that women were the backbone of agriculture and that they supplemented the low urban wages of males. In the last decade, the migration of women has been resented, particularly by the urban men who do not want to lose the second income—in Uganda, the poorest man is said to be one without a wife to generate wealth for him.

Women in some societies have used threats to withdraw their labour to bargain for greater latitude in other areas.[17] In the south of Uganda, the 1900 agreement between Great Britain and the Buganda, among other provisions, radically transformed the system of land tenure from communal ownership to freehold. In 1904, cotton was introduced by the Church Missionary Society, and coffee followed about 1914. Overzealous chiefs whipped their subjects to make them grow cotton. The men resented being treated like women and complained that they did not want "to stoop and dig the ground like a woman,"[18] even though men's hoes have long handles so they, in fact, dug from a relatively upright position. Married men saw their job as one of supervising, occasionally helping the women and children, and above all, strolling empty handed or headed to the trading posts to spend the proceeds from the sales.[19] The women complained that their work load had increased, they demanded plots from their husbands so they could grow their own cash crops, and they threatened to stop growing bananas and instead seek wage labor like the men.[20]

By the 1940s, women were acquiring land in their own right through allocations from their husbands, inheritance, and purchase. In the 1960s, the government of independent Uganda called upon every man, woman, and child to assist in the task of nation building. As far as agricultural work was concerned, the unspoken stress was understood by everyone to be on the women, but the extension officers who visited the farms demonstrated the pruning and spraying of coffee trees and the destruction of potato and banana root worms to the men. The women were advised to attend related extension courses at subcounty community centers. There was enthusiasm among the women as they planned their activities so that at least once a week they had an afternoon free to go and learn sewing, chicken and vegetable farming, and balancing and cooking meals the proper way to retain nutrition. However, they continued to use their hoes to bash banana root worms because those who had tried to use the chemical *dudumaki* managed to destroy the trees because they had not learned the proper application methods. They also continued to curse the potato root worms. This case study shows that women were willing to learn new ideas and techniques but they had to be taught.

As the population increased, the pressure on land grew, and the urban areas seemed much more attractive in terms of being rewarded for labor. In 1974, the low-income women I interviewed in Nairobi and Kampala stressed, among other things, that they had left the rural areas because farm work took too much time and was back breaking, yet the harvests were poor. Women as producers at least wanted their labor to be reflected in output. In the cases in which the women, after a lot of arguments, had decided to accompany their migrant husbands to town, they realized immediately on arrival that everything costs money and since the husband's wages were not adequate, they had to earn money. These women sell food, vegetables, beer, etc., and the issue of who should control their income surfaced in each case I examined.

The majority of the women, however, have stayed in the rural areas and do the best they can. In a village in the East Kano District of western Kenya, Luo women stressed that they needed to own land. I recorded cases in whch women refused to cultivate the so-called husbands' gardens and spent their energies growing corn and sugarcane for the nearby sugar mill. The corn that was not budgeted for feeding the family was sold at market, and the cash was used to buy clothing and milk for the children as well as paying for grinding corn at a diesel power mill owned by a local politician. Some enterprising women took their corn to nearby South Nyanza where they sold it, then bought groundnuts, baskets, and pots, which they took by bus to Nairobi. In some cases, they retailed the items or sold them to Indian or other traders. These trips were usually combined with visiting their husbands. Three women had bought land, but since land technically belongs to men, their brothers had conducted the transactions for them.

Although rural trading is one way women generate income to support their families or to ease the insecurities they feel in not controlling land, the phenomenon of women who earn money by agricultural labor has also increased in the rural areas of Buganda. Between 1971 and 1974, while conducting research, there were a few women from Ruanda and Burundi who were employed as agricultural wage earners—previously, only their men had been engaged in this international search for a monetary income. By 1979, many Ganda women were employed to weed food crops, harvest coffee, cook, and fetch water and firewood for relatively rich rural elites. Meanwhile, the urban elites complained that it was difficult to find domestic servants, even when they brought someone from a village, and many female ex-domestics could be seen weeding municipal flower beds, cutting grass, and pruning bushes. Despite the fact that the wages were low, they claimed they preferred to work for the urban authorities, with fixed hours and clearly defined duties, than to work for the elites who made them work long hours for a pittance.

Those women whose labor power has become a commodity no longer have the option to refrain from work. The married rural women in this category continue to produce food and in many ways subsidize urban wages, which serves to lower the urban wages of men and women alike. But women have further to contend with sexual discrimination, which means that they are always receiving lower wages than men. The proletarianized or independent women, who have overcome subordination to men within the family, often find themselves subordinate to men in the marketplace (Bryceson 1980, Obbo 1980). These women are economically self-supporting while others rely on "boyfriends" to pay the rent, but in both cases, they usually depend on relatives or friends or neighbors in regard to cooking, babysitting, housekeeping, and income generation (Bryceson 1980, Obbo 1980).

It will appear that although "what in a group of countries is called the issue of sexism" has been reduced to a footnote in international dialogues, it cannot be denied that "the unfavourable status of women is aggravated in many countries, developed and underdeveloped, by *de facto* discrimination on the grounds of sex."[21] Worldwide, the condition of women may be changing constantly, but it still remains less advanced than that of men. In the Third World, generally, and Africa in particular, there is an increasing number of elite women who enjoy a high visibility and earning power that dilute their experiences of sexism, but the majority of peasant women in the rural areas and the semi-illiterate and illiterate women in the urban areas live within a structure that limits their options and strategies. The women express their desire to share fairly the resources of their societies, and the working women speak of their need for decent wages and for work other than self-employment using traditional skills and battling against city officials and regulations.

The idea of integrating women into the development process as equal partners with men has been floating around, but its adoption by some member states of the United Nations was the result of the UN Programme of Action. However, in many countries it is assumed that women are automatically beneficiaries of development policies simply because of their contribution to their society's economy. Recent studies have documented that the opposite is true: Women in many countries, although indispensable in agricultural production, are denied resources (training, credit, and even land) that are made available to male producers. In the North-South dialogue, there has been a tendency to argue that women are not an isolated group with special needs because men also suffer from uneven development. But what seems to remain unmentioned is that even in Third World countries, the political leaders are men with the authority to define which activities carry prestige and which deserve and which do not deserve remuneration. Through policies and practices they impose the type of advancement they will allow women to have, in ways very similar to the way the industrialized world influences the rate of modernization in the developing countries. Through their policy decisions, political leaders have erected parallel ladders for men and women, but the condition of men and women is not uniform even upon their respective ladders. Any discussion that leaves out class or other social distinctions such as marital status, age, and caste does not give a complete picture.

The persistent dilemma facing Third World elite women is how to achieve autonomy while uniting with men to face broader economic and social issues. It is worthwhile to remember that sexism, unlike class or racial oppression, did not come out of imperialism or capitalism. Many societies have ideologies that allow male authority and control over a woman's person and her reproductive capacity. The sexual division of labor and the possession of women by men is a precapitalist phenomenon— and so is the fact that women lag behind.

To remedy this state of affairs, recent research and policies have emphasized "women's projects" or "women's components" in development projects. The Percy Amendment to the Foreign Assistance Bill of 1973 states that foreign assistance "shall be administered so as to give attention to those programs, projects and activities which tend to integrate women into the national economies of foreign countries, thus improving their status and assisting the total development effort."[22] This approach is important in attempting to correct the disadvantaged position of women, but in some countries, women's issues can be swept under the carpet by arguing that with "modernization" (national development) and increased education, the social attitudes toward women will change (Papanek 1981: 219). In addition, widespread caution has been reported among development agencies when it comes to women's programs, which is shown by the fact that agencies demand "strong documentation" that a program for women is really needed since there is lack of knowledge about women (p. 220).

As knowledge accumulates, it becomes relegated to a special "women in development" section. These departments of women in development in agencies are essential for documentation, but often their data do not become incorporated into the planning and policy decision stages of development programs. The planners who often engage in the most incredible national projections based on flimsy data appear awkward in planning with empirical data on women (Papanek 1981: 220). The emphasis on special projects for women underscores the ignorance regarding women's work. There is no precise information about domestic work, which explains why it has never appeared in economic models. The sexual division of labor tells us who is doing what. Many microstudies on working women have documented that irrespective of geographical region or economic system, women cross-culturally work longer hours than men. And although women are said to compose only one-third of the world's official labor force, the nonmarket activities that consume most of their energy and time are not considered. The knowledge, for example, that women prepare food does not necessarily include knowing the complexities involved. In fact, in most places, the preparation of food is regarded as leisure and a waste of productive time.

In a village in Buganda, I tried to find out why women who had joined literacy and other self-improvement programs such as sewing and cooking had dropped out. The men told me they did not know what the women did with their time since farm work (gardening) ended at 9:00 or 10:00 A.M. It turned out that the men were talking about when *they* finished gardening and returned home to drink some tea before visiting with friends or fixing things around the homestead. In actual fact, most of the women hoed until 12:00. Some harvested bananas, which took up to thirty minutes or an hour depending on whether the stems had to be stripped and laid out for mulch, and others dug out potatoes, using sharpened sticks, which took about half an hour—in the case of new potatoes, it took up to one and a half hours. On returning home, they would rush to get water, if they had not done so the day before or if they had no child old enough to help them. They would have a mug of tea while peeling the bananas and potatoes, and as soon as the food had been wrapped up and put on the fire, they would go and collect spinach or other vegetables to be cleaned and cooked. By three o'clock, the women would have washed themselves, and lunch would be ready. After-lunch chores varied depending on the season. During the weeding season, the women spent their siesta time preparing the evening meal and occasionally working on their handicrafts such as baskets and mats. During the coffee harvesting period, they usually had to cook cassava with the evening meal for lunch the next day, or those with children would have them cook while the adults picked coffee between 3:00 and 6:00 P.M. This schedule meant that the evening meals would not be eaten until 10:00 P.M. or midnight.

I have elaborated on this case study because it illustrates the misconceptions regarding women's work. In another study done in the Bukoba area of Tanzania to determine the constraints on labor time available to small farmers, it was found that there was a tendency to regard domestic activities, which occupied most of the women's time, as a principal constraint on female agricultural labor (Kamuzora 1980: 131–132). Like Ganda women, these women allegedly stopped agricultural work early in order to prepare food, and the men take exception to the amount of time women spend on domestic activities (p. 132). The study leaves little doubt that women have no leisure except that necessitated by sitting down to eat, caring for the sick, or attending funerals of relatives and neighbors. Men who had no cattle to care for rested, visited their neighbors or the bar, or attended political meetings while their wives prepared food (p. 130). It turns out that the real constraints on the availability of labor time are the high rates of morbidity and mortality (p. 133). Thus social activities, meaning attending the sick or funerals, take up between 13 and 14 percent of the farmers' time (p. 132). Women's domestic work is essential. In Western countries, all the substitutes for domestic work such as cleaning, cooking, babysitting, repairing all sorts of things, and craft production are regarded as premium labor and command high pay.

A paper by the International Labor Organization (ILO) Office for Women has pointed out that some of the difficulties involved in the development process are due to inequalities of access to technical education and technological knowledge, and it calls for specific policy measures to improve the technological level of women for higher productivity in employment (ILO 1981: 34). Technology as an issue relating directly to women cannot be left out in any meaningful decision of development or the strategies for different approaches to basic needs.

In any discussion of women and technology, illiteracy stands out as a major obstacle. Although more girls are attending school than before, their dropout rates continue to be higher than those of boys. Although reasons like poor academic performance or pregnancy are important factors in accounting for the dropout rates, the widespread preference for boys means that girls are the ones who are more likely to drop out to help with economic activities such as farming or trading. Thus, school intake and graduation figures do not reflect the ratio of the sexes in the population.

The World Bank is helping various countries improve the educational opportunities for women. In Papua, New Guinea, radio programs will be used to promote positive attitudes toward female education, and it is hoped that the recruitment and training of local women as teachers will provide a role model for girls and encourage them to go to school. In the pipeline are projects to increase the number of women teachers in Yemen, Syria, and Pakistan. In Mauritius, in an attempt to redress previous enrollment inequalities, 60 percent of the new places being provided in junior secondary schools will be for girls, and in Tanzania, a new education project plans to increase boarding facilities for girls at technical schools—the university entrance requirements had already been adjusted to facilitate the education of women. In Morocco, an educational center for women in Rabat will combine craft and vocational training with reading, writing, and elementary mathematics.

The ILO report has shown that in most developing countries, not only are few girls enrolled in technical and vocational education but those who are enrolled learn sewing, dressmaking, housecraft, child care, and embroidery (ILO 1981: 37). It is clear that the women are being trained to be nothing more than skillful contributing dependents; the roles of wife and mother are always foremost in the minds of the planners (Ellickson 1975: 81). Although home economics is important in the development process, women must also be trained to be skilled users of modern technology. In Africa, the number of women technicians in medicine and industry is growing, but it is still small. Agricultural extension officers need to know home economics, but they are more valuable if they have skilled technical knowledge on how to increase production using the simplest and most efficient methods.

Women's lack of access to technical education and the practice of overlooking women lead to erroneous assumptions such as that appropriate modern labor is that performed by men because women are backward. The real issue is selective exposure. Policies continue to regard men as the main agents of technological change while the women learn by hearsay from less informed people. Women generally have limited or no access to technological input at any level, and using muscle power instead of animal or horse power, the women have been unable to meet the demands of feeding increasing populations. Often when the producers are not assumed to be male, women's labor and production problems are made invisible by pretending that the sex of the producer is not a relevant factor.

In Upper Volta, Conti (1980) has found that women were resisting a multimillion dollar resettlement project financed by the World Bank and others. The pilot project aimed at restructuring the local economy by increasing the commercialization of production, but the women found that they were more dependent upon men for their personal needs and that their labor had also increased. The scheme was based on the assumption that the nuclear family would be the unit of production and use "appropriate technology," but it was reported that many women were leaving the settlement scheme because facilities that they regarded as essential in their home villages had not been thought of, including land to grow the family food, a village well, grain mills, and marketplaces (*Economist*, April 1979). Perhaps the extended family to help with the labor and to mediate the male control was also an important missing factor!

It has been claimed that one of the aims of appropriate technology is to ease the burden of the domestic chores. For example, thin-walled cement tanks, simple hand pumps, and better food storage facilities have been proposed, and the use of solar energy and wind power is being considered by international and local experts. The emphasis in the appropriate basic technology approach is on local generation and relevance, but in the case of the Upper Volta resettlement scheme just referred to, the appropriate technology has not bridged the gap of access privilege between men and women. Access to technology reflects not only the division of labor but also the ownership of land upon which relationships of production and redistribution depend. The Upper Volta case also raises the issue of the need for socioeconomic research that examines women's needs, wants, and problems as part of the problems of development. The question of when the technology is appropriate must also be addressed and not assumed by technologists and developmentalists.

African women have often been chastised for rejecting technological ideas that domestic elites and foreigners thought would be good for them. For example, in Ethiopia the introduction of cooking with solar energy, which would have reduced the hours women spent on collecting wood was rejected by the women for three reasons. First, by the time women finished the activities connected with animal husbandry, food processing, trading, and medical and spiritual health, daylight had ended, and the ovens were useless for cooking. Second, the women objected to cooking outside—it goes without saying that it is extremely difficult to prepare bread and meat outside. Third, the women did not want to cook in the sun as doing so caused certain illnesses and skin complaints. In this instance, the women's complaints expose the fallacy of the presumption that Third World people are so poor they will adopt any Western idea. It is harmful to stand in the hot sun for a long time, and cooking outside all the time is awkward in Africa, just as it would be in other areas.

In neighboring Egypt, however, in the village of Baseisa it seems that the peasants have been receptive to the idea of solar energy. It took three years for a Cairo-raised ("grand son of the village"), Princeton-trained young university professor to persuade the villagers to use it, but when they watched the 1977 meeting between Sadat and Begin on a television set powered by a solar cell placed on top of a cow dung barn, the excitement spread to nearby villages. When local politicians tried to bring in electricity, the people snubbed it in favor of solar energy. If the idea of solar power is ever implemented, not only will women have some of the cooking time reduced but other changes will result as well. For instance, they will be able to enjoy activities away from the house after the farming hours.

Another instance in which the technologists and developmentalists assumed they knew better than the users was in West Africa. Scythes seemed appropriate because they would save some of the time women spent harvesting the millet with the small knife. However, the women did not take kindly to the extra weight of the implement or the cuts and bruises produced by the longer stalks left after harvesting.

Technologies, whether aimed at women or the general population, seem to have the propensity to affect women adversely. Many interpretations have been suggested to account for the 1929 Aba riots, which took place in eastern Nigeria, but "development" seems to have been at the heart of it all. A large commercial venture to produce palm oil more efficiently involved taking the whole palm fruit to the mills where the men were paid and the nuts were thrown away. Previously the women had taken the nuts as payment for their labor and sold them, which generated some income.[23] The mills were taking away women's incomes. The women rioted, and everyone expressed surprise.

Property and Class Relations

In the course of this chapter, I have attempted to pinpoint the issues connected with women and development. The issues are interrelated, and they are all important. Policies and programs that are serious about development and women will have to try to identify, first, precisely which ideologies perpetuate the dominance of men over women and the property relations that result, and, second, the class relations that determine the local allocation and exploitation of resources. The factors of capitalism and imperialism are also important as they influence the rate of development.

Men, Women, and Property Relationships

The condition of women in any society can be meaningfully evaluated by comparing them to the men in that society. In Africa, the women are not begging for a stake in their society's future, for they are deeply entrenched as citizens, wives, and mothers, but almost any African woman will raise the issue that women are disadvantaged with regard to the society's resources. Because Africa is still predominantly agricultural, the resource women want to have equal access to is land. Women already provide labor power, and they wish to control the products of their labor because they learned from experience that owning the land gives men the prerogative over women's labor and what they produce. Rural women who manage to establish some way of reaping the fruits of their labor also usually use complex arrangements to overcome their ignorance as well as the tendency of others to overlook them. However, women farmers who acquaint themselves with new ideas and practices usually fail in implementing them because the people in charge of giving them credit erroneously assume that only men are farmers, despite the fact that they personally may know significant numbers of married, widowed, or unmarried women whose men (husbands, fathers, or brothers) only spend a total of a few days a year in the village.

The women who manage to migrate to the cities usually find that unless they are lucky, their lack of education and skills in the modern sector condemns them to the informal sector where they have to rely on their own initiative and skills to create employment for themselves. The daughters of ordinary rural and urban women sometimes receive an education that prepares them for white-collar jobs, but because they often drop out before they have acquired all the papers they need, they are not employed. When they are employed in light or heavy industries, they often find that upgrading their skills or their income is difficult.

because men are pushed to pursue the new ideas that improve their skills and increase their incomes. When hard times come, the women lose their jobs or are not hired because male labor is more valuable than theirs.

It has been pointed out that while the introduction of technology introduces new avenues of employment for women, in most cases it pushes women into less-skilled or low-skilled occupations that are less mechanized and command low wages. Also, whenever employment opportunities for all workers are in short supply, the women are the most likely to lose their jobs or to be denied jobs by male managers and employees who fear female competition (Mbilinyi 1976). This situation results from the myth that greater employment of women leads to even greater male unemployment. Women's employment is further resented because "their place is at home" and they can work only at the expense of domestic chores. This attitude leads to another that I have encountered many times: What do women need money for? Are they not satisfied with marriage?

Women in Uganda, rural and urban, elite and illiterate, find that segregated savings systems make their lives easier. The low-income women I studied followed their husband's practice of keeping their income or savings a mystery because, "When my husband sees me with money he suddenly claims to have no money for a cigarette or beer," or, "Since I started working, the children are sent to me if they need school fees, uniforms, or money for lunch." Also, the husbands start projects or engage in schemes that inevitably involve the wives' bailing them out, that is, "if domestic relations are not to be disrupted." In addition, women are expected to take care of the little domestic expenses like buying salt, milk, charcoal, etc.

Perhaps the presupposition that women do not need money is best illustrated by a Mauritius case related by A. Seidman (1981: 118). A U.S. factory manager complained that the women did not produce enough. When it was brought to his attention that they might be malnourished, he was willing to give them a slight increase in wages, but it was pointed out that the food bought with the extra money would probably be consumed by the husband and the rest of the family. Instead, the manager provided lunches, and productivity noticeably improved. This was a classic situation in which the women probably ate last at home and it was assumed that they had no use for money, hence the low wages.

There is also an implicit assumption that working women are married as well—it does not matter that this idea is contrary to even the domestic experiences of most people. Suffice to say that this assumption ignores a significant number of women. The market women who operate in official markets (for example, 80 percent of the Ghanian traders are women) or the informal-sector women who trade without licenses and have no legal protection are frequently unmarried or divorced. In Jamaica, many urban households are said to be headed by women, in Benin the number is as high as 30 percent, and in Kenya, 33 percent of the rural and urban households are in that category. In some parts of Uganda, the category of single women is an established social one.

It is going to be difficult for women to upgrade their skills or their income-generating activities when in country after country they are considered to be unproductive workers. The ILO report found that even in the textile industry, which employs many of the world's women workers, when new machines are installed, the tendency on the whole is to train the male workers to use them and to keep the women workers on the older nonautomatic machinery (ILO 1981: 46). In most cases, women using traditional technologies are pushed out by new techniques. In Zambia, female bakers in the small towns were displaced when the government introduced modern bakeries (Seidman 1981: 116). In Indonesia, women lost their only source of income when a rice mill that greatly reduced the number of work hours was introduced, and women spinners and weavers in various parts of India have suffered the same fate.

Class Relations

Some of the women who persevere and become professionals find that their earnings are on a par with those of their male colleagues, and those who are shrewd or are well connected to influential men may have access to the societal resources such as credit, land, or business. Uneducated women do not see any difference between elite men and women in their attitudes toward workers. Elite women are accused of being just as exploitive as elite men when dealing with employees who are domestic servants, farm laborers, and the like. In all stratified societies, men too are the victims of progress or development, but the women often see themselves as "victims of victims." As one woman put it, "however poor a man may be, he still lords over women." Also, however desperate the situation gets, the women must do their chores. Everyone needs a helper ("a wife"), but only men get to have wives in most cultures.

Technology will not play a decisive role in the process of development if policies do not aggressively deal with the traditional division of labor between the sexes; the relationship to production, i.e., land ownership and earnings from production; and ideological reasons that inhibit women from acquiring technology and skills. The declining status of women will not be corrected, and they will continue to be a wasted resource. This situation is best illustrated by looking at Tanzania where government policies have intervened to make education more accessible to women, to encourage women in technological training, to encourage women's participation in political offices, and to make women's membership meaningful in religious and village life by opening the mosques to women and registering women as independent landowners. Yet even in Tanzania the contradictions continue. In some areas the village council does not allocate land to women, in other villages women's groups are denied land for planting permanent crops, and women continue to migrate to the urban areas as an escape from male control. But in the towns, unless they engage in self-employment, they find that they have exchanged domestic male control for that of the work situation. Their willingness to put up with the discrimination and harassment will determine to a large extent whether their skills and salaries are upgraded.

The contradictions in the lives of Third World women require serious examination and multipronged solutions. The causes are domestic and foreign, so the solutions will have to be likewise.

Notes

1. The colonial governments in Uganda and Tanzania had development plans that seem progressive even today, but there is no evidence that they were ever implemented on a national scale. See, for instance, E. Barry Worthington, *The Uganda Development Plan* (Entebbe: Government Printer, 1946).

2. See N. J. Hafkin, *Women and Development in Africa: An Annotated Bibliography* (Addis Ababa: ECA, 1976).

3. For example, J. L. Brain, "Less Than Second Class: Women in Rural Settlement Schemes in Tanzania," in *Women in Africa*, ed. Nancy J. Hafkin and Edna G. Bay (Stanford: Stanford University Press, 1976), pp. 271–273.

4. ILO, *A Research Note on Technology and Rural Women* (Geneva, April 1978), and ILO, "Appropriate Technologies for Employment Generation in the Food Processing and Drinks Industries, mimeograph (Geneva: World Employment Programme Research, September 1977).

5. The North-South dialogue calls for a new economic arrangement between the industrialized nations and the Third World countries. At the heart of the issue is the widening gap between the rich ("have") and the poor ("have not") nations. The exploitation by the former has led to the underdevelopment of the latter.

6. Quoted in Kenneth Little, "African Women: Traditional or Liberated?" *West Africa*, July 14, 1975.

7. One comes across many Western academic women who fervently use feminist rhetoric to condemn the deplorable situation Third World women find themselves in, but the latter resent non-Westerners pointing out intolerable aspects of sexism in their lives or in the society generally. A woman who was about to set off on a development mission to Africa told a group of Africans attending the University of Wisconsin: "I love Africans. They are so easy to understand." Raised eyebrows caused her to mutter, "eh, . . . they laugh and they are friendly." Still, an expert on Zimbabwe felt it necessary to sprinkle her lecture with comments like, "The women are so muscular they violate our standards of beauty."

8. "Statement by a Group of Women from Africa and of African Descent Attending the Wellesley Conference on Women and Development," Wellesley, Massachusetts, June 2–6, 1976.

9. Ibid.

10. Ibid.

11. "Building New Knowledge Through Technical Cooperation Among Developing Countries: The Experience of the Association of African Women for Research and Development" (Paper presented at the United Nations Meeting on

Technical Cooperation Among Developing Countries, Geneva, May 26–June 2, 1980; henceforth referred to as AAWORD).

12. AAWORD, p. 4.

13. Ibid., p. 13.

14. In a book on Bangladesh women, it was pointed out that the only three studies on rural women had been done by foreigners. "This is an indication of the present limits within which Bengalese women operate in their own society, and the freedom from such constraints enjoyed by foreign research workers," (*Women for Women* [Bangladesh: Bangladesh University Press, 1975], p. xi).

15. The official statistics usually ignore women when discussing remuneration of the agricultural labor force precisely because they are not paid employees and their work is regarded as traditional. This situation does not change the fact that their tasks make up the bulk of the agricultural labor work.

16. The importance of industrial products in the material well-being of people cannot be underestimated. In recent years, smuggling has affected many African countries with scarce industrial goods. For example, along the Tanzania-Kenya border, the smuggling of clothing became particularly acute as goods became scarce and the currency weakened in Tanzania. On the Kenya-Uganda border, smuggling was the only way to get foreign goods. A trucker who invested 42 Kenya shillings in bags of maize flour sold them for 600 Kenya shillings at the border. This story has been repeated many times over.

17. See, for example, Ronald Cohen, *The Kanuri of Bornu* (New York: Holt, Rinehart and Winston, 1971), and Harold K. Schneider, *The Wahi Wanyaturu: Economics in an African Society* (Chicago: Aldine Publishing Company, 1970).

18. *Mengo Notes* (Kampala) 4:4 (April 1903): 21; quoted in P. G. Powesland, "The History of the Migration in Uganda," in *Economic Development and Tribal Change*, ed. Audrey I. Richards, rev. ed. (Nairobi: Oxford University Press, 1973), p. 18.

19. Powesland, "History of Migration in Uganda," p. 22.

20. Ibid., p. 21.

21. See 1975 International Women's Year Conference, Programme of Action, paragraph 12.

22. U.S. Congress, Senate, *Congressional Record*, S. 18423, October 2, 1973.

23. Personal communication, October 1980, with Dr. G. Jones, administrator of Eastern Nigeria in 1927–1947.

References

Bryceson, Doborah Fahy
    1980   The Proletarization of Women in Tanzania. *Review of African Political Economy*, no. 17 (November).

Conti, Anna
    1980   Capitalist Organization of Production Through Non-Capitalist Relations: Women's Role in a Pilot Resettlement in Upper Volta. *Review of African Political Economy*, no. 16 (July).

Dumont, R.
    1966   *False Start in Africa*. New York: Praeger.
    1969   *1969 Tanzanian Agriculture After the Arusha Declaration: A Report*. Dar es Salaam: Ministry to Economic Affairs and Development Planning.

Ellickson, Jean
  1975   Rural Women. In *Women for Women*, pp. 814–889. Dacca: Bangladesh University Press.

International Labor Organization (ILO), Office for Women
  1981   Women, Technology, and the Development Process. In Roslyn Danker and Melinda L. Cain, eds., *Women and Technological Change in Developing Countries*, pp. 33–47. Boulder, Colo.: Westview Press for the American Association for the Advancement of Science.

Kamuzora, C. Lwechungura
  1980   Constraints to Labour Time Availability in Smallholder Agriculture: The Case of Bukoba District, Tanzania. *Development and Change* 11(1): 123–136.

Mbilinyi, M.
  1976   Women as Labour in Underdevelopment. Paper presented at Wellesley Conference on Women and Development, June 1976, Wellesley College.

Obbo, Christine
  1980   *African Women: Their Struggle for Economic Independence.* London: Zed Press.

Papanek, Hanna
  1981   The Differential Impact of Programs and Policies on Women in Development. In Roslyn Danker and Melinda L. Cain, eds., *Women and Technological Change in Developing Countries*, pp. 215–220. Boulder, Colo.: Westview Press for the American Association for the Advancement of Science.

Seidman, Ann
  1981   Women and the Development of "Underdevelopment": The African Experience. In Roslyn Danker and Melinda L. Cain, eds., *Women and Technological Change in Developing Countries*, pp. 109–123. Boulder, Colo.: Westview Press for the American Association for the Advancement of Science.

Sullerot, Evelyne
  1971   *Women, Society, and Change.* London: World University Library.

12
The Social Impacts of Differential Access to New Health Programs in Northern Nigeria

Robert Stock

"Who gets what where?" D. M. Smith's statement of theme from his study of the geography of inequality, *Where the Grass Is Greener* (1979), might profitably be rephrased, "Who gets what where, and with what consequences?" Expenditure on the development of social services like health care facilities, whether undertaken by governments or private enterprise, occurs within a spatial frame of reference. Decisionmakers reflect in their attitudes and priorities their own class and educational backgrounds and other factors such as available information and political considerations. Spatial inequalities have grave consequences for those people who are denied adequate access to basic human needs such as sufficient food, safe water, and health care. These consequences include an increase in the rate, duration, and seriousness of disease; increased mortality risk; and reduced productivity.

The actual impact of health care provision on health cannot be measured accurately, and health care is only one of many interrelated factors affecting levels of morbidity and mortality. The quality of food, available safe water, the elimination of disease vectors and hazardous environmental conditions, and personal variables associated with life-style and education also have profound effects on human health. In fact, historical demographic research suggests strongly that the quality of medical care is significantly less important than life-style and environmental factors (McKeown 1976). Nevertheless, modern medicine provides effective remedies for the prevention and treatment of conditions that formerly were routinely fatal.

Disease and Underdevelopment

The burden of disease in Africa remains not only the cause of excessive suffering and death but a significant impediment to development. Ironically, disease was a major factor protecting the interior of Africa, "the white man's grave," from European penetration and colonization until the latter part of the nineteenth century. The World Health Organization (WHO) categorizes Africa as the least healthy continent:

> Available data showed that over most of middle Africa malaria infected virtually every child by its third year of life, accounting for probably one third of those who failed to survive that critical hurdle; that although human trypanosomiasis had been largely contained, its reservoir in animals and the ever-present tsetse posed a constant threat of resurgence; that schistosomiasis would probably spread even further as hydro-agricultural and industrial schemes developed, that onchocerciasis continued, unchecked, to create human suffering, while forcing the abandonment of extensive fertile areas the loss of which, even temporarily, the countries could ill afford; that tuberculosis and leprosy pursued their course among a heavy proportion of the population; that although considerable progress had been made in reducing yaws endemicity, the goal of eradication had become more difficult to achieve; and that other diseases such as measles, smallpox and cerebrospinal meningitis added each year to the toll of morbidity and. mortality. In addition to this heavy load, the prevalence of kwashiorkor and other manifestations of protein deficiency was also known, as was the general inadequacy or total absence of sanitation facilities and safe water supplies, particularly in the rural areas. [WHO 1968, 4]

The diseases usually categorized in medical science as being "man-made and degenerative," such as cardiovascular diseases, malignant neo-plasms (cancers), and diabetes, are relatively unimportant as causes of death in Africa. The infectious diseases and conditions associated with undernutrition are the primary causes of morbidity and mortality. With an estimated average of two infections per person, Africa is the most parasitized of all the continents (Hughes and Hunter 1970). These organisms cause many types of debilitating and potentially fatal diseases, of which malaria and schistosomiasis are but two examples. The impact of these vector-borne infections and of nonvectored infectious diseases such as diarrhea and measles is exacerbated by the prevalence of general protein-calorie malnutrition as well as various specific nutritional deficiencies.

Although it is universally recognized that African health problems are both varied and severe, there is some disagreement concerning the explanation of this situation. Are these problems primarily environmental or anthropogenic? Are they primarily a reflection of local or of global relationships? In the past, the debilitating environments of the tropics were viewed deterministically as the essential cause of African ill health (e.g., Gourou 1966). Tropical environments, which facilitate the survival, rapid proliferation, and dissemination of disease organisms, are still recognized as being important, but few people would still claim that environment is more important than human influences. The most popular mankind-related explanations have ranged from culture-specific criticisms of traditional beliefs such as food taboos and reliance on traditional medicine to very general explanations focusing on the poverty and lack of development of the continent. Such explanations are of little value if the nature and perpetuation of poverty and lack of development are not explored. This fact accounts for the emergence of a growing body of literature that sees original African health problems as being perpetuated by and new problems as being generated by the processes of development and underdevelopment. Whereas earlier contributions stressed the detrimental side effects of development schemes (e.g., Hughes and Hunter 1970), later writers such as Elling (1981) stress that the persistence of excessive morbidity and mortality is no accident but, rather, is the inevitable consequence of capitalist activity in underdeveloped countries.

Capitalist underdevelopment and the underdevelopment of health integral to it began with colonial policies such as the alienation of land and the recruitment of labor away from subsistence agriculture by force or the imposition of taxes. The migrant workers were exposed to a variety of new health hazards and unwittingly acted as diffusion agents for disease. Meanwhile, food shortages became chronic in the villages as a result of the loss of land and productive manpower (Wisner 1980–1981). On the regional and national levels, very weak and dependent economic and potential structures were a universal part of the colonial legacy, and African countries remain unable to generate sufficient resources to effectively change the health status of their populations. Moreover, available resources are disproportionally consumed by the urban elites, who have the fewest unmet health-related needs but the greatest political power. The active underdevelopment of health is now particularly evident in the marketing activities of multinational corporations selling health-threatening infant formulas and other processed foods, dangerous drugs, and pesticides in the Third World.

Investment in health care delivery programs cannot fundamentally change the health status of Africans without concurrent programs dedicated to changing the structures and processes responsible for the deepening underdevelopment of health. More hospitals will not mean less infant malnutrition and mortality if the ill-advised use of infant formulas continues to increase. Rather, efforts to improve living conditions and alleviate the fundamental causes of suffering and death must go hand in hand with programs to improve the accessibility and quality of health care. Whereas better water supply, sanitation, and housing generally alter the *incidence* of disease, curative medicine generally has more impact on its *effects* than on incidence (World Bank 1975).

Many studies have shown that relatively large and rapid benefits can be obtained through increased expenditure on basic health services in very poor countries where basic needs remain unmet (Basch 1978). Immunization programs to protect infants from diseases like measles and whooping cough, when combined with supportive measures like health education, can significantly reduce infant mortality. For example, infant mortality in a southern Nigerian locality was reduced from 295 to 72 per 1,000 live births and child mortality from 69 to 28 per 1,000 with the provision of physician-staffed primary care and some nutritional assistance (Morely 1973). "Poor people usually have inexpensive possessions and this includes their illnesses. . . . Disease cheaply acquired may also be relatively cheaply prevented" (Basch 1978, 248).

The extent of colonial neglect of the health and well-being of Africans varied greatly, and it is equally hard to generalize about the effectiveness and social justice of health-related programs since independence. Certain countries such as Tanzania and Mozambique have concentrated on providing basic health services, both preventative and curative, for everyone, as well as reallocating resources so as to reduce class-based and spatial disparities in access to care. The health services of many other countries show little evidence of restructuring but are characterized instead by a perpetuation of the colonial model of health service provision and a deepening of disparities in health and access to health care.

The case study that follows is an example of the latter situation, namely, continued neglect of the health problems of the majority of people. The extent, origins, and consequences of unequal access to Western scientific medicine are considered. In the absence of appropriate data on health status and levels of morbidity and mortality, the impact of unequal access to health care is approached through an examination of patterns of health service utilization, especially the relationship between traveling distance to health facilities and the per capita utilization of those establishments.

Study Area

This study focuses on the utilization of Western scientific medical facilities in Kano State, Nigeria. It is based primarily on fieldwork conducted in 1976–1977 and 1982 in the vicinity of Hadejia, a town of 40,000 people located 200 km. east of the city of Kano. The initial research project included interviews with 4,260 patients at health facilities about their illnesses and the therapeutic strategies employed. These interviews yielded solid evidence about the nature of spatial variations in the utilization of the facilities as well as considerable information about the utilization of other types of medical treatment.

Kano State (Figure 12.1) had an estimated 9,467,000 people in 1981, of whom approximately 870,000 lived in the four Hadejia local government areas (L.G.A.s)—Hadejia, Kafin Hausa, Birniwa, and Kaugama (Kano State 1981). Metropolitan Kano, with some 800,000 people, is the only urban center exceeding 40,000 people.

The great majority of the population, consisting of Hausa and Kanuri farmers and Fulani herdsmen, lives in smaller rural settlements. Close to 100 percent of Kano State's indigenous population is Muslim, although there are small pockets of Maguzawa (Hausa speakers who practice

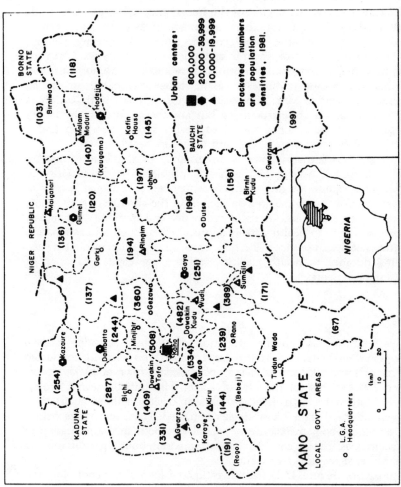

Figure 12.1 Population map of Kano State. Since the 1980 local-government reform, Kano State has had twenty-nine L.G.A.s. This figure also shows urban centers and variations in population density. The "close settled zone" (Mortimore and Wilson 1965) of very high rural densities near Kano is evident.

traditional forms of worship) on the western and southern borders of the state.

Although Kano was a very productive agricultural region during colonial times, there was little investment in modern development. For example, the four L.G.S.s surrounding Hadejia had only six primary schools and about 1,500 children in school at independence in 1960. This neglect is largely explained by Britain's decision to govern by indirect rule, leaving indigenous political, economic, and social structures essentially intact. In recent years, oil revenues have provided a financial basis for the expansion of rural infrastructure, ranging from roads and irrigation schemes to schools and health clinics. Opportunities for primary education were massively increased with the 1976 universal primary education scheme; modern development in other sectors has been more gradual.

Health Care Systems

Although one may legitimately speak in general terms about the existence of two contrasting health care systems, namely, traditional and Western scientific medicine, it is important to be aware of the diversity of each. Each system provides a considerable range of choice in terms of cost, professionalism, degree of specialization, and mode of practice.

The distribution system for Western-type medicine is very diverse. There are various government-provided health services, a small voluntary agency sector, and a private sector with both formal and informal components. Government services may be further subdivided between those administered by local governments (mainly dispensaries and leprosy clinics), the Kano State hospitals and health centers, and federal institutions. The picture is further complicated by the top-down flow of both policy directives and funds for health programs.

Privately owned clinics and pharmacies have recently been proliferating in metropolitan Kano, while the number of patent medicine stores has been growing rapidly in rural areas as well. Although these commercial outlets for drugs are visible and usually licensed, other sources are unregulated and illegal. Injection salesmen, itinerant medicine hawkers, and table traders are responsible for the distribution of large quantities of drugs, with potentially dire consequences for individuals and the legitimate health care system. Silverman et al. (1982) and other scholars have described the massive dumping of substandard and prohibited drugs in Third World countries.

Traditional medicine is characterized by even greater diversity. Not only are there more than ten distinct Hausa healing traditions (Stock 1981), but there are very substantial differences within each group. For example, while some healers practice only from their homes, others visit periodic markets or travel about as itinerants in seach of customers. Professional commitment, reputation, degree of specialization, and approach to healing also vary greatly among traditional healers.

Virtually all Hausa know about the preparation of some herbal home remedies, which they use within the household and occasionally share with neighbors. Persons identifying themselves as professional healers are ubiquitous, so access to traditional health care is easy. Moreover, many healers will travel to their patients' homes to provide treatment. This easy spatial accessibility is an important contrast with the official Western-type system, which is very unevenly distributed.

Polgar (1963) has warned about the "fallacy of the empty vessels," namely, the common mistake of assuming that the absence of Western scientific health facilities is the same as the absence of health care. The decision to focus attention on modern health services is not to deny the importance of traditional medicine in both rural and urban Kano State. People patronize traditional healers because of convenience or spatial accessibility, but also because traditional medicine is generally preferred for most illness and is deemed essential for some conditions. Many traditional practitioners are highly skilled in both the psychological and the physical aspects of healing, and scientific research is beginning to provide concrete evidence about the chemotherapeutic properties of Hausa traditional herbal medicines (Etkin 1979, Etkin and Ross 1982).

Bonesetting and childbirth are two areas in which traditional therapy is strongly preferred. There is one family of bonesetters in a remote village near Hadejia who alone set more fractures in a month than Hadejia Hospital does in a year. Traditional midwives are preferred because the birth can take place at home where the prescribed traditional regimen may be followed. In 1976, only 102 normal deliveries took place at Hadejia Hospital, which ostensibly serves four L.G.A.s. Of those 102 cases, 91 came from the town of Hadejia, a total of nine came from two relatively modern towns, and only two came from other parts of the region (population over 700,000). Almost 30 percent of the normal deliveries involved women from nonlocal ethnic groups. Rural women experiencing serious complications in childbirth may be brought to the hospital, although often not until a critical stage has been reached.

Despite the ubiquity of traditional healers and the efficacy of many of their treatments, the unequal access to Western scientific medicine is a critical problem. Such disparities in access are not only contrary to the fundamental principles of social justice, but they have important health consequences. Extremely high infant mortality rates—sample surveys have shown that over one-third of infants die before the age of five years (e.g., Launiala 1974)—demonstrate that Hausa medicine has not been very successful in controlling the deadly diseases that afflict infants and small children. Unequal access to modern health care means that the majority of children will not receive life-saving immunizations, nor are they likely to receive adequate care in times of emergency. It is a question of choice for the people who live near a hospital or a health center, because they may choose from the full range of therapeutic possibilities, but those in the more remote areas lack effective access to competent Western-type care.

Evolution of the Modern Health Care System

The Colonial Period

British colonial rule left a legacy in the health care field of highly unequal care and a virtual neglect of rural health care needs. The initial priority for the colonial health services was the protection and care of Europeans (Schram 1971), both through the implementation of public health measures, such as the segregation of lepers, and through the provision of health care for Europeans. The Northern Nigeria *Annual Medical Report* for 1913 clearly reflects colonial priorities: "the public health principles which had been laid down by the end of 1913 extended the same safeguards to the health of unofficial Europeans as to that of Government officials," (Northern Nigeria 1913, 47). Five years after the establishment in 1903 of a European clinic in Kano, the first "native dispensary" was opened (Fika 1978). The rural dispensaries were opened at Gaya, Bichi, Dambatta, and Ringim, and hospitals were established in Kano and Hadejia during the 1930s (Fika 1978).

Colonial policy also restricted the activities of Christian missionaries in solidly Muslim areas like Kano State. The Sudan Interior Mission was given permission to open an eye hospital in Kano plus only eight dispensaries in rural areas. Thus, the missions were unable to contribute significantly to the development of a health system, as they did in many other parts of Nigeria.

The colonial legacy extended far beyond the failure to construct more than a token number of health care facilities, few of which were located outside the largest towns. The colonial administration left a model of health care that remains fundamentally unchanged. The model is elitist, favoring the wealthy and powerful over the poor and especially favoring urban centers over rural areas. These disparities occur in terms of both per capita provision of services and the quality of care. The colonial approach of choosing particular diseases like leprosy, sleeping sickness, and malaria for special attention has also continued to exert a strong influence, despite the lip service paid to more holistic approaches that emphasize health education and comprehensive development programs. During colonial times, traditional medicine was virtually ignored, except for disparaging references to its primitiveness. Despite tentative efforts to establish lines of communication with traditional healers and increasing scientific interest in the efficacy of traditional remedies, there is still very little cooperation between the two types of practitioners in Kano State. Finally, the colonial neglect of education left Kano State with virtually no indigenous medical doctors, pharmacists, or nurses. This lack of

TABLE 12.1
State and local government health institutions in Kano State (1965–1974)

	1965	1968	1971	1974
All Institutions	346	346	384	416
Hospitals	6	6	8	10
Rural Health Centers	0	0	2	6
Dispensaries	102	102	115	121
Child Welfare Clinics	4	4	8	8
Leprosy Clinics	234	234	241	247
Dental Clinic	0	0	1	1

Source: Kano State Yearbook, 1975

qualified manpower remains critical more than twenty years after independence.

Postindependence, 1960–1974

Independence did not bring any significant policy changes. The organizational structure remained the same, and there was no increase in the pace of facility construction. Between 1965 and 1974, for example, the number of state and L.G.A. government-run health care facilities increased by 20.2 percent, from 346 to 416 (see Table 12.1). The entire state outside of metropolitan Kano had only seven hospitals in 1974, and fewer than ten medical doctors were posted outside of metropolitan Kano to serve 8 million people. There were more hospital beds in Kano City Hospital, now Murtala Mohammed Hospital (597 beds) in 1973 than in all of the hospitals outside of Kano combined (461 beds) (Kano State 1973). The concentration of private and voluntary agency clinics and hospitals in Kano heightened the rural-urban disparities.

The Mid-1970s Reforms

Despite the persistence of massive rural-urban disparities, increased attention has been focused on rural health needs since the 1970s. This change reflects the impact of much-increased government revenue during the 1970s from petroleum sales, as well as two significant reforms. These were the inclusion of a Basic Health Services (B.H.S.) scheme in the Third National Development Plan of 1975–1979 and a sweeping reform of local governments in 1976.

The B.H.S. plan envisaged the establishment of a hierarchical network of health facilities covering Nigeria: Health clinics would feed primary.

health centers, which, in turn, would feed comprehensive health centers. Each unit of one comprehensive and four primary health centers plus twenty clinics was to serve 150,000 people (Battersby 1979). Priority was allocated to health education and preventative programs. The impetus and 70 percent of the funding for the plan were federal, but state governments are implementing the program.

Progress in implementing the B.H.S. plan has been slow in Kano State. By 1982, only 61 of the proposed total of almost 600 clinics had been built; some of these remained closed because of staff and equipment shortages. The standard design health clinics are essentially very expensive dispensaries. Each unit of twenty health clinics and associated health centers has cost 8 million Naira, sixteen times the original estimate of 500,000 Naira per unit (*New Nigerian*, April 24, 1980). Despite the stated emphasis on preventative work, curative medicine takes the great majority of resources. B.H.S. has done little to alter the status quo.

Local government reform was initiated throughout Nigeria in 1976. Twenty L.G.A.s were established in Kano State; this number was increased to twenty-nine in 1980. The new, elected L.G.A.s were given more resources and assumed more responsibilities than the old emirate administrations. They have responsibility for public health and shared responsibility for primary health care (Federal Republic of Nigeria 1976). L.G.A. reform has meant a quickening of the pace of dispensary construction. For example, there were thirteen dispensaries in the four Hadejia-area L.G.A.s in 1976 and thirty in 1982, plus eight under construction.

The Early 1980s: Restraint

Nigeria has suffered increasing financial pressure as a result of the tightening of the world oil market. The result has been forced restraint and cutbacks in most development programs. The timetable for constructing new health facilities is being extended, and some constructed clinics remain closed. Restraint has necessitated reduced purchases of drugs, causing extensive and chronic drug shortages.

There is some eivdence that new directions in health care are under serious consideration. It is now Kano government policy to encourage the development of private-sector health care and especially to encourage the establishment of patent medicine stores in rural areas. The government apparently believes that these shops will supplement the official health care system. For the first time, there seems to be serious interest in actively cooperating with the traditional healers. Meanwhile, the government has contracted for the construction of 1,000 new bore-holes (*West Africa*, June 13, 1983), possibly indicating increased emphasis on the prevention of ill health.

The Spatial Distribution of Health Services

Kano State's health care infrastructure grew significantly between 1974 and 1981. The total number of facilities increased from 426 to 636 (49.3

percent), and the number of dispensaries more than doubled, from 129 in 1974 to 263 in 1981, reflecting the new L.G.A.s' increased resources and commitment to expansion. Higher-order facilities opened between 1974 and 1981 consisted of seven hospitals, three rural health centers, and twenty-six B.H.S. clinics. The number of leprosy clinics increased only marginally from 257 to 264.

Figure 12.2 shows the distribution of the various categories of health care facilities by local government area and highlights the concentration of services in the Kano Municipal L.G.A. Although all rural L.G.A.s have several dispensaries and leprosy clinics, the location of higher-order facilities is much more scattered. Birniwa, with only four dispensaries and three leprosy clinics in 1981 for a population of 177,000, was especially underserved. As an interim measure, the state government gave mobile clinics to several of the underserved L.G.S.s; they appear to have operated only sporadically. The 1974–1981 period was characterized by a more rapid growth of medical infrastructure outside of metropolitan Kano than within the city. Nevertheless, the urban-rural gap remains enormous, especially with respect to health centers and hospitals providing inpatient care. About one-eighth of Kano State's area is located within eight km. of an inpatient facility; only one-thirtieth of the state is within a 4 km. radius.

The location of medical doctors and the provision of inpatient beds may be used as indicators of the distribution of higher-quality care. As of 1981, 85 percent of Kano State's 204 medical doctors were located in the capital city. Thirty doctors were divided between the twenty-eight "rural" L.G.A.s, resulting in a doctor-patient ratio of 1:290,000. With 4,574 inhabitants per doctor, even the Kano Municipal L.G.A. is hardly overprovided with physicians. Seventy percent (143 of 204) of Kano State's doctors are employees of the government. Since government employees have no choice in their postings, the distribution of state-employed doctors summarized in Table 12.2 essentially documents the continuing neglect of the so-called rural areas—so-called since 22 of the 30 doctors outside the city of Kano were posted to places with populations of 10,000 to 40,000. Two-thirds of the 39 additional physicians employed by Kano State between 1978 and 1981 were posted to metropolitan Kano.

The distribution of hospital beds gives further evidence of extreme urban bias, with the per capita provision in 1981 being ten times greater in the Kano Municipal L.G.A. than in the rest of the state. Despite a 243 percent increase in "rural" beds between 1973 and 1981, there were still only 1.83 hospital beds per 10,000 people outside Kano, i.e., 1,583 beds to serve 8,671,000 people (Kano State 1981). Clearly the chances of obtaining adequate emergency care or of choosing to give birth in a hospital setting vary greatly within rural Kano State. Most people live too far from a hospital or health center to be able to effectively use its services.

Table 12.3 and Figure 12.3 attempt to provide summary measurements of access to health care. In the four Hadejia-area L.G.A.s, 41 percent of

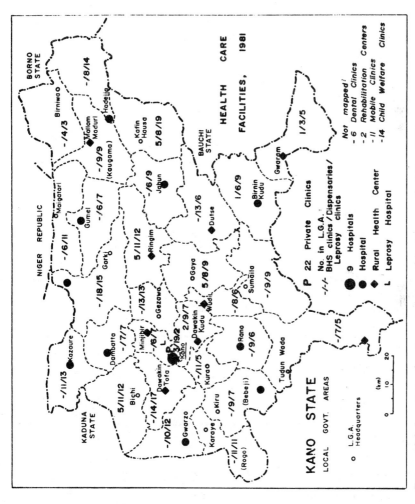

Figure 12.2 Location of major categories of health care facilities, 1981

TABLE 12.2
Medical doctors in Kano State, 1978 and 1981

	Kano State 1978	Kano State 1981	Kano Municipal 1978	Kano Municipal 1981	Rest of Kano State 1978	Rest of Kano State 1981
All Medical Doctors	149	204	133	174	16	30
Private Sector Doctors	29	38	29	38	--	--
State Government Doctors	104	143	88 (62*)	113 (73*)	16	30
Other Employed Doctors	16	23	16	23		
Doctors per 100,000	1.57	2.15	16.71	21.86	0.18	0.35
Population (1981) (000)	9,467		796		8,671	

*Doctors posted to Murtala Mohammed Hospital, Kano.

Source: Based on Annual Medical Statistics Bulletin, 1978: Statistical Yearbook, 1979; unpublished Ministry of Health data.

TABLE 12.3
Accessibility* of health care facilities in four Hadejia-area L.G.A.s, 1976 and 1982

Type of Facility	Distance to Nearest Facility of Given or Higher Order			
	0-4 Km 1976	0-4 Km 1982	0-8 Km 1976	0-8 Km 1982
Hospital	6%	6%	10%	10%
Rural Health Center	9%	9%	14%	14%
BHS Health Clinic	--	21%	---	43%
Dispensary	27%	41%	59%	83%

*Percentage of total 1976 population served. Possible redistribution of population between 1976 and 1982 has not been taken into account.

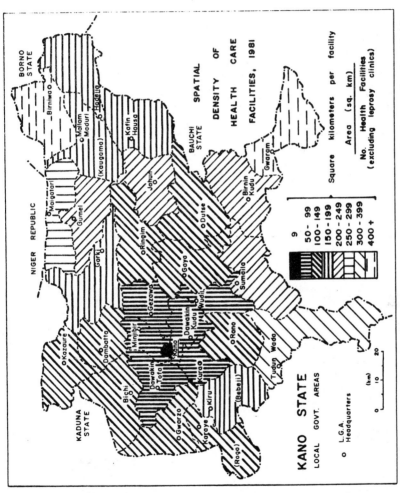

Figure 12.3 The spatial density of health facility provision is closely correlated with the pattern of population density (see Figure 12.1); densities in peripheral areas are much lower than those near Kano.

the population was with 4 km. of at least a dispensary in 1982, compared to 27 percent in 1976. The proportion within 8 km. of basic care increased from 59 to 83 percent. However, the only improvements in access to higher-order facilities came from increases in the frequency and range of commercial transportation. Only 14 percent of the study population was within 8 km. of inpatient care. Planners have too often relied on measures of health care per capita as the ultimate measure of service provision. Such measures are valid only when applied spatially, analyzing the accessibility of health services to the entire population to be served.

Figure 12.3 provides a rough statewide measure of the spatial accessibility of at least basic outpatient care. Leprosy clinics have been excluded since they provide treatment for only one disease. The density of facilities is greatest close to Kano and is generally much lower in peripheral areas. This allocation of resources is partially justifiable because of the extremely high population densities near Kano (Figure 12.1). However, since the peripheral areas seldom have densities below 100 per square kilometer, these are areas of "underpopulation" only in relation to central Kano State. A 4-km. radius encompasses 50 sq. km., and an 8-km. radius 201 sq. km.; even assuming perfect spacing of facilities, most L.G.A.s have very inadequate spatial coverage of health care. In reality, the calculated average figures for service areas are underestimates because of the duplication that results when facilities are spatially clustered. For example, three of the five B.H.S. clinics in Kafin Hausa are in towns with functioning L.G.A. dispensaries.

Impact of Disparities in Access to Health Care

The ideal approach to measuring the impact of unequal provision of health care would be to determine patterns of spatial variation in health status, and in particular to distinguish variations that are attributable to health care disparities from those that are attributable to other factors. Unfortunately, such data are not available. As mentioned earlier, improved health services have been shown to be capable of significantly reducing mortality in previously underserved areas. Empirical knowledge of the efficacy of Western medicine in "killing" certain diseases, most notably smallpox, is widespread among the Hausa. Another common perception in Hausaland is that infant mortality is falling in towns but remains very high in rural areas. However, this difference is attributed as often to the changing behavior of spirits as to the actual impact of Western medicine.

Some cultures have clearly ordered preferences for the treatment of illness; if the first treatment fails, the next choice in the "hierarchy of resort" is likely to be tried (Schwartz 1969). There is no evidence that the Hausa have clearly ranked hierarchies of resort. For most illnesses, there is no commitment to any particular strategy. Rather, there is a variable and empirical approach to the medical treatment of most conditions. There are exceptions, i.e., illnesses that are believed to require very specific forms of treatment, usually traditional ones. Among the clusters of factors commonly identified as influencing the choice of treatment, namely, illness characteristics, predisposing factors, and enabling factors (e.g., Andersen 1968, Wan and Soifer 1975, Wolinsky 1978), distance as an enabling factor is particularly crucial in the Hausa choice of therapy. Overcoming the barrier of distance involves various costs including time, energy, and money, so people living several kilometers from a health facility are likely to delay their journey, hoping the symptoms will wane, or to use an alternate type of treatment.

The impact of distance as a cause of delay in seeking treatment is shown in Figure 12.4. The figure relates the duration of illness prior to seeking Western-type medicine to distance from the facility. Whereas 38 percent of the patients living closer than 2 km. to a dispensary sought treatment within two days and 80 percent of them did so within a week of illness onset, far fewer of the more distant patients seek such prompt treatment. Only 20 percent of patients traveling 4–6 km. and 10 percent of those traveling from 15–20 km. sought treatment within two days of illness onset. When specific diseases such as malaria are analyzed similarly, the same positive relationship between distance and delay in seeking treatment is evident.

As distance from a facility increases, patients are more likely to first use some other form of treatment (Table 12.4). Only 35.2 percent of those traveling over 10 km. reported no previous treatment of their illness. The reported use of traditional therapies increased from 0.24 per person at 0–2 km. to 0.57 per person beyond 10 km. Two notes of caution are necessary. Many respondents underreported their previous use of traditional medicine. Moreover, these data refer only to those patients who eventually sought care from a Western-type health care facility and excludes those who successfully treated their illnesses with traditional remedies, self-administered patent medicines, and/or patience.

Calculations of per capita utilization rates at different distances from a health care facility provide a better insight into the varying impact of the facility. Table 12.5 provides indices of utilization for Hadejia-area health care facilities. Dispensary attendance falls to 32 percent of the "local" (adjacent to the facility) level after only 4 km., and at 8 km. the figure is only ten percent of the 0-km. rate of utilization. For higher-order facilities, where the perceived quality of care is better, the rate of distance decay in per capita utilization is less, but still amounts to more than 20 percent per kilometer. Given distance decay gradients of this magnitude, it is apparent that outpatient departments have relatively little impact beyond about 4 km.; beyond about 8 km., they approach being irrelevant to the regular health care needs of the population. Inpatient departments get the most serious cases, so it is not surprising that utilization per capita falls more gradually. However, admission rates at 8 km. are less than half, and at 12 km. they are only one-third, of the "local" rate. Only 14 percent of the study area population lives within 8 km. of facilities that provide inpatient services (Table 12.3).

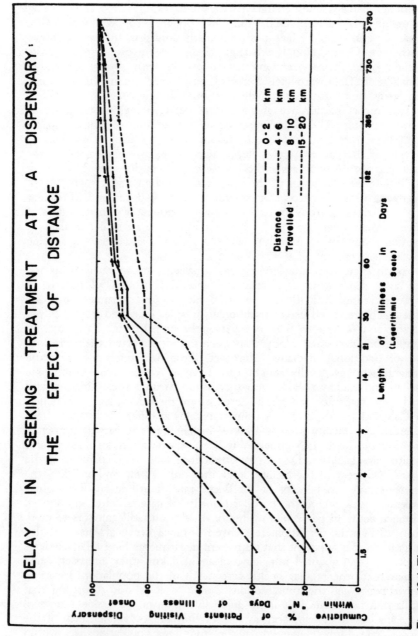

Figure 12.4 There is a strong positive relationship between the duration of illness prior to se care facility and patients' traveling distance.

TABLE 12.4
Previous treatment used, by distance from a health facility

Distance (km)	No. In Sample	No Previous Treatment	Previous Treatments, Per Person*	
			All	Traditional
0-2	2,470	51.5%	.67	.24
2-10	1,180	49.0%	.70	.36
10+	610	35.2%	1.11	.57
TOTAL	4,260	48.5%	.75	.33

*Many patients used more than one type of treatment. The reported use of previous treatments is significantly less than the actual use.

Source: Sample survey

TABLE 12.5
Indices of utilization* of Hadejia-area health care facilities (visits per capita), 1976-1977

	Distance from Facility				
	0 Km	2 Km	4 Km	8 Km	12 Km
Hospital & Health Center: Inpatients	100	83	69	47	32
Hospital & Health Center: Outpatients	100	64	41	17	7
Dispensaries	100	56	32	10	3

*Relative to the per capita utilization adjacent to the facility (0 Km).

Source: Regression lines computed from sample data.

The extra difficulties of mobility experienced by women in this strict Muslim society are reflected in the male-female disparities in visits to health care facilities. Women may be denied permission to leave the household if strict purdah is in effect, and women usually must make the journey on foot—rather than by bicycle, motorcycle, or donkey—if commercial transport is unavailable. At all distances, the number of visits by male patients significantly outnumber those by female patients, and this disproportion increases with distance due to the higher rate of distance decay for females than for males (see Table 12.6). In the Hadejia study (1976–1977), 64.0 percent of the adult outpatients and 74.8 percent of the inpatients were male.

Although the rates of distance decay in utilization are generally great, they do vary in relation to illness (see Table 12.7). Relatively minor symptomatic illnesses such as conjunctivitis and skin rashes are characterized by very steep distance decay gradients and a usual reliance on self-treatment as a first resort. Chronic infections such as gonorrhea and tropical ulcer, and acute conditions such as urinary stricture and snakebite, are characterized by gentler rates of distance decay. These variations in distance decay gradients show conclusively that the impact of distance on utilization is not absolute and fixed but varies in relation to the perceived needs and benefits associated with the use of health services in particular situations.

Planning Implications

There are no magical prescriptions to correct the problems of disease and death attributable to health care systems that provide grossly inadequate care distributed unequally, particularly in the absence of any fundamental reordering of societal values and priorities or the structure of decision making. As a starting point, the Alma-Ata declaration of the World Health Assembly in 1978 provides a clear and concise statement on the essential characteristics of socially just and appropriate basic health care:

> Primary health care is essentially health care based on practical, scientifically sound and socially acceptable methods and technologies made universally accessible to individuals and families in the community through their full participation and at a cost which the community and country can afford to maintain at every stage of their development in the spirit of self-reliance and self-determination. [Mahler 1981, 21]

Nevertheless, the Alma-Ata declaration is vague about the actual implementation of the principles it espouses. Thus, strategies have to be developed to achieve the goals set at Alma-Ata; the objectives still have to be given spatial form.

As a first step toward designing health systems that are both effective and efficient in the use of scarce resources, planners and policymakers

TABLE 12.6
Distance decay in per capita utilization, by sex

	Rate of Distance Decay	Visits per 100 persons annually at:				
		0 km	2 km	4 km	8 km	12 km
Male	14.5%/km	57.6	42.1	30.8	16.4	8.8
Female	16.0%/km	37.6	26.5	18.7	9.3	4.6
Ratio of Male to Female users		1.53	1.58	1.65	1.76	1.91

Source: Regression lines computed from sample data.

TABLE 12.7
Rates of distance decay in per capita utilization of health
facilities for treating selected illnesses

	Rate of Distance Decay	
Illness	Outpatients	Inpatients
Skin Rashes	28.6%/km	-
Conjunctivitis	26.0%/km	-
Diarrhea	22.6%/km	10.3%/km
Malaria	19.7%/km	11.7%/km
Measles	18.3%/km	10.2%/km
Gonorrhea	12.6%/km	-
Urinary Stricture	-	3.7%/km

Source: Regression lines computed from sample data.

must become more sensitive to the constraints imposed by distance on
the effective utilization of health care services. Much can be learned by
studying actual patterns of utilization of health services. How far are
people willing to travel, given certain constraints, for the treatment of
various health problems? How effective, therefore, are health facilities in
positively affecting the health of people in successively distant parts of
a country's catchment areas? What disparities are evident in the health
care behavior of different sex, age, class, and ethnic groups in the society?
What, then, is the appropriate density for basic health care, as well as
more specialized services, to achieve the objective of providing accessible
care for all?

The Kano findings reported in this chapter suggest that a relatively dense network of facilities is needed there. Existing outpatient facilities have relatively little impact beyond about 4 km.; the effective range for inpatient departments is not much more than 8 km. Beyond these distances, rural Kano people are clearly "voting with their feet" against the common rule of thumb that suggests 8-km. or 16-km. radii in estimating health facility catchment areas (see Walker and Gish 1977). This conclusion is not to imply that 4 km. or 8 km. should become the new standard, but rather that empirical investigations of patient utilization behavior should be an integral part of regional-scale health care planning in the rural Third World. Although time-consuming, such studies can provide substantial benefits in terms of improved effectiveness and efficiency as well as a better appreciation of the strengths and weaknesses of the health care system in reaching its target population.

The Kano State findings provide strong support for initiatives toward highly decentralized systems for the delivery of basic health services as well as a significant decentralization of first-line inpatient care. Nigeria's B.H.S. scheme is too expensive in terms of manpower requirements and both capital and recurrent costs to be able to achieve universal coverage of primary health care in the foreseeable future. The top end of the hierarchy, namely, the major hospitals, consume a particularly dispro-portionate share of the resources. The concentration of more than one-third of all the doctors in Kano State in Murtala Mohammed Hospital exemplifies this imbalance. In moving toward universal access to primary health care, it will be necessary to mobilize new resources such as community-based and community-supported primary health workers and traditional healers as well as to find ways of reallocating presently employed resources in a more equitable and effective manner.

The importance of improving the quality as well as the quantity of health care must also be stressed. The common reluctance of rural Kano people to use official health services is related to widespread dissatisfaction with the quality of care. Health care professionals are commonly seen as being intolerant, rude, and looking for bribes. It is believed widely that the "proper" drugs will not be available, due to chronic drug shortages. There is much room for improvement in the quality of care; such improvements would encourage more potential users of health facilities to invest their time, money, and energy in overcoming the distance barrier.

Notes

The Social Sciences and Humanities Research Council of Canada provided funding for the research. The invaluable help of Ahmadu Bello University and Bayero University is gratefully acknowledged. Babangida Ahmed Tage assisted in the data collection.

References

Andersen, R.
  1968   *A Behavioral Model of Families' Use of Health Services.* Chicago: Center for Health Administration Research.

Basch, P.
  1978   *International Health.* New York: Oxford University Press.

Battersby, A.
  1979   "Planning Basic Health Services in Nigeria." *Disasters* 3: 179–183.

Djukanovic, V., and E. P. Mach
  1975   *Alternative Approaches to Meeting Basic Health Needs in Developing Countries.* Geneva: World Health Organization.

Elling, R. H.
  1981   "The Capitalist World-System and International Health." *International Journal of Health Services* 11: 21–51.

Etkin, N.
  1979   "Indigenous Medicine Among the Hausa of Northern Nigeria: Laboratory Evaluation for Potential Therapeutic Efficacy of Anti-malarial Plant Medicinals." *Medical Anthropology* 3:401–429.

Etkin, N., and P. Ross
  1982   "Food as Medicine and Medicine as Food: An Adaptive Framework for Interpretation of Plant Utilization Among the Hausa of Northern Nigeria." *Social Science and Medicine* 16: 1559–1573.

Fika, A. M.
  1978   *The Kano Civil War and British Over-rule, 1982–1940.* Ibadan: Oxford University Press.

Gish, O.
  1973   "Resource Allocation, Equality of Access, and Health." *World Development* 1(12): 37–44.

Gourou, P.
  1966   *The Tropical World.* 4th ed. New York: John Wiley.

Hughes, C. C., and J. M. Hunter
  1970   "Disease and 'Development' in Africa." *Social Science and Medicine* 3: 443–493.

Kano, State of
  n.d.   *Medical Annual Statistics Bulletin, 1973.* Kano: Ministry of Health and Social Welfare.
  n.d.   *Annual Medical Statistics Bulletin, 1978.* Kano: Ministry of Health.
  n.d.   *Annual Medical Statistics Bulletin, 1979.* Kano: Ministry of Health.
  1981   *Statistical Yearbook 1979.* Kano: Governor's Office.

Last, D. M.
  1981   "The Importance of Knowing About Not Knowing." *Social Science and Medicine* 15B: 387–395.

238   Robert Stock

Launiala, K.
1974   "Preliminary Report of 1973." Unpublished report, Institute of
         Health, Ahmadu Bello University, Malumfashi Paediatric Field Ser-
         vices and Training Unit, Kano.

McKeown, T.
1976   *The Modern Rise of Population.* London: Edward Arnold.

Mahler, H.
1981   "The Meaning of Health for All by the Year 2000." *World Health
         Forum* 2: 5–22.

Morley, D.
1973   *Paediatric Priorities in the Developing World.* London: Butterworth.

Mortimore, M. J., and J. Wilson
1965   "Land and People in the Kano Close-Settled Zone." Occasional
         Paper no. 1, Department of Geography, Ahmadu Bello University.

Nigeria, Federal Republic of
1976   *Guidelines for Local Government Reform.* Lagos.

Nigeria, Northern
1913   *Annual Medical Report, 1913.* London: Colonial Office.

Polgar, S.
1963   "Health Action in Cross-Cultural Perspective." In H. E. Freeman
         et al., eds., *The Handbook of Medical Sociology,* pp. 379–419.
         Englewood Cliffs, N.J.: Prentice-Hall.

Schram, R.
1971   *A History of the Nigerian Health Services.* Ibadan: Ibadan University
         Press.

Schwartz, L. R.
1969   "The Hierarchy of Resort in Curative Practice: The Admiralty
         Islands, Melanesia." *Journal of Health and Social Behavior* 10: 201–
         209.

Silverman, M., et al.
1982   "The Drugging of the Third World." *International Journal of Health
         Services* 12: 585–597.

Smith, D. M.
1979   *Where the Grass Is Greener: Living in an Unequal World.* Harmonds-
         worth, Eng.: Penguin.

Stock, R.
1980   "Health Care Behaviour in Rural Nigerian Setting." Ph.D. Thesis,
         Department of Geography, University of Liverpool.
1981   "Traditional Healers in Rural Hausaland." *Geojournal* 5: 363–368.
1983   "Distance and the Utilization of Health Facilities in Rural Nigeria."
         Social Science and Medicine 17: 563–570.

Walker, G., and O. Gish
    1977   "Inequality in the Distribution and Differential Utilization of Health Services: A Botswana Case Study." *Journal of Tropical Medicine and Hygiene* 80: 238–243.

Wan, T., and J. Soifer
    1975   "Determinants of Physician Utilization: A Casual Analysis." *Journal of Health and Social Behavior* 15: 100–112.

Wisner, B.
    1980–1981 "Nutritional Consequences of the Articulation of Capitalist and Non-capitalist Modes of Production in Eastern Kenya." *Rural Africana*, nos. 8–9: 99–132.

Wolinsky, F. D.
    1978   "Assessing the Effects of Predisposing, Enabling, and Illness-Morbidity Characteristics on Health Service Utilization." *Journal of Health and Social Behavior* 19: 384–396.

World Bank
    1975   *Health.* Sector Policy Paper. New York.

World Health Organization (WHO)
    1968   *The Second Ten Years of the World Health Organization.* Geneva.

13
Policy and Praxis: Planning for Health Care in Nicaragua

John M. Donahue

Introduction

In 1978, at Alma Ata in the Soviet Union, member nations of the World Health Organization (WHO) set for themselves the goal of providing health care to all by the year 2000. In 1982, WHO chose Nicaragua as one of several countries whose efforts in primary health care delivery could serve as a model for attaining that goal (MINSA 1982b:57, Barricada 1983).

This chapter seeks to demonstrate how popular participation in the planning process has shaped the Nicaraguan health system since the Revolution of 1979. The analysis focuses upon health policies that have evolved since the revolution, the specific actions undertaken to implement those policies, and their social and epidemiological impact. Policy changes in that period are traced to the ascendancy of groups both within and without the Ministry of Health (MINSA) who successfully promoted a primary health care policy based upon popular or noninstitutional strategies over one that favored professional and institutional control. Several conclusions are drawn as to the applicability of the Nicaraguan planning process and health strategies to other developing countries.

The Nicaraguan health sector prior to the Revolution of 1979 was characterized by fragmentation, poor distribution and duplication of services, and vertical political control by the dictator (Escudero 1980, Bossert 1982, Donahue 1983). The revolution did not immediately initiate radical new plans in the health sector. In fact, the first eighteen months witnessed a general effort to return the health infrastructure to its prewar condition (Bossert 1982:269). Even the National Unified Health System (Sistema Nacional Unico de Salud—SNUS), created three weeks after the revolution, had been first proposed in 1976 (Donahue 1983). The structural changes in the health bureaucracy did set in motion a series of organizational changes that would have a long-term effect on the planning process and the eventual ascendancy of primary care and preventive medicine over secondary care and a more institutional approach.

to health delivery. Before turning to an analysis of the planning process and its social impact, it is important to place those policy changes in their historical context.

Background

Several studies document the extreme conditions of poor health in which the great majority of the Nicaraguan people lived prior to the revolution (INCAP 1966, Holland, Davis, and Gangloff 1973, USAID 1976), and two indicators suggest how critical the state of poor health had become. In the first place, Nicaragua had the highest infant mortality rate in Central America (121/1,000 live births) (Teller 1981:10). Second, between 1965 and 1976, a period of time in which many countries made strides in combating malnutrition among children under four years of age, Nicaragua recorded a 105 percent increase in malnutrition, the second highest rate of increase in Central America during that time (Teller 1981:11).

Several studies (Booth 1982, Walker 1982) have documented the events that led to the general insurrection of 1978 and 1979. The insurrection had important consequences, both negative and positive, for the health of the Nicaraguan people. On the negative side, 50,000 lives were lost in what turned out to be a street-by-street and house-by-house struggle of the people against the National Guard. Before the guard retreated from a city or town, its members would often turn their guns on public works such as sewage plants, water pumping and treatment plants, and hospitals and clinics. The United Nations estimated that during the war, Nicaragua lost $700 million in capital flight and some $200 million in lost cotton exports and suffered some $500 million in physical damage, including $5 million in damages to hospitals and clinics. Before he left, Somoza plundered the national treasury, leaving only $3.5 million and a foreign debt of $1.6 billion.

Reconstruction and Health

Given the extensive damage to health facilities, one of the priorities of the Sandinista Government of National Reconstruction was rebuilding the damaged hospitals and clinics as well as constructing new facilities. Yet other and at times conflicting priorities emerged from the experience of the insurrection. Each was to have its impact on the new national health plan.

Three weeks after the Sandinista victory, the Government of National Reconstruction created the National Unified Health System (SNUS). Health as a national priority was itself defined within the context of three more immediate agendas of the government: defense, the economy, and education.

The defense of the revolution was placed above all other priorities. The experience of the extended insurrection as well as the high price paid in human lives and property damage was only part of the motivation behind this priority. The structural changes envisioned necessitated a strong defense against those interests, domestic and international, that were threatened by the reforms. In addition to the regular troops, the Sandinistas organized a civilian militia, which after three years numbered 80,000 men and women. In 1983, a compulsory military draft was instituted.

The second priority as defined by the Government of National Reconstruction was the economy, including price supports for basic commodities, an increase in the production of export crops, the refinancing of the national debt, and an agrarian reform. Workers on the 1 million hectares of former Somoza family lands (20 percent of Nicaragua's total arable land) were organized into cooperatives and state production units (UPEs). Some 12,000 peasant farmers received title to their own land. Basic grain production was given more priority and increased from 10 percent of the 1977 total agricultural production to 16 percent in 1980 (UNAG, ATC, and CIERA 1982:18). The changes made in the agricultural and market economy have important implications for health inasmuch as nutritional levels are directly affected by policies affecting food production and distribution as well as by the ability of the population to purchase staples.

The third priority area of the government was education. Like defense and the economy, education has important implications for the health status of the population. The illiteracy rate in Nicaragua prior to the revolution was 50.3 percent, and school enrollments stood at about 501,000. In early 1980, the government trained 100,000 literacy workers, many of whom traveled into the countryside to teach the peasants to read and write. By August 1981, the illiteracy rate had dropped to 12 percent. By 1982, some 613,000 persons had been taught to read and write, and school enrollments have doubled to over 1,000,000.

The fourth priority area was health. The National Unified Health System (SNUS) brought under one organizational framework some twenty-three semiautonomous health bureaucracies that had duplicated and fragmented health services before the revolution. The SNUS put forward six principles, which were to be the basis of health planning and organization:

1. Health is a right of every individual and a responsibility of the State and the Popular Organizations.
2. Health services ought to be accessible to the entire population, geographically, economically and culturally.
3. Health services should function to integrate the physical, mental and social dimensions of health and to address the conditions of work and residence as they affect health.
4. Health care ought to be delivered in a multi-professional team effort.
5. Health activities are to be planned.

6. The community ought to participate in all activities of the health system. [MINSA 1981:17–21]

The health planning process in Nicaragua has provided for the inclusion within the Ministry of Health of several different constituencies and points of view on health delivery. In addition to the physicians, who generally represent a medical and institutional perspective, the planning function also involves the Division of Communication and Popular Education in Health (Division de Comunicacion y Educacion Popular en Salud—DECOPS). These health educators tend to define health in social as well as biological terms and stress a more popular and preventive strategy rather than an institutional and curative one. Finally, health planning has been given both a professional and a public forum. The analysis and summary workshops (*jornadas de analysis y balance*—JABs) are regular meetings held at the regional and national levels in which health professionals discuss previously set health objectives, actual performance, and continuing needs. Discussions evolve around why objectives have or have not been met, and corrective strategies are agreed upon. The first JAB was held in 1979 after some months of experience in meeting the health needs of the population immediately after the insurrection. One result of that experience was the decision to decentralize the health bureaucracy. The Emergency Plan of 1980 called for the creation of nine health regions and, within each region, the creation of health areas (MINSA 1981:79). The health regions were redefined in May 1982 to conform to the National Plan of Regionalization, which brought all government agencies under the same regional jurisdictions. The new alignment resulted in six health regions and three special zones on the Atlantic Coast (see Figure 13.1).

The creation of popular health councils (*consejos populares de salud*—CPSs) as well as face-the-people meetings (*cara al pueblo*) provided for direct input by the popular organizations and by the local communities into the health planning and evaluation process. Before turning to an analysis of the impact of these various bodies on the planning process, a more detailed description of the popular organizations and their experience in health delivery is in order.

Popular Organization and Health

The Sandinista government organized the population into associations, called mass organizations (*organizaciones de masas*), each of which would participate in activities related to the four priority areas of defense, the economy, education, and health. The most active organizations in the health sector have been the Sandinista Defense Committee (Comite de Defensa Sandinista—CDS) and The Luisa Amanda Espinoza National Association of Nicaraguan Women (Asociacion de Mujeres Nicaraguenses Luisa Amanda Espinoza—AMNLAE). The CDS has a geographical con-

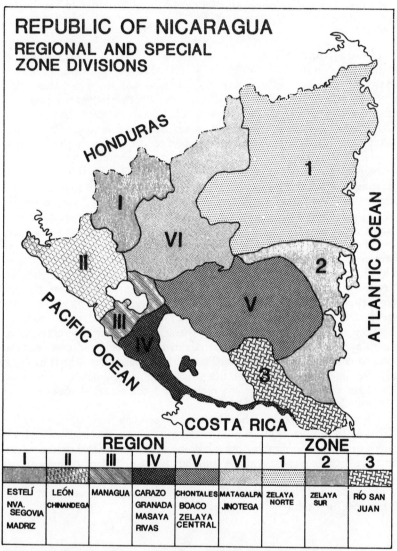

Figure 13.1 Health regions and special zones in Nicaragua

stituency on the neighborhood or rural sector level, and AMNLAE focuses its concerns directly on how women might contribute to the revolutionary process.

Other organizations have occupational memberships, such as the Federation of Health Workers (FETSALUD), the Confederation of Sandinista Workers (CST), the National Association of Nicaraguan Educators (ANDEN), and the Association of Agricultural Workers (ATC). The

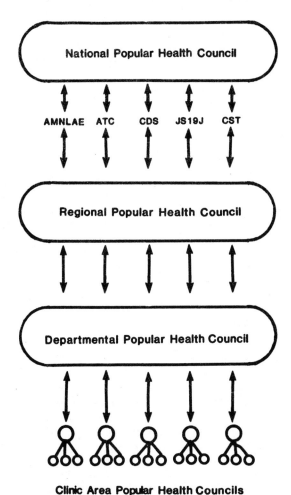

Clinic Area Popular Health Councils

Figure 13.2 Structure of popular participation in
health in Nicaragua

Sandinista Youth "19th of July" (JS19J) and the Sandinista Children's
Association (ANS) incorporate children and young people into the reform
programs. The Parent's Association (APF) addresses educational and other
familial matters.

The popular organizations have each participated in reforms in the
four priority areas. The Ministry of Health developed a particular structure,
the CPSs, to ensure popular participation in the areas of health planning
and health delivery. Figure 13.2 illustrates the organization of participation
in health within these popular health councils.

One of the early contributions of the popular health councils was the organization and implementation of the popular health work days (*las jornadas populares de salud*—JPSs). In fact, the decision to mobilize the population nationally in a mass vaccination and environmental sanitation effort set the tone for popular participation that would have an impact long after the programs themselves ended.

The organization of the popular health days emerged from the experience of the civil defense committees (*comites de defensa civil*—CDCs) during the insurrection. Many of the CDCs provided emergency health care as access to health facilities became severely restricted by the fighting and the intimidation of the National Guard. As a result, some physicians and nurses went into the barrios and trained people in the CDCs to provide emergency care to combatants and civilians. Small clandestine clinics were set up in homes, and the health workers organized pharmacies in their neighborhoods. Both clinics and pharmacies were moved from home to home as necessitated by the search and seizure operations of the guard. Physicians provided medicines from hospital stores by means of this clandestine network of mobile clinics and pharmacies. Some health workers were also trained to perform emergency surgery in the event that a serious wound needed suturing. Volunteers were likewise instructed on how to dispose of corpses so as to minimize health hazards. Emergency plans were provided in the event that water supplies became contaminated or were cut off.

There emerged from this experience a group of health workers who had firsthand experience in health care and sanitation. Physicians and medical professionals had provided training in health care strategies accommodated to nonprofessional volunteers. The success of the civil defense committees provided the basis for the formation of the Sandinista defense committees (CDSs), which emerged after the triumph. Along with the organizational continuity, there continued to exist a group of people at the neighborhood level who had health care training and experience. In some cases, these people became the health coordinators (*responsables de salud*) on the neighborhood CDSs.

Several health care initiatives were organized in the first months after the revolution. In August 1979, the popular organizations and the Ministry of Health agreed to set up oral rehydration posts nationwide to serve those children who suffered from the effects of diarrhea. Over the next three years UNICEF provided $400,000 for equipment, training, popular health education, and oral rehydration salts in a total of 330 posts (UNICEF 1983).

In September and October of 1979, an antipolio and antirabies vaccination campaign was carried out in which the CDS health workers actively participated. In early 1980, the Division of Communication and Popular Education in Health (DECOPS) was created within MINSA, and between March and August of 1980, DECOPS prepared 200,000 copies of "Health Lessons for Literacy Workers" and trained 12,325 literacy workers in malaria prevention and treatment (MIPLAN/MINSA 1981:7). The policy decision to organize several national vaccination and sanitation campaigns, or popular health work days, emerged from these successful organizing efforts in health care during and immediately after the insurrection.

The decision also provided an opportunity for the entire country to experience the strategy of popular participation on which the new health system would be built (DECOPS/MINSA 1982:1). The Government of National Reconstruction viewed the JPSs as an opportunity to organize national and regional government bodies and popular organizations around a common activity. This experience would serve as a lesson for organizing in areas other than health (DECOPS/MINSA 1982:1), and the JPSs would prove to have a major effect on the organization of the Ministry of Health (MINSA) and in the setting of health care priorities.

Major organizational responsibility for the JPSs resided in DECOPS, which had been instrumental in the organization of the CPSs in early 1980. Originally, the CPSs were to be made up exclusively of the popular organizations to ensure an independent forum for the discussion of community health concerns and strategies. The popular organizations could thereby better negotiate with the MINSA as a partner in planning. However, with the emergence of the popular health day campaigns in 1981, the CPSs became joint bodies of representatives from the popular organizations and the MINSA. During the JPSs, the CPSs were subordinated to the centralized planning of the MINSA. The popular organizations were more involved in the implementation than in the planning of the JPSs, but their participation was crucial for the success of the campaigns (Keyzer and Ulate 1981:133).

In 1981, four national popular health campaigns were carried out. These included an antipolio campaign in two phases (March 28 and 29 and May 9 and 10), an environmental sanitation campaign (June 1 through July 15), an antidengue campaign (the last three weekends in August), and what was the most ambitious of the four, an antimalaria campaign (November 4 through 6). In 1982, the JPSs continued at the national level. The first was an antipolio, diptheria-whooping cough-tetanus, and measles vaccination campaign on May 15 and 16, and the second was a combined environmental sanitation and antimalaria/antidengue campaign in June. In November and December, there was a national effort to train 8,000 health workers (Brigadistas de Atencion Primaria Salud—BAPSs) in the basic concepts of primary health care for mothers and children and first aid. The summary statistics presented in the Table 13.1 suggest the extent of the organizational effort of the JPSs.

The number of persons immunized and the doses administered is reported in Table 13.2. UNICEF assisted in equipping the network that facilitated the national distribution of the vaccines for each campaign (UNICEF 1983:1). The impact of the vaccination program can be observed in Table 13.3, which reports the number of cases and morbidity rates for five common childhood diseases.

TABLE 13.1
Summary statistics of the 1981 popular health campaign

	Antipolio First (March)	Antipolio Second (May)	Clean-up (June-July)	Antidengue (August)	Malaria (November)
Workshops	753	539	1269	1509	4062
Multipliers[a] trained	2170	2201	3716	8906	10,429
Brigadistas trained	17,687	15,073	19,755	77,619	73,594
Pamphlets distributed	500,000		1,200,000		
Vaccination posts	4911	4397			
Children vaccinated	341,975	301,160			
Persons medicated					1,892,746
Packages of Abate[b] distributed				1,000,000	
Tablets[c] Distributed					35,000,000

Source: MINSA 1982A unpublished report. MINSA 1982B.
a   Multipliers are volunteer health workers who in turn train Brigadistas
b   Packages which contain an insecticide (temephos) that kills mosquito larvae
c   Included 8 million packages of 25 million chloroquine and 10 million primaquine tablets

Policy Changes

The experience of the popular organizations in health in the first eighteen months of the revolution coincided with a second and quite different focus within the MINSA. Although the popular organizations were engaged in massive vaccination campaigns, popular education in health, and other preventive strategies, much of the institutional support within the MINSA was going to the reconstruction of hospitals and the construction of new primary care clinics. Primary care efforts focused upon the expansion of clinic and health post services and the preparation.

TABLE 13.2
Number of persons vaccinated and doses provided in Nicaragua,
1980, 1981, and 1982

Type of Vaccine	1980		Year 1981		1982	
	Persons	Doses	Persons	Doses	Persons	Doses
B.C.G.	81,228	81,228	139,327	139,327	211,275	211,275
Polio	n/a	538,178	n/a	1,163,853[a]	n/a	1,492,109[a]
Measles	101,829	101,829	225,932[a]	225,932[a]	205,825[a]	205,825[a]
D.P.T.	n/a	384,949	n/a	410,693	n/a	705,955[a]
D.T.	46,817	156,411	56,722	155,229	85,088	401,192
T.T.	168,457	527,748	131,388	449,362	167,606	738,545
Total	n/a	1,790,343	n/a	2,544,396	n/a	3,754,901

Source: MINSA 1983:59,60. Tables 19 and 20
a   Includes the activities of the Popular Health Work Days

TABLE 13.3
Transmittable diseases reported in Nicaragua and rates per
100,000 inhabitants, 1980, 1981, and 1982[a]

Disease	Number of Cases			Rate per 100,000		
	1980	1981	1982	1980	1981	1982
Poliomyelitis	21	46	0	0.7	1.6	0
Diphtheria	5	2	2	0.1	0.0	0.0
Whooping Cough	2,469	1,935	377	90.03	68.5	12.9
Tetanus	89	132	98	3.2	4.6	3.3
Measles	3,784	224	219	138.4	7.9	7.5

Source: MINSA 1983:61. Table 21
a   Includes data from January to November

of volunteer health workers (BAPSs) who would work under the supervision of the clinic director and the area nurses.[1]

By mid-1980, however, the popular health constituency within the
MINSA and in the popular health councils were able to challenge the
more institutional approach to primary care. The neurosurgeon minister
of health was replaced by a member of the Sandinista leadership, Lea
Guido, who was a nonphysician and social scientist. The change in
ministry leadership signaled a new policy direction in the health sector
that was more in keeping with the government's own efforts to contain
costs and promote popular participation. The Government of National
Reconstruction initiated the National Austerity and Efficiency Plan in
1981. This plan was, in part, a response to the embargo on bilateral
government aid that the Reagan administration had imposed upon Nicaragua, which affected the yet-unspent money allocated by the Carter
administration for the construction of five new hospitals. With the
termination of USAID funding, the Nicaraguan government had to divert
funds from other sources to complete the construction, but cost overruns
further delayed the completion of the new hospitals.

Funding restrictions, increases in construction costs, and a change in
Ministry of Health leadership allowed DECOPS and the popular organizations to argue for a more popular, broad-based, and cost-effective
approach to primary health care. The result was that the new hospital
and clinic construction program, begun in 1980, was curtailed in 1981.
(New clinic and health post construction would resume in 1982.) Although
financial constraints in 1981 favored a cost-effective primary care model,
the fact that DECOPS and the popular organizations had already successfully trained health workers and organized thousands of Nicaraguans
in vaccination and malaria campaigns provided credibility to their strategy.
At the same time, WHO and UNICEF offered technical and financial
assistance to expand the primary care program and the training of health
workers throughout the country (UNICEF 1983).

Social Impact

The impact of the health policy changes initiated by the revolution
and carried forward during the first two years of the revolution are visible
in the changing profile of medical care and epidemiological indicators.[2]

Medical Care

One of the objectives of the SNUS has been to make health care
more accessible to all, and a priority of the MINSA has been to provide
more service to the medically underserved areas of the country and to
increase medical encounters. The number of medical encounters has
doubled since 1977, and the most significant increases have occurred in
those areas of greatest need: Region I (Estelí), Region V (Chontales,
Boaco), Region VI (Matagalpa, Jinotega), and in the special zones of the

Atlantic Coast (see Figure 13.1 and Table 13.4). Managua (Region III) continues to lead the country in medical encounters, although there was a slight drop in 1982. Indeed, Managua's share of the total medical encounters of the country decreased from 64 percent in 1977 to 38 percent in 1982, which reflects the redistribution of medical personnel to more underserved areas of the country (see Table 13.5).

There is a concern with the quality of care in this rapid expansion of medical encounters. There is no universally accepted triage system in the area clinics; whoever walks in the door will see a physician. This policy is not a cost-effective use of professional resources, but it seems to be deliberate. The popular health councils may support the policy because of people's preference for seeing physicians and obtaining prescriptions. The policy also reaffirms the medical model of healing and physician control over health care. The policy might therefore reflect a convergence of professional and patient interests. Clinics are crowded, and many physicians seem overwhelmed by the patient load. In some cases encounters are perfunctory, and since no one will be turned away on a given day, there is no incentive for patients to schedule appointments. Nor are physicians guaranteed that they will have a minimum amount of time to see each patient.

Hospital Care

Hospital construction has not kept up with the growth of population. In 1977, there were 588 persons per hospital bed as compared to 625 persons per bed in 1982 (see Table 13.6). In 1980, the number of hospital beds had increased by more than 300 over the number available in 1977—after the revolution, the MINSA took over operation of three private hospitals. The net increase over the next two years was only 88, as hospital construction already under way fell behind schedule and new construction was restricted. Meanwhile, there was a redistribution of hospital bed capacity in an attempt to achieve greater equity in the allocation of those scarce resources (see Table 13.7). The greatest increases in the number of hospital beds since 1977 are to be found in the most underserved regions of Estalí/Nueva Segovia (I), Rivas (IV), Chontales/Boaca (V), and Zelaya Norte (Special Zone 1).

During 1981 and 1982, several hospitals were closed as an economy measure. A new hospital is being built by the Soviets in Chinandega to replace the one destroyed in the May 1982 floods, but four other constructions are large clinics with added inpatient care.

The restrictions of new hospital construction is paralleled by a decrease in the number of surgical procedures performed in the country. The number of surgeries increased from 36,052 in 1977 to 54,457 in 1980, in part because of the large number of war casualties. The number remained virtually unchanged in 1981 and 1982, and in fact, the number of surgeries per 100 people actually declined from 1.99 in 1980 to 1.87 in 1982 (MINSA 1983:81 Table 27). It may be that the demand for

TABLE 13.4
Number of medical encounters[a] in Nicaragua by health region and
special zone, 1977, 1980, 1981, and 1982

Regions and Special Zones	Number of Medical Encounters				Encounters per Inhabitant			
	1977	1980	1981	1982	1977	1980	1981	1982
I	56,882	387,622	484,772	597,671	0.2	1.4	1.7	2.0
II	372,758	713,122	655,725	765,904	0.9	1.5	1.4	1.6
III	1,565,820	2,201,115	2,353,420	2,291,777	2.1	2.8	2.9	2.7
IV	197,742	820,800	864,157	917,090	0.5	1.7	1.8	1.8
V	42,459[b]	347,573	291,298	351,583	0.2	1.4	1.1	1.3
VI	80,391	233,556	446,631	598,395	0.3	0.7	1.3	1.7
S-Z 1	116,873[c]	132,884	145,992	295,062	0.9	1.8	1.9	3.7
S-Z 2	-	140,028	163,196	175,077	-	2.6	2.9	2.9
S-Z 3	-	5,923	6,241	30,075	-	0.2	0.2	1.0
National Totals	2,432,925	4,982,623	5,411,432	6,022,634	1.0	1.8	1.9	2.1

Source: MINSA 1983:28. Table 2
a   Includes encounters in hospitals and area health clinics.
b   Includes Special Zone 3
c   Includes Special Zones 1 and 2

TABLE 13.5
Distribution of physicians[a] in Nicaragua by health region and special zones, 1980[b] and 1982[c]

Region and Special Zone	No. of Physicians per 10,000 Inhabitants	
	1980	1982
I	1.98	2.86
II	3.93	4.37
III	7.0	7.9
IV	3.3	4.7
V	1.17	3.5
VI	2.0	3.42
S-Z 1	d	8.2
S-Z 2	2.2	5.1
S-Z 3	5.7	e
National	4.4	5.24

Source: MINSA 1981:87,1983:89. Table 31.
a   Figures include only Nicaraguan physicians
b   The 1980 total of 1212 physicians includes 34 assigned to administrative duties.
c   The 1982 total of 1541 physicians includes 34 assigned to administrative duties.
d   Included in Region V
e   Included in Region V

surgical procedures declined once the wartime casualties were cared for. The poor distribution of surgeons in the country, combined with deteriorating equipment and lack of supplies, has also contributed to the decline. As a result, some patients have been sent overseas for needed surgery.

As inpatient hospital bed capacity stabilized, there was an increase in hospital usage as measured by the number of discharges (see Table 13.6). On the other hand, a comparison of medical encounters in outpatient clinics and hospitals indicates that there are three medical encounters in primary care facilities for every one in a hospital (see Table 13.8). In fact, in 1980 and 1982, one can note what may represent a gradual shift in medical encounters from hospitals to community health centers (the decrease in clinic and health post encounters in 1981 may reflect the building moratorium in that year).[3] The decrease in hospital encounters

TABLE 13.6
Hospital capacity and usage in Nicaragua, 1977, 1980, 1981, and 1982[a]

Year	Number of Beds	Number of Persons/Bed	Number of Discharges	Number of Discharges/100 Pop.
1977	4313	588	120,952	4.8
1980	4677	588	178,017	6.5
1981	4729	625	190,577	6.7
1982	4765	625	197,214	6.8

Source: MINSA 1983:80,82. Tables 26 & 28
a   Includes acute and chronic care hospitals and health centers with beds for all years.

TABLE 13.7
Hospital bed capacity[a] in Nicaragua, 1977, 1980, 1981, and 1982

Health Region/ Special Zone	Number of Beds				Change	
	1977	1980	1981	1982	77-82	80-82
I	298	420	388	392	+94	-28
II	882	752	784	844	-38	+92
III	1561	1687	1639	1607	+46	-80
IV	699	733	750	790	+91	+57
V	185	279	289	294	+109	+15
VI	512	471	498	508	-4	+37
1	47	127	168	133	+86	+6
2	129	157	153	130	+1	-27
3	b	51	60	67	n/a	+16
National Totals	4313	4677	4729	4765	+385	+88

Source: MINSA 1983:80. Table 26
a   Includes acute and chronic care hospitals and health centers with beds.
b   Included in Region V

may be due to an increase in the number of health centers and posts and to more effective care at the local level (see Table 13.9). The 1982 total of 453 health clinics and posts represents a 24 percent increase over the 366 built in the first eighteen months of the revolution and almost a 300 percent increase over the 115 in existence in 1975 (USAID 1976:91).

TABLE 13.8
Medical encounters in Nicaragua in health centers and
hospitals, 1980, 1981, and 1982

Type of Facility	Medical Encounters					
	1980		1981		1982	
	No.	%	No.	%	No.	%
Health Center and Post	3,013,824	(60.5)	3,093,595	(57.2)	3,782,690	(62.8)
Hospital	1,968,799	(39.5)	2,317,837	(42.8)	2,239,944	(37.2)
Total	4,982,623	(100)	5,411,432	(100)	6,022,634	(100)

Source: MINSA 1983:28-30. Tables 2, 3 and 4

TABLE 13.9
Health clinics and health posts in Nicaragua by health
regions and special zones, 1980, 1981, and 1982

Variables	Year	National Level	I	II	III	IV	V	VI	1	2	3
				Regions and Special Zones							
Number	1980	366	40	67	42	71	75	43	13	15	a
of	1981	373	40	67	44	71	75	47	14	15	a
Units	1982	453	54	80	62	85	79	40	24	15	14
Number of	1980	1.3	1.4	1.5	C.5	1.5	2.6	1.3	1.8	2.8	a
Units per	1981	1.3	1.4	1.4	0.5	1.5	2.6	1.4	1.8	2.7	a
10,000 Population	1982	1.5	1.8	1.6	0.7	1.7	3.0	1.1	3.0	2.5	4.6

Source: MINSA 1983:27. Table 1
a   Data for Special Zone 3 appears in that of Region V for the years
1980-1981

After the flurry of construction in 1980, only seven new health clinics
and posts were opened in 1981. Another eighty were built in 1982, and
twenty-six were reconditioned; seven were closed in Region VI (Matagalpa/
Jinotega) because of border conflicts with the *contras*. Rural areas in
Regions I, II, III, IV, and Special Zone 1 benefited from most of the
health clinic expansion in 1982.

TABLE 13.10
Dental encounters in Nicaragua, 1977, 1980, 1981, and 1982

| Year | Dental Encounters | |
	Number	Percent of Increase
1977	203,540	-
1980	258,742	27%
1981	331,821	28%
1982	430,643	30%

Source: MINSA 1983:34. Table 7

The expansion of dental services parallels the establishment of primary care facilities during the same period (see Table 13.10). The major expansion of dental services between 1977 and 1982 occurred in Region V (Chontales and Boaco) and Region VI (Matagalpa and Jinotega), which registered an increase of over 400 percent (MINSA 1983:34 Table 7).

The above analysis suggests that health care, as measured by access to institutional care facilities, is much greater now than it was before the revolution. Policy changes that favored clinic over hospital construction greatly enhanced accessibility, and those changes reflect the participation of the popular organizations in the planning process both within the analysis and summary workshops (JABs) and the popular health councils (CPSs). The National Association of Nicaraguan Women (AMNLAE) was especially active in the area of maternal-child care.

Maternal-Child Care

The expansion of clinics and hospitals has had a significant impact on children. Child medical encounters increased from 36 percent of total encounters in 1977 to 41 percent in 1982 (MINSA 1983:31,32 Tables 5 and 6), and much of the increase is due to maternal-child care programs. For instance, the number of pregnant women enrolled in the prenatal program rose from 82,599 in 1981 to 133,132 in 1982 (MINSA 1983:41 Table 9).

Between 1977 and 1982, the percentage of institutional births nationwide increased from 37 percent of all births to 43 percent (MINSA 1983:43 Table 11). Most of that increase took place in the first year of the revolution. Households and child care responsibilities, distance from hospitals, and the availability of local midwives may explain the large number of home deliveries. In 1982, the MINSA organized a national board to formulate a policy for the selection and training of midwives. Several meetings were held, a training manual was published, and training programs were piloted in Estalí and León/Chinandega. By mid-1983,.

more than 100 midwives had been trained and provided with birthing kits by UNICEF.

Postpartum visits rose from 55,024 in 1981 to 111,288 in 1982, or from 67 percent to 84 percent of the participants in the prenatal care program (MINSA 1983:41 Table 9). By contrast, postpartum care in Special Zone 1 (Zelaya Norte) declined between 1981 and 1982 as the result of the increased hostilities along the Honduran-Nicaraguan border and the migration of the local population (MINSA 1983:42 Table 10).

A program to monitor child growth and development has widespread acceptance in the country, but underregistration of children affects estimates of the degree of coverage. Some 316,807 children participated in the program in 1982, up 80 percent from 176,072 in 1981 (MINSA 1983:52 Table 14).

An analysis of the program for malnourished children suggests that malnutrition will continue to be a serious health problem as the Nicaraguan population continues to grow. In 1982, a total of 143,602 children were examined for nutritional deficiencies and provided with 148,826 follow-up examinations. Yet, this figure represents only 32 percent of the possible beneficiaries. Of the total number of children examined in 1981 (72,904), 67 percent were classified as suffering from first-degree malnutrition (MINSA 1983:48), and the percentages of the prevalence of second- and third-degree malnutrition among Nicaraguan children ages zero to four years old for the periods of 1965-1967, 1974-1976, and 1981-1982 were 15.0, 22.6, and 34.0 percent, respectively (Teller 1981:11, MINSA 1983:53 Table 15).[4] An increasing birthrate will demand greater and greater efforts to actually decrease the percentage of malnourished children in the population. In 1980, a supplementary feeding program was initiated with the assistance of the World Food Program, and by the end of 1982, a total of 408,730 children and 76,808 pregnant women had participated in it.

In the first three years of the revolution, hospital deaths of children under the age of four due to diarrhea was reduced in the rankings from first to third place, partly because of the 330 oral rehydration units. It is hoped that this treatment will be given within the home and that mothers will be trained to utilize the salts on an early and a routine basis (UNICEF 1983:1). Data indicate that utilization of the oral rehydration posts has begun to decrease in most regions (MINSA 1983:51 Table 13), and given the declines in hospital infant mortality, it may be that more mothers are now preparing the rehydration salts at home. Other public health measures taken since the revolution include environmental sanitation, rabies, tuberculosis, goiter, and malaria control programs.

Environmental Sanitation

Sanitation programs include potable water programs, liquid and solid waste disposal, and school and work place sanitation. Water control activities included 1,240 site inspections in 1981 and 1982 and 2,509 water sample tests. From 1980 to the end of 1982, 29,631 latrines were installed (MINSA 1981:55, 1983:66). In 1981–1982, waste disposal site inspections reached 7,697, garbage site inspections numbered 1,867, and garbage collection supervisions numbered 1,155. Food sanitation included 89,448 inspections of meat processing and packing plants, food processing plants, and food warehouses and distribution centers in that two-year period. Both environmental sanitation and rabies control programs received major support in the popular health work days carried out during those two years (MINSA 1983:58–75).

Tuberculosis Control

The tuberculosis program includes four elements: immunization, search for cases, treatment, and control of contagion. There were 81,228 childhood immunizations in 1980, 139,317 in 1981, and 211,275 in 1982. The ministry calculated that 2,817 new cases of tuberculosis would need to be treated in 1982, but only 1,330 were found. Of those, only 23 percent underwent the year-long treatment (MINSA 1983:56).

Malaria Control

The popular health campaign provided the organizational structure for a mass drug administration program in November of 1981 to control the transmission of malaria. One objective was to inhibit the transmission of the infection from humans to mosquitoes. If the infection could be eliminated in the general population for a period of three weeks, the mosquito could not acquire the malaria organism from human hosts and spread the infection. A three-day drug administration program was devised, and a total of 25 million chloroquine and 10 million primaquine tablets were packaged in 8 million color-coded envelopes of doses appropriate to each day and the age of the recipient (Garfield and Vermund 1983a:12). Popular participation was massive, and it has been estimated that one in ten Nicaraguans was involved in promoting the campaign and disseminating information. Altogether, 70 percent (1,900,000) of the total population was treated (Garfield and Vermund 1983b:502). Monthly data collection showed that malaria incidence was considerably reduced for the four months following the campaign and that a total of 9,200 new cases of malaria were avoided (Garfield and Vermund 1983a:15). The total number of malaria cases in 1982 was 15,601, down from 17,434 in 1981 and 25,465 in 1980 (MINSA 1983:107 Table 38).

Goiter

Goiter was endemic in the country before the revolution (USAID 1976:189). Although no statistics are available on the current incidence of the disease, since 1980 the MINSA has supervised seventy-six salt mines, thirteen salt iodinization factories, and the wholesaling of iodized salt in the country.

Conclusion

The process of health planning in Nicaragua since the revolution reveals several lessons about efforts of developing countries to provide "health to all by the year 2000." The first is that a government's political will to provide such care is extremely important. Comparisons of government efforts in public health before and after the revolution suggest significant differences in political commitment (Donahue 1983), and the linkages between politics and health have been strong whenever countries with scarce resources have experienced rapid and significant improvements in the health of the general population—as in China (New and New 1975) and Cuba (Roemer 1976, Danielson 1979).

A second lesson is that if elimination of hunger and preventable diseases are made priorities, the state must organize its people for those tasks. Manpower and financial constraints make it impossible for health professionals and bureaucracies in most poor countries to carry out those programs by themselves.

A third lesson is that once people are independently organized for massive public health programs, their organizational base can allow them to make further demands on the state for health care. Faced with scarce resources and the need to be cost-effective, the state must reconcile the institutional interests of those health professionals who practice in hospital settings and the demands of the organized people for a more broadly based and accessible primary care delivery system. The success of primary care delivery will depend on how much popular health organizations are able to participate in the health planning process. To be popular, participation must allow people, once organized, to initiate and formulate national and local health policies in ways that take them well beyond the tasks of implementation.

Notes

1. Primary health care is essential health care that includes education, promotion of basic food production and nutrition, potable water and sewage disposal, maternal and child care, immunizations, prevention and control of locally endemic diseases, simplified care of common diseases and injuries, and provision of essential drugs. Primary health care should be made universally accessible to individuals and families in the community by means acceptable to them, through their full participation, and at a cost that the community and country can afford (WHO 1978:6).

2. Where possible, data from the prerevolutionary period (pre-1979) has been included for comparative purposes. Data from the MINSA includes only public sector services.

3. The use of medical encounters to compare health care delivery in hospitals and clinics understates the reality inasmuch as nursing encounters are not counted. Prenatal and postnatal care in the clinics as well as well-baby visits supervised by nurses are not included. As a result, clinic activity is much greater than is suggested by medical encounters alone.

4. Malnutrition, as measured by the Gomez classification, refers to the adequacy of a child's body weight as compared to the desirable standard for his or her age and sex. For example, second-degree malnutrition is 60-74 percent of the standard; third-degree malnutrition is below 60 percent.

References

Barricada
1983   Nicaragua es Modelo de Salud para America Latina. July 13, p. 14.

Benno de Keyzer and Jeanette Ulate
1981   Educacion, Paticipacion en Salud e Ideologia: Nicaragua pasado y presente. *Revista Centroamericana de Salud*, no. 17.

Booth, John A.
1982   *The End and the Beginning: The Nicaraguan Revolution.* Boulder, Colo.: Westview Press.

Bossert, Thomas J.
1982   Health Care in Revolutionary Nicaragua. In *Nicaragua in Revolution*, ed. Thomas W. Walker, pp. 259-272. New York: Praeger.

Danielson, Ross
1979   *Cuban Medicine.* New Brunswick, N.J.: Transaction Books.

DECOPS/MINSA
1982   Las Jornadas Populares de Salud. Unpublished report. Managua: MINSA.

Donahue, J.
1983   The Politics of Health Care in Nicaragua Before and After the Revolution of 1979. *Human Organization* 42(3):264-272.

Escuerdo, J. C.
1980   Starting from Year One: The Politics of Health in Nicaragua. *International Journal of Health Services* 10(4):647-656.

Garfield, R., and S. Vermund
1983a   Malaria Control in Nicaragua: Health Promotion Through a Mass Drug Administration Campaign. Columbia University, Department of Epidemiology. Mimeograph.
1983b   Changes in Malaria Incidence After Mass Drug Administration in Nicaragua. *Lancet*, August 27, pp. 500-503.

Holland, B., J. Davis, and L. Gangloff
1973   *Syncrisis: The Dynamics of Health*, vol. 11, *Nicaragua.* Washington, D.C.: Government Printing Office.

Instituto de Nutricion para Centroamerica y Panana (INCAP)
1966   Evaluacion Nutricional de la Poblacion de Centro America y Panama: Nicaragua. Report.

Keyzer, Benno de, and Jeanette Ulate
1981   Educacion, Participacion en Salud e Ideologia: Nicaragua pasado y presente. *Revista Centroamericana de Salud*, no. 17.

MINSA
1981   *Informe 1980*. Managua: Ministerio de Salud.
1982a   Las Jornadas Populares de Salud. Unpublished report. Managua: Division de Comunicacion y Educacion Popular en Salud (DECOPS).
1982b   *El Sistema Nacional Unico de Salud: Tres Anos de Revolucion 1979–1982*. Managua: Ministerio de Salud, Republica de Nicaragua.
1983   *Plan de Salud 1983*. Managua.

MIPAN/MINSA
1981   *Estrategias de Atencion Primaria de la Salud en la Republica de Nicaragua*. Managua: Ministerio de Planificacion y Ministerio de Salud.

New, Peter Kong-Ming, and Mary Louie New
1975   The Links Between Health and the Political Structure in New China. *Human Organization* 34(3):237–251.

Roemer, M. I.
1976   *Cuban Health Services and Resources*. Washington, D.C.: Pan American Health Organization.

Teller, C.
1981   The Demography of Malnutrition in Latin America. *Intercom* 9(8):8–11.

UNICEF
1983   UNICEF Programme: Nicaragua. Managua. Mimeograph.

Union Nacional de Agricultores y Ganaderos (UNAG), Asociacion de Trabajadores del Campo (ATC), and Centro de Investigaciones y Estudios de la Reforma Agraria (CIERA).
1982   *Produccion y Organizacion en el Agro Nicaraguense*. Managua.

United States Agency for International Development (USAID)
1976   *Health Sector Assessment for Nicaragua*. Managua: USAID Mission to Nicaragua.

Walker, T., ed.
1982   *Nicaragua in Revolution*. New York: Praeger.

World Health Organization (WHO), United Nations Children's Fund
1978   Primary Health Care. Report of the International Conference on Primary Health Care, Alma-Ata, USSR, September 6–12, 1978, p. 6.

14
Social Impact, Socialism, and the Case of Mozambique

Ben Wisner

Introduction

Discussions of social impact analysis tend to treat the subject universally, that is, ahistorically. If recent historical experience gives the term "social" a different meaning in different parts of the world, is it not reasonable to expect that the social impact analysis of a road building project in, for instance, Guatemala, Romania, or the United States will take quite different forms? There are a number of reasons why social impact analysis (SIA) is discussed and written about in universalistic terms. The very currency of the abbreviation suggests one of the reasons. People concerned with SIA are, for the most part, talking about a technical bureaucratic task defined as part of later-day "project assessment" activities. In the present crisis of development planning, atomized assessment procedures laid down in the manuals by a series of relatively isolated "expert" bureaus are used to evaluate the feasibility and suitability of atomized "projects." This activity has come to substitute for integrative, formative development planning, with its higher political risks. Project assessment, on the other hand, covers the bankruptcy of planning with a veneer of social legitimacy, the hard gloss of technique, while at its core lies enshrined the calculation of internal rates of return.

When all else is said, the purpose of project planning is to minimize risk to capital. To the extent that SIA has become part of this "technical" procedure, it has taken on its own technical vocabulary and assumptions. One of these assumptions, derived from the uncompromisingly positivistic orientation of the investment and environmental calculuses with which SIA serves as a minor partner in project assessment, is the universal applicability of a checklist or calculus of social changes, the consequences of projects. This assumption, in turn, rests on the assumed legitimacy of separating the "social" from the "economic" and the "environmental."

Development planning in the People's Republic of Mozambique has proceeded differently according to different assumptions.[1] In Mozambique, development planning is consciously framed within the scheme of national reconstruction. In this chapter, I shall show how the focus on national reconstruction tends to give planning a holistic character while injecting social content into aspects of projects and programs that might elsewhere appear narrowly economic. I will then discuss the structures within state and party in Mozambique that seemed, by late 1980, to be accepting responsibility for safeguarding this social content in the face of urgent needs for rapid industrial growth and a reorganization of much of the country's infrastructure.

National Reconstruction

Historical Context

The Front for the Liberation of Mozambique (FRELIMO) fought a long war of national liberation against the Portuguese colonial state, and in 1975, independent Mozambique inherited an economy and people scarred by that war. On one level, national reconstruction refers to efforts to heal those war wounds, and I shall return to this immediate priority a little later. On a deeper level, national reconstruction refers to the task of reversing the effects of several hundred years of colonialism on social, economic, and even spatial structures.

Over the years, Portuguese colonial capitalism had produced a de facto dichotomy between North and South and a strong distinction between town and country, and among the towns, it had established the primacy of Lourenço Marques (now Maputo) in the extreme South. Infrastructural investment in the cities served a minority of whites, who lived in small replicas of the tree-lined, sidewalk cafe scenes of the Mediterranean cityscape surrounded by vast shantytowns. In the countryside, infrastructure served the needs of white settler farmers and plantation owners. Irrigation and hydropower projects, road networks, and the distribution of service towns all followed this pattern. The major railroad and port facilities were oriented toward the export and import needs of South Africa and white-ruled Rhodesia.

In effect, the southern third of the country (present-day Maputo, Gaza, and Inhambane Provinces) was dominated socially and economically by the export of mine labor to South Africa. The central provinces around the Zambezi River were dominated by the large, foreign-owned plantations growing sugar and coconuts and raising cattle. The North— where the liberation struggle was fought out between 1964 and 1974— the dominant influence over social, economic, and spatial structures was a regime of forced smallholder cultivation of cotton for export to Portugal's domestic textile industry.[2] Thus, in a sense national reconstruction means the task of reworking this entire sociospatial and economic structure in such a way that the needs of the masses of peasants and workers are served. It is also a matter of realizing the forces of production that are latent in a population of 13 million in a territory of which two-thirds is fertile alluvial plain crossed by a hundred rivers.[3]

One can see the broad scope of this perceived challenge as well as a realization of its combined social/economic/territorial character in the analysis resulting from the first national seminar on agriculture held just three months after independence in 1975. This seminar noted that 5,000 "entrepreneural" enterprises (less than 0.3 percent of a total of more than a million and a half farms) worked half of the cultivated land. It went on to point out that

1. There are insufficient instruments of labor in the rural areas;
2. Agriculture is individualistic, dispersed, disorganized, and itinerant;
3. There is a vicious circle in the countryside of poor nutrition and low agricultural productivity;
4. The majority of farmers are ignorant of technical aids;
5. There does not exist a commercial structure capable of ensuring fair prices;
6. Transportation routes in the countryside are poor and poorly maintained;
7. Most farmers are helpless before the irregularities and vagaries of rainfall;
8. There does not exist a fair and standard credit system in the rural areas;
9. Illiteracy and obscurantism are widespread;
10. There are few schools, health facilities or any sort of sanitary provisions. [translated in Wisner 1977: 14]

Rural development is conceived in this analysis as a total territorial, economic, and class transformation. The notion of a communal village (*aldeia communal*), developed pragmatically in the daily administration of life in the northern liberated zone and crystallized as an integrated development policy between 1975 and 1978, is the focus of such transformation. These rural settlements of up to a thousand families are seen, not only as service centers and points where productive forces are magnified and transformed, but also as communities where interaction and discussion will increase political consciousness and channel political activity. This combined social, economic, and territorial role sets the communal village apart from its Tanzanian counterpart, to which it is sometimes compared. The contrast became very clear in the 1980 national seminar on communal villages in which an attempt was made to define complementary roles for village co-op and state farm as the economic counterpart of the "peasant-worker alliance" at the heart of FRELIMO, the party's political philosophy.

Further evidence of the holistic view of development as national reconstruction comes from the 1979 national conference on cities. Although representatives from the country's twelve largest urban areas discussed numerous concrete problems of daily life—poor food distribution, price speculation, lack of water supplies and sewers, poor transport and garbage collection, lack of recreational areas, overcrowding, and unemployment—the whole discussion was placed in the context of an analysis of the Mozambican city as a focus of postcolonial class struggle (RPM 1979: 7–10, 11–12). The city was understood to be a social, not merely geographic, concentration of petty bourgeois interests that colonialism had created and encouraged. Many of the problems of urban life, such as hoarding in shops and corrupt practices in the allocation of nationalized housing, were traced back to the contradiction between urban working-class and petty bourgeois interests. The solution to these problems was believed to lie in the creation of units of class-conscious urban community, the communal township (*bairro communal*), which would parallel the creation of communal villages in rural areas.

The *bairro communal* was to support through political mobilization the efforts of existing state initiatives such as the consumption cooperatives and popular vigilance groups that had been created to deal with the problems of urban supply and crime, respectively. The *bairro communal* was also supposed to be a focus of infrastructural development through self-help projects (e.g., installation of water mains), the basic participatory planning unit for even more ambitious urban renewal projects (Pinsky 1981), and was supposed to develop craft production (carpentry, shoe-making, poultry keeping, horticulture in peri-urban swamps) on a cooperative basis.

I will discuss some of these recent developments in more detail later, but this introductory overview of rural and urban policy should suffice to establish the holistic and, hence, necessarily social character of Mozambique's approach to development planning. National reconstruction requires a thorough reorganization of all of the social, economic, and territorial relationships colonial capitalism put in place to ensure an exportable labor supply for South Africa; docile and low-cost labor for the Portuguese settler farmer and foreign plantation owner; low-cost production of cotton, cashews, and peanuts for export; and docile and low-cost labor for limited manufacturing, construction, and service industries in the few large towns. Reorganization of these relationships requires, above all, political consciousness and mobilization.

The territorial implications of national reconstruction alone give the sociopolitical aspect top priority because so much population resettlement is called for as colonial demographic patterns, patterns of urbanization, and labor migration are reorganized into patterns serving socialist construction and not colonial accumulation. Without the aid of class consciousness, it is impossible to explain to a group of peasant farmers with several generations of attachment to the soil and elaborate survival economies built around their locale that they actually live there because of the old settlers' need for cheap labor. Peasants who live on the site proposed for a dam to be constructed to enlarge urban water supply must appreciate the worker-peasant alliance on some day-to-day level in order to accept resettlement as more than a sacrifice.

Priority Focuses

Before continuing to treat the social impact analysis that is implicit in the task of complete social, economic, and territorial reconstruction, I must return briefly to war reconstruction as a special, though immensely important, case of national reconstruction. The war was fought in the three northernmost provinces of Cabo Delgado, Niassa, and Tete. A million people lived in the liberated zones (*zonas libertatas*) thus created, but they suffered from Portuguese air raids, bombing, napalming, and defoliation (the use of Agent Orange obtained through NATO links has been documented).[4] Further south, another 800,000 Mozambicans were relocated into population centers much like the strategic hamlets created in South Vietnam or the "protected villages" in Rhodesia. Called *aldeamentos*, these settlements were placed to maximize control by the Portuguese military over infiltration by FRELIMO, not necessarily on or near good agricultural land. In some cases, even agricultural implements were confiscated lest they be used as weapons, and people were marched out daily to cultivate under supervision. These people were literally abandoned to their fate during the Portuguese withdrawal in 1974, a situation complicated by serious flooding. There were reports of cholera and malnutrition, and tragic famine conditions were averted only by concentrated FRELIMO and international efforts (Wisner 1975).

In one specialized sense, therefore, national reconstruction means focusing special attention on the people and areas of the country that suffered especially during the war. Indeed, early efforts to develop communal villages socially and infrastructurally were focused on the North, where some 75 percent of the 1,500 communal villages were concentrated by 1979. Similarly, the president, Samora Machel, made many references to the suffering of the *zonas libertatas* during his sojourn there in 1979 as he launched a major regional planning effort aimed at "making of Niassa a model for the struggle against underdevelopment."[5] War orphans, the disabled, and former prostitutes have likewise been singled out for special programs of education and reintegration into society. On behalf of orphans, especially, an elaborate parallel education system has been constructed. Smaller children are raised in three children's centers (*infantarios*) in Cabo Delgado, Niassa, and Tete by trained teachers and health workers as well as women from the famous women's detachment of the former liberation army (*destacamento feminino*). The children go to various residential pilot centers (*centros pilotos*) for intermediate education from about age eleven and afterward are tracked into one of three FRELIMO secondary schools in the North, Center, and South of the country.

Programs with a priority focus on such special places or people clearly do not follow the project assessment sequence that is so common in the Third World, within which the methodology in SIA, as usually discussed, is embedded. The causes of these problems are social, the programs are social, and the achievements of the programs, monitored continuously.

by politically responsible structures (usually the FRELIMO cell) are social. To talk of SIA in this context, implying the conventional sequence of technical, financial, environmental, *and* social feasibility, would be absurd. It is as important to note the way in which conventional capitalist assumptions about "the social" are absent from such policy and program decisions as to note how another, more organic notion of social life is implied.

Democratic Centralism

All planning in Mozambique should be participatory. The theory of democratic centralism implies a voluminous flow of suggestions, initiatives, reactions, and information up and down from national center to local units of work and residence and back through means of the party, FRELIMO, and its associated system of mass organizations (e.g., for youth, women, workers); residential dynamizing groups (*grupos dinamizadores*); and the state, through the hierarchy of legislative assemblies reaching from the locality (*localidade* of perhaps 100,000 people) through the district and major town level to province (there are ten) and the national People's Assembly (Assemblia Popular). Discussion of policy and projects by units in these parallel hierarchies is the basic way in which technology should be socialized. The interventions suggested by the logic of national reconstruction should be discussed at the various levels of this system of mass democratic communication, and the possible consequences for people at the grass roots should be articulated.

The People's Assembly has a history of taking care to safeguard individuals against the presumption of technical omniscience. For instance, Article 13 of the national Land Law (1979) allows compensation for any farmer whose land lies in a zone of planned agrarian development who suffers from the implementation of such agricultural plans. The process of formulating the Land Law took three years and several cycles of formulation, discussion at the grass roots, and reformulation before it was promulgated.

Democratic centralism and national reconstruction are the two frameworks within which a focus on the social nature of development initiatives, while not fully ensured, is generally more likely than in the case of perfunctory SIA produced by a subcontractor or some other "professional" player in the development game.

Planning Structures and Experience

Structures

Among the technical ministries and national directorates making up the apparatus of the state there are, of course, certain defined responsibilities for translating social policy into concrete project and for monitoring the social consequences of such actions. These governmental structures (*estructuras*) are highly variable, and in these early years of independence, responsibilities often overlap. Some of these units such as the National Directorate of Statistics (DNE), the National Directorate of Water (DNA), and the National Directorate of Housing (DNH) are direct, though reorganized, descendants of fairly elaborate colonial statistical and physical planning units. The old statistical service, for instance, had 300 employees and facilities, including automatic data processing, at the time of independence (Egerö 1977). By the end of 1976, this facility was down to 50 employees. It has since been reorganized and rebuilt, serving as the hub of preparations for the 1980 national population census, and is now an integral part of a new National Planning Commission (CNP). Other units, such as the CNP just mentioned or the National Commission for Communal Villages (CNAC),[6] formed in 1978, are entirely new organizations conceived of as complements or even counterbalances to the older technical organs of the state.

In all such bureaucratic entities, whether old or new, there is widespread acceptance of FRELIMO's notion that the seizure of state power requires a long, continuous struggle *within* the organs of state power even as they are supposed to carry on with their "technical" tasks. The year 1979 was officially dedicated as the year of the structuring (*estructuração*) of the party. A long process, which continued into 1984,[7] of nomination of party members and public discussion of their past activities, especially under the colonial regime, took place within most units and subunits of government as well as in factories and on state farms.

There is a long history in Mozambique of the use of political organizations to monitor and criticize the activities of technical organizations. During the transition year of power sharing between FRELIMO and the Portuguese, 1974, mass organizations called dynamizing groups (*grupos dinamizadores*), usually referred to as GDs, were formed in many units of production and neighborhoods. Industrially based GDs carefully scrutinized the actions of foreign firms with an eye to possible economic sabotage and worker safety, and many interventions by the independent state since 1975 have originated in the vigilance of GDs, as is documented by the cases of the cashew processing industry and heavy engineering (Wisner and Kruks 1977) as well as the steel rolling mill (Sketchley and Lappé 1980). In industry, the function of the GD was assumed in 1979 by branches of a newly established mass democratic organization (similar in structure to those for women and youth) called production councils. Party membership is not required for belonging to such mass organizations. In addition, also beginning in 1979, party cells were created in industry and in the state apparatus.

What these political and organizational developments have meant is an intensification of the struggle between technocratic and the more political approaches to planning and administration. This struggle is an uneven one, varying from institution to institution, but its general effect has been to keep social issues in the center of public debate during a period of economic stress that might have subordinated such discussion to the need to push through the urgent program of national reconstruction. Most striking examples of this debate took place in the Ministry of Agriculture over the proper balance between state farms and peasant co-ops (Hanlon 1984, Harris 1980) and in the Ministry of Health over primary health care and participation of nonhealth professionals from the community in health care planning (Walt and Melamed 1984). In both cases, the long internal as well as public debate resulted in removal of the ministers.

Table 14.1 overviews the organizational responsibilities for monitoring the social aspects of national reconstruction as of late 1980. For the sake of illustration, national reconstruction has been broken down arbitrarily and nonexhaustively into tasks related to the reorganization of the forces of production (divided into "means of production" and "labor") and the reorganization of rural and urban settlement. In each case, I have given the year from which an explicit concern with the social implications of policy can be dated, the units of government in which the social data are centralized, the units in which this and other data are specifically analyzed in ways that reveal the conflict between technical and social factors, and the units that carry the main planning responsibility.

In each case, the dates correspond to the emergence of the kind of internal and public debate discussed earlier of either new bodies or reorganized bodies within which the sociopolitical aspects of their technical missions came to be clearly articulated. In regard to the inventory and reorganization of Mozambique's natural forces of production—the land, water, forests, wildlife, minerals, etc.—as well as its stock of factories, dams, bridges, and instruments of production (tractors, hoes), data are collected primarily by the research sections (*gabinete do estudo*) of various national directorates of the Ministries of Agriculture, Public Works, Industry, and Internal Commerce. The date 1980 is significant because in that year were created separate secretaries of state for fisheries and for the cotton industry (*secretariado do estado*) in response to a long debate about the lack of support for the small-scale, artisanal fishing industry and increasing evidence of conflict between food production and the production of cotton in the northern parts of the country. Also in that year, the Ministry of Agriculture reorganized its National Directorate of Forests (DNF) to absorb freshwater fisheries and wildlife management. This action marked an advance for those people who were worried about the strong technocratic bias in wildlife management (there had been strong links with South African game park administrators before independence).

Data on the Mozambican population in general, and the labor force in particular, are centralized in the National Directorate of Statistics. In the period 1979–1980, two debates took place that profoundly affected thinking about the qualitative side of what is often treated as merely quantitative "manpower planning." The first was the culmination of three

TABLE 14.1
Focuses of social analysis of projects in RPM

SECTOR	YEAR	WHO STUDIES (GEN)?	WHO STUDIES (SPECIFIC)?	WHO PLANS?
Forces of Production (Means of Production)	'80	DINAGECA Plano Min. Industry FRELIMO	DN Florestas Sec. Est. de Pescas Centro de Ecologia(UEM) DNA	CNAC Min. Agric. Plano DNA
Forces of Production (Labor, its quantity and quality)	'79-'80	FRELIMO Plano DNE	Min. Health Min. of Ed. CEA/UEM DNE	Min. Labor Plano
Rural Settlement	'78	CNAC FRELIMO	CEA/UEM CNAC	CNAC Min. Internal Commerce Min. Agric. Plano
Urban Settlement	'79	Plano FRELIMO	DNH	DNH CZV City Councils

ABBREVIATIONS: DINAGECA = Nat. Directorate of Geodesic and Cadastral Survey. Plano = Nat. Planning Commission. DNE = Nat. Dir. of Statistics. CNAC = Nat. Comm. for Communal Villages. DN Florestas = Nat. Dir. of Forests. Sec. Est. de Pescas = Sec. of State for Fisheries. UEM = Univ. Eduardo Mondlane. CEA = Centre of African Studies. DNH = Nat. Dir. of Housing. CZV = Comision for Green Belts. DNA = Nat. Dir. of Water Resources.
N.B.: This was the situation as of mid-1981.

years of research on the effects of wage migration to South Africa by the Center of African Studies at Eduardo Mondlane University (First 1983) presented by the Mozambican delegation to a regional conference in Lusaka, Zambia, in connection with the issues surrounding labor flows from independent African states to South Africa.

The other debate accompanied preparations for the 1980 national population census. The lines were drawn between the people in the National Directorate of Statistics who wanted to replicate the Portuguese colonial census procedure for reasons of technical comparability and statistical "standards" and those, including Marcelino dos Santos, the vice-president and head of the National Planning Commission, who said the national census was a political offensive in the class struggle that would require a political approach to census taking as well as new and different questions to be asked of the population. Dos Santos predicted publicly that petty bourgeois opposition to the revolution, particularly in the cities, and other enemies (*inimigo*) in the rural areas would oppose the census because a successful census would push the organization of the masses to a new level, and every increase in the level of social organization makes destabilization and the maintenance of special privilege more difficult. He pointed to similar opposition to the campaign to structure the party and even to the national vaccination campaign.

Rural settlement had been the responsibility of the National Directorate of Housing (of the Ministry of Public Works) until 1978. This organ of the state received increasing criticism for dealing with rural settlement exclusively in terms of street patterns, house types, and sanitation and not considering socioeconomic transformation. In 1978, the National Commission for Communal Villages (CNAC) was created. It was directly responsible to the president and had the responsibility of coordinating all efforts in the various technical ministries (Agriculture, Public Works, Health, Education, Information) concerned with the communal village program. Throughout 1979 and 1980, CNAC became more and more of an arbitrator between the mass of unorganized peasants who were still producing on family farms and a few hundred peasant cooperatives on one side and the rapidly expanding state farm sector on the other. CNAC did not have executive power in these increasing disputes over land and other resources, nor did it assume anything like the role of an ombudsman, but it did provide a forum for debating these issues.

It was possibly because CNAC really lacked power to resolve such conflicts that it was abolished in another round of reorganization preceding the Fourth Congress of the Party FRELIMO. The latter took major steps to ensure that the social content of these debates be continued and deepened, and congress documents reaffirmed the importance of the family and the cooperative sectors alongside the state farm sector. They also affirmed the significance of small-scale, locally initiated development efforts alongside large-scale, state-initiated ones. Most significantly, the congress expanded the Central Committee of the Party to include more representatives of the peasantry and the working class—a move that could increase the articulation of grass-roots impacts of development efforts. Finally, in mid-1984, Mozambique requested and received a high-level follow-up mission from the United Nations to monitor progress since the World Conference on Agrarian Reform and Rural Development in 1979 (WCARRD).

The WCARRD mission will have certainly found that a major factor shaping Mozambique's rural resettlement program has been the significant increase in terrorist counterrevolutionary attacks on the rural population and infrastructure since the independence of Zimbabwe in 1980, when contras shifted their base of operations to South Africa and began to receive increased financial and material support. Popular mobilization for self-defense against these *bandidos armados* has been a major social reality that has impressed itself on virtually all aspects of rural resettlement since 1981, reinforcing the social and political nature of such planning already established by the urgencies of national reconstruction and the evolving structures of democratic centralism.

Finally, urban reorganization was politicized in 1979 in the course of the national conference on cities. Since that conference, considerable success has been reported in a deeply participatory approach to urban renewal, and a National Commission for Green Belts (Commissao National de Zonas Verdes) has been created to oversee a reorganization and an expansion of peri-urban horticulture, which is conceived of as much as a program for mobilizing unemployed youth as well as one for increasing urban food supply and for improving environmental health.[8] These recent developments have brought a new sensitivity to sociopolitical dimensions to the DNH as well as to the reorganized city councils (*camara municipal*). The latter became city executive councils (*consehlo executivo municipal*) responsible to city assemblies, further enlarging the democratic base of administration within the framework of the People's Assembly discussed earlier.

It was upon such a mobilized social basis that steps were taken in 1982 to resettle unemployed urban youth in the sparsely settled, fertile North, especially in Niassa Province where by mid-1984 around 13,000 such "unproductive youth" (*improdutivos*) had been integrated into agricultural production.[9] This was a very controversial move, and a full discussion of Operação Produção (Operation Production) would require more space than I have here. It is significant in the context of this argument to note, however, that the execution of this program of resettlement was carried out with a massive involvement of the urban population organized in their neighborhood and township structures. Whatever one may think of forced resettlement, one must still be struck by the highly socialized nature of the urbanism that was achieved as a precondition for implementing this program: The urban people had been organized and were in a position to discuss each case publicly, expose misuses of power (e.g., cases in which resettlement was used to settle a personal grudge), etc.

Experience: Socialization of Resource Planning

Water resources planning in Portuguese Africa was technocratic, one might even say antisocial. Numerous reports by such Portuguese consulting firms as Hidrotecnica Portuguesa from the late 1960s and early 1970s contain very little reference to environmental impacts and virtually no reference to people. When people are mentioned, as in the lengthy sections of a plan for the Zambezi valley devoted to identifying possible irrigation sites,[10] local livelihood systems are not taken into consideration. According to one recent reassessment of this ambitious plan, which was modeled on the U.S. Tennessee Valley Authority, "behind the schemes lay the assumption that the customs, attitudes, and practices of the local population could be manipulated to fit the plans in the same way as the various physical parameters" (Bolton 1978: 10). By contrast, recent hydrological development in Mozambique has included a careful study of the economy, society, and environment of the people to be displaced and the people themselves have been involved in quite timely discussions of possible relocation sites.

A case in point is the Pequenos Limbombos dam on the Umbeluzi River in southern Mozambique. This dam was considered to be an urgent priority because of the need to expand Maputo's water supply in response to greatly expanded access to the municipal water supply since independence—in part the result of successful self-help water projects in the peripheral shantytowns.[11] In 1979, more than five years before scheduled completion of the dam, contact was initiated through party representatives and the two district administrations involved with the roughly 1,000 families to be affected. Data were gathered on the origin and recent history of the residents, their farm and nonfarm employment, access to services, and, above all, preference for relocation. A wide range of alternatives emerged in small informal discussions during random visits to groups of homesteads and in formal mass meetings organized through the party and the state farm that turned out to be a major employer of many of the families on a permanent or part-time basis.

Depending on their circumstances, some of the people preferred moving to a *bairro communal* composed of the families of full-time state-farm workers in one or two centralized places on the state farm. The former large white settler farms, which had been abandoned by their owners at independence and put together to form the state farm, had settlements of workers on wasteland within them, looking very much like nucleated villages—an illusion since the majority of the workers came from the extreme South where no "traditional" villages had existed for 150 years. Some improvement and consolidation of these settlements was envisioned as constituting a *bairro communal*. Other residents preferred to join a fairly well established communal village some miles away. A delegation visited that village and was told they would be welcomed since there was still a lot of land to clear. The establishment of a new communal village on the other, less-accessible and less-developed side of the river was proposed, but this proposal received little enthusiasm. Finally, certain families preferred to continue to live by themselves in sites outside the area to be flooded, which they would choose by themselves.

Although not an ideal approach in some ways, one thing is certainly clear in this case: Social impact analysis was implicit in this project from the beginning. Although irrigation and flood control were seen by planners as additional benefits, the motive behind the dam in the first place was social: response to the political demand for connection to the former elite system of urban water distribution. This demand arose in turn from the quite successful mobilization of shantytown residents in campaigns to reconstruct not only urban space but also the alienated attitudes implicit in colonial urbanism. The existence of a network of GDs and other party structures in the area to be flooded facilitated the early involvement of the majority of its residents in a discussion of the dam and its implications. No one would deny that part of the colonial heritage is a rather technocratic attitude on the part of engineers and other professionals, yet the political framework created by the focus on national reconstruction and democratic centralism seems, in this case at least, to have forced this latent arrogance into the background.

Wildlife management provides further examples of the socialization of resource planning and the way in which SIA is embedded in the structure of the current situation. In colonial times, the Portuguese established a large number of reserve areas: four national parks, five nature reserves, forest reserves, and sixteen "recreational hunting zones." African settlement, cultivation, and herding were rigidly excluded from these areas. Not surprisingly, Africans resisted to varying degrees and developed clandestine ways of using the forbidden resources—vegetation, fresh- and brackish-water fauna, and wildlife.

The new government became aware of these practices when it took power, and in addition, considerable numbers of people felt that one of the fruits of independence was freedom to settle wherever they pleased, and they entered the reserves. FRELIMO was faced with a dilemma. Completely unregulated settlement and land use, including charcoal production, would soon ruin the character of these reserves, precluding, among other options, a tourist industry FRELIMO did not want to rule out as a future possibility. Heavy-handed administrative action against these people, on the other hand, would appear no different from the colonial approach. Who were these people in the nature reserves anyway? Where had they come from? How did they live? Were systems of multiple use conceivable under existing social and ecological conditions? If not, what alternative sites for these people were available and how could they be made attractive?

These were some of the questions a team based in the Ecology Center of Eduardo Mondlane University was asked to answer by CNAC. The starting point was the opinion of professionals working for the Wild Animal Division of the Ministry of Agriculture (since absorbed into the

National Directorate of Forests). They believed these people were "primitive hunters," an opinion that is very revealing of a technocratic substratum commonly encountered in the apparatus of the state—in this particular case exaggerated by long association with South African "white hunters" and other game mangement technicians. The results of the team's contact with the residents of the Special Elephant Reserve of Maputo—chosen as a pilot project—revealed something quite different.

Again through a combination of formal and informal meetings with residents (somewhat more difficult on the formal side since the party was less well established in this case), a socioeconomic profile was built up. Far from being hunters, these people were, strictly speaking, proletarians. The senior male in the household most often had worked in South Africa—in the mines, for white farmers, or in industry—and was now unable to return. These people were generally fairly recent arrivals and were dealing with the general disruption of the southern Mozambican rural economy caused by the dramatic decrease in South African employment and the breakdown of Portuguese dominated rural marketing in the best way they could. They farmed a little, poached a little, fished a little, and made charcoal for sale in Maputo. Contrary to expectations, they were usually open to alternatives. Jobs were what they wanted.

Investigations were launched into regional employment possibilities in expanding state farms, possible cooperative fishing in the lakes within the reserve to be overseen by wildlife authorities, the possibility of multiuse plans incorporating a reserved core with corridors for North-South elephant migration, a buffer zone of soft woods for commercial exploitation (and jobs), and an outer zone of limited human settlement in communal villages about a fifth the usual size (in accordance with the carrying capacity of the sandy soils) (Wisner 1984). These reports and suggestions were not universally accepted in ministry circles, but some party officials and CNAC employees were pleased that at least the terms of the debate had been shifted and a very stale corner of the inherited bureaucratic apparatus been forced to see the political-economic and social sides of the issue. In 1983, some five years after investigation was begun into the social realities of the squatters in the Special Elephant Reserve of Maputo, long discussions between residents and political workers resulted in the first significant resettlement of the population outside the reserve.

Experience: Socialization of Urban Settlement Planning

Despite the heavy distortions in service access, morphology, and social development produced by colonial urbanism, major successes have been registered in reorganizing urban space and life-style. The task of shanty upgrading might well have been tackled in a heavily technocratic manner but for the political statement of the urban problem by the national conference in 1979 and serious efforts that same year to extend and deepen party membership in shanty areas. Self-help shanty upgrading efforts described by Pinsky (1981) in the Maxaquene section of the capital, Maputo, are typical.

Liaison between the DNH and Maxaquene's GD produced an ad hoc planning commission composed of local representatives and DNH employees. The commission began by identifying quite straightforward-seeming deficiencies:

1. Water—only four public taps and six owned by water vendors for 10,000 people.
2. Access—no street system or system of addresses. Buses, fire engines, and ambulances could not penetrate the area.
3. Housing materials—80 percent were constructions of wood and reeds (caniço). These materials were very light and temporary, and inhabitants aspired to more permanent clay or cement-block construction.
4. Sanitation—pit latrines hand dug in sandy soil collapsed easily. Materials and new construction methods were repaired.

After a series of discussions in mass meetings, it was decided that no improvements could be made unless the area was opened up by 12–18-meter corridors, which would give access to service vehicles as well as provide the alignment for water mains and eventually street lighting, electricity and drainage. Housing would be reorganized in blocks of from sixty to eighty homes laid out on either side of the corridors. Each block was to have a central plaza containing a water standpipe and an outside light. Blocks were to be numbered, and the residents would name the new streets.

Bulldozing these corridors meant that some caniço structures had to be moved, which was done, by popular decision in mass meetings, without compensation to owners. These sacrifices were tolerated because of the huge social benefit perceived in the security of tenure to be enjoyed under the new arrangements. No such security had existed under the Portuguese, and it is a testimony to the insight of the ad hoc planning commission that this social dimension was properly grasped, without which no number of physical improvements, such as those mentioned as well as the allocation of plots for future schools, parks, small industries, etc., would have been convincing.

The very popularity of the idea of secure family plots produced a breakthrough from technocracy to mass participation. In Pinsky's words:

One of the first problems facing the new committee (committees now representing each new block, emphasing fifty-fifty male-female representation) and the DNH team was a growing demand to parcel each block into plots. The DNH initially resisted this idea because its technical resources, particularly surveyors, were extremely limited. It also feared that plot division would provoke unnecessary demolition and that certain socio-cultural values inherent in the existing arrangement would be destroyed. Nevertheless, with minimal assistance from the DNH team, one of the block committees, working with the residents, succeeded in redividing its block into plots of approximately equal size. It was thus concluded that plot division could be done by the residents without major technical inputs. [Pinsky 1981: 4]

In the end, 90 percent of the blocks were subdivided by self-help means with more "expert" block committees helping the others. There followed other self-help activities such as digging trenches for water mains (recall the tremendously increased demand for water, provoking the plan to dam the Umbeluzi River), weekly cleanups, and fruit and shade tree planting. By September 1979, 36,000 people had been legalized on 300 hectares of former squatter settlement, and there were further plans for cooperatives for renting construction tools, courses in home improvement, and small-scale industry.

Within the general argument of this chapter, such a transformation of urban space and social being serves as a clear example of national reconstruction in its territorial, social, and economic sense, and it further demonstrates the inherently social nature of such interventions, transcending the need for bourgeois SIA *as long as* the process is sufficiently political and democratic.

Experience: Socialization of Rural Settlement Planning

Rural settlement provides another set of examples illustrating the central thesis of this chapter and also raises open and unanswered questions about the limits of national reconstruction and democratic centralism as guiding principles. Precolonial Mozambique had areas of dense agricultural settlement, principally in the fertile river valleys such as the Zambezi (Issacman 1972) and the Limpopo (Young 1977). Although the Portuguese had been present on the coast since the sixteenth century and had penetrated up the Zambezi, establishing the system of estates known as *prazos*, it was not until the turn of the twentieth century that competition with other colonial powers forced them to establish "effective occupance" in the form of increased control over African labor power and, later, land. This expansion of colonial control precipitated a demographic crisis and dispersion of settlement. For instance, increased mortality, constraints on fertility such as disrupted home life, and emigration caused the population of Inhambane Province in southern Mozambique to fall by more than 25 percent between 1907 and 1930 (Wisner 1982). Policies emphasizing forced labor and/or the imposition of cash-cropping requirements and high taxes tended to reinforce a tendency toward dispersion of settlement as a way in which people could minimize enforcement and control. In some parts of the country, including the Limpopo valley, this manner of passive resistance had existed since precolonial times, when numerous settlements of over a thousand persons each were abandoned to avoid the billeting and tribute demands of invading Nguni warlords from the 1880s onward.

The Portuguese supplanted the Nguni as masters of land and labor in the southern interior at a time when the exodus of men to the South

African gold mines was accelerating the breakdown of communal structures in the South. Much of the labor power used to construct the roads and other infrastructure in the Limpopo valley, which was to support the expansion of white farming on alienated land, was that of women and children as a result of the wage migration of men. Dispersion, dependency, and poorly developed forces of production have characterized this zone up to the present. As recently as 1974, Portuguese farmers continued to expand their farms, pushing Africans further and further up the sandy valley sides.

At independence there was a rush to reoccupy land that had been alienated from Africans within living memory and abandoned at independence by the white farmers. Ironically, this spontaneous peasant reoccupance resulted in great vulnerability to flooding of the rivers in the South (Wisner 1979), and after the floods in 1977, victims were resettled in communal villages on higher ground. The model for such settlements came from the experience of the liberated zones in the North. Implementation of these plans was rigid and static at this stage as the responsibility lay with the physical planners and architects in the DNH, and they gave little thought to the productive basis of this new life or to social relations. Criticism of DNH had been developing for some time and resulted in the establishment of CNAC in 1978 to deal with the social and the economic as well as infrastructural issues. Since CNAC was directly responsible to the president, it was thus free of the established channels that had been inherited in the apparatus of the state, which was undergoing transformation at uneven speeds from within as it carried on with "business as usual."

The establishment of CNAC represented a major victory of the holistic and political over the fragmented and technocratic. Since then, however, a new set of problems has arisen that may constitute the ultimate test of democratic centralism and the national reconstruction model of development.

The main problem centers around the relationship between the mass of settled families, who remain dependent on private food production and wage remittance, and the state farms (mashamba estatal) that have increasingly come to dominate the economy and land use in the Limpopo valley. The Portuguese had created, at present-day Chokwe, a massive agroindustrial complex to crown their efforts at "effective occupance." FRELIMO understandably sees the continued development of the irrigation potential of the Limpopo system and the related industrialization of the valley through processing and agrotechnical industries as a model of development in the Mozambican context. For FRELIMO, the agroindustrial complex embodies the worker-peasant alliance; it focuses on basic needs, especially food as a wage good for the urban worker; and it concretizes the important FRELIMO watchword: "agriculture is the base, and industry is the dynamizing factor." Yet, at the moment, the state farms employ a minute percentage of the population and offer wages far below what the men had been used to getting in South Africa. Cooperatives have been created in the villages, but the typical membership so far is predominantly female, and these co-ops have serious problems of organization, credit, and marketing. Conflicts over access to land have arisen as state farms have sought to expand into areas set aside for communal villages.

CNAC has been active in studying these conflicting needs, but the formula arrived at in a national conference on communal villages in 1980 is really too generalized to help adjudicate these problems. According to the conference, communal villages near state farms are to be seen, in the first instance, as providing workers for agroindustry. When such proletarianization is not possible, cooperative agricultural production is to be the basis of life. The problem is that in the short run, these two alternatives do not exhaust the array of real possibilities. Much as their counterparts in many more recently formed Tanzanian *ujamaa* villages, the vast majority of the population is still an aggregate of individual peasant families, surviving much as they have in the past through a combination of farming, herding, laboring, remittances from town, and *briccolage* ("tinkering about"). This is a terribly brutalized and fragmented peasantry with little acquaintance with FRELIMO before independence. Ways must be sought to ease the transition from family to collective survival and development.

Especially in southern Mozambique, family food production is in the hands of women because of 100 years of history of male labor migration to South Africa. A recent review of the impact of state and party policies on this "female peasantry" (Kruks and Wisner 1984) concludes that this majority of food producers has been largely unengaged in the process of cooperative formation and the strengthening of state farms. This is perhaps the weakest point in the evolution of an organic (versus mechanical) social impact analysis of projects and policies. The answer, however, does not lie in the mechanical application of a checklist of questions about women in the planning process. The logic of the argument advanced so far is that technology and planning in general are socialized in Mozambique through the day-to-day political process within the overall priorities of national reconstruction and the emerging structures of democratic centralism. Women are slowly gaining more voice in assemblies (25 percent of the representatives to local assemblies were women in 1980, and 15 percent of the delegates to the Fourth Congress of the Party in 1983 were women) (RPM 1980, FRELIMO 1983), and if steps are taken to accelerate rapidly the involvement of *rural* women in such discussions and debates, one could be more optimistic about the incorporation of rural women's realities in the rural planning process.

The state farms must function in ways that are seen as directly beneficial to the mass of resettled families even if doing so means, in the short run, less efficient operation. The state farms could function as centers of mechanization, social services, and cultural life. Some steps in this direction are being taken, but it remains to be seen if the constant struggle between the "technical" and the "political" will favor such a gradual transition, given the economic urgency focused on the state farms. The state farms are, after all, the major source of food for the urban areas. Drought has shown that food imports from Zimbabwe cannot always be counted on, and the United States has already used its "food weapon," canceling food shipments in 1980 (Wisner 1981).

In the long run, however, the balance between the technical and the political in criteria for judging such actions as expansion of state farms, access to irrigation water for cooperatives, or the level of state farm wages will be decided by the level of organization of the grass roots of the party and the legislative assembly. The campaign to structure the party (1979–1980) did not proceed as quickly in rural areas as it did in towns and in units of industrial production and the bureaucracy. It was a very uneven process, but it continues, and there are signs that such activities as the 1980 population census have helped to draw in many rural dwellers who were formerly uninvolved in GDs. Similarly, the whole legislative assembly system is new, and its operation and representativeness on the local level (localidade) are uneven. Given FRELIMO's continued emphasis on strengthening these two vital communication and decision networks, and given the many examples of ways in which "social consequences" have time and again been injected into Mozambican planning since independence by the day-to-day functioning of GDs, party cells, and the People's Assembly, one can perhaps afford to be guardedly optimistic about the resolution of these rural issues.

FRELIMO's long-term structural plan calls for the creation of peasant cooperativist associations (associaçoes dos camponeses cooperativistas) as a complement to the existing mass democratic organizations (CEDIMO 1978: 51). Perhaps activation of this plan would be the next hopeful sign one should look for in addition to signs that the other democratic structures in place are being strengthened and that the class struggle FRELIMO explicitly refers to as the "motor force of the revolution" is continuing.

Notes

This chapter was originally prepared as a paper given at a conference on social impact analysis, Michigan State University, East Lansing, 1981, and has been revised for inclusion in this book.

1. Some attempt has been made to bring the argument against a "technical" bureaucratic SIA up to date, but this has not been done in-depth nor is the more recent period covered by firsthand experience. The major events since 1982 (accelerated terrorist war against Mozambique by South Africa, drought, devastating coastal storms, the Fourth Congress of the Party, mobilization, and forced resettlement of the urban unemployed) have only served to reinforce the dominance of "national reconstruction" as a socializing influence in project planning. Thus,

the argument that social impact analysis is "built in" to the fabric of political life in Mozambique still holds, but that does not mean that projects and policy decisions formulated in Mozambique cannot be criticized on a social basis "from the outside." It does mean that there is a struggle at work in Mozambique between technocratic and popular planning and that the "inside" of this struggle is rooted in the history of the liberation struggle and its continuing evolution in southern Africa. For recent overviews, see Issacman and· Issacman 1983, Munslow 1983, and Hanlon 1984.

2. See Wuyts 1978 and Wield 1983 on the colonial political economy.

3. The irrigation potential of the country is very large but is mirrored by a correspondingly large hazard of flooding (see Wisner 1979).

4. From 1969 up until the first half of 1972, the United States exported 561,000 pounds of herbicides and herbicidal products to Portugal (including Angola and Mozambique) and more than 12 million pounds to South Africa, from where defoliation flights were also made in aid of the Portuguese colonial war (see Roder 1973).

5. Tempo, December 1979.

6. CNAC was abolished later. See discussion later in the chapter and also Hanlon 1984.

7. For instance, *Tempo*, no. 714 (June 17, 1984), reports reinitiation of the process in Gaza Province in the South.

8. *Noticias*, May 13, 1979.

9. *Tempo*, no. 716 (July 1, 1984), pp. 12–16.

10. The huge Cabora Bassa dam provides a classic case (see Middlemas 1975).

11. Because of conflicts with Swaziland over the water in the Umbeluzi River, this project was never executed. Studies of economic and social impacts of nearby dam sites continued, however, according to information graciously provided by Dr. Philip Raikes, Centre for Development Research, Copenhagen.

References

Bolton, Peter
   1978   "Cabora Bassa." University of Edinburgh, School of Civil Engi-
           neering, Programme in Science and Society, Discussion Paper.

Centro Nacional de Documentação e Informação
de Moçambique (CEDIMO)
   1978   "Documento Informativo: Repúbica Popular de Moçambique." Doc.
           inf. no. 24. Maputo.

Egerö, Bertil
   1977   "Mozambique and Angola: Reconstruction in the Social Sciences."
           Scandinavian Institute of African Studies, Research Report no. 42.
           Uppsala.

First, Ruth
   1983   *Black Gold: The Mozambican Miner, Proletarian, and Peasant.*
           Sussex, Eng.: Harvester.

FRELIMO
   1983   "Report of the Credentials Commission." In *Building Socialism:
           The People's Answer.* Maputo: National Printer.

Hanlon, Joseph
1984   *Revolution Under Fire.* London: Zed Press.

Harris, Lawrence
1980   "Agricultural Cooperatives and Development Policy in Mozambique."
            Journal of Peasant Studies 7(3).

Issacman, Alan
1972   *Mozambique: The Africanisation of a European Institution—The
            Zambezi Prazos, 1750-1921.* Madison: University of Wisconsin Press.

Issacman, Alan, and Barbara Issacman
1983   *Mozambique: From Colonialism to Revolution 1900-1982.* Boulder,
            Colo.: Westview Press.

Kruks, Sonia, and Ben Wisner
1984   "The State, the Party, and the Female Peasantry in Mozambique."
            Journal of Southern Africa Studies, in press.

Middlemas, Keith
1975   *Cabora Bassa: Engineering and Politics in Southern Africa.* London:
            Weidenfeld and Nicolson.

Munslow, Barry
1983   *Mozambique: The Revolution and Its Origins.* London: Longman.

Pinsky, Barry
1981   "Self-Help Shanty Upgrading." *Development Forum* (March).

República Popular de Moçambique (RPM)
1979   *Síntese da Resolução sobre a Organização da Direcção Estatal das
            Cidades. 1.a Reunião Nacional sobre Cidades e Bairros Comunais.*
            Maputo: National Printer.
1980   "Relatório da Comissao de Eleições." Report. Maputo: National
            Printer. (Citation thanks to Dr. Bertil Egerö, personal communi-
            cation, 1983).

Roder, Wolf
1973   "Effects of Guerilla War in Angola and Mozambique." *Antipode*
            5(2).

Sketchley, Peter, and Frances Lappé
1980   *Casting New Moulds.* San Francisco: Institute for Food and De-
            velopment Policy.

Walt, Gillian, and Angela Melamed, eds.
1984   *Mozambique: Towards a People's Health Service.* London: Zed Press.

Wield, David
1983   "Mozambique: Late Colonialism and Early Problems of Transition."
            In R. Murray, C. White, and G. White, eds., *Socialist Transformation
            and Development in the Third World.* Sussex, Eng.: Harvester.

Wisner, Ben
   1975   "Famine Relief and People's War." *Review of African Political Economy* 3.
   1977   "Agriculture in Mozambique." *Science for People* 34.
   1979   "Flood Prevention and Mitigation in the People's Republic of Mozambique." *Disasters* 3(3).
   1981   "The Food Weapon." *Commonweal* 9 (October). ·
   1982   "Migration, Dürre, und Hungersnot in Ost und Sud-Ost-Afrika." In G. Elwert, ed., *Afrika zwischen Subsistenzökonomie und Imperialismus.* Frankfurt am Main: Campus Verlag.
   1984   "Ecofarming and Ecodevelopment in Mozambique." In B. Glaeser, ed., *Ecodevelopment: Concepts, Projects, Strategies.* Oxford: Pergamon.

Wisner, Ben, and Sonia Kruks.
   1977   "Science and Technology in Mozambique." *Science for People* 36.

Wuyts, Marc
   1978   "Peasants and Rural Economy in Mozambique." Discussion paper, University Eduardo Mondlane (Mozambique), Centre of African Studies.

Young, Sherilyn.
   1977   "Fertility and Famine: Women's Agricultural History in Southern Mozambique." In A. Parsons and N. Palmer, eds., *The Roots of Rural Poverty in Southern and Central Africa.* London: Heinemann.

About the Contributors

George H. Axinn has served as the associate coordinator of the Center for Advanced Study of International Development, codirector of the Non-Formal Education Information Center, and professor of agricultural economics at Michigan State University. Since writing this chapter he has been the representative of the United Nations Food and Agriculture Organization in Nepal.

Nancy W. Axinn is a specialist on issues in women in development and has served as a consultant to UNICEF and FAO.

Peggy F. Barlett is an associate professor of anthropology at Emory University and has done fieldwork in Costa Rica, Ecuador, and the United States. She received her doctorate from Columbia University and is the author of *Agricultural Choice and Change: Decision Making in a Costa Rican Community* and editor of *Agricultural Decision Making: Anthropological Contributions to Rural Development.*

Jack Corbett received his degree in political science from Stanford University. He has published extensively on local-level politics, environmental politics, and rural development. He is director of the Public Administration Program at Southwest Texas State University.

William Derman is professor of anthropology at Michigan State University and socioeconomic team leader of the Gambia River Basin Studies carried out by the University of Michigan. The studies focus upon dam impacts and irrigation potential in the nations of The Gambia, Guinea, and Senegal. His published works include *Peasants, Serfs, and Socialists: A Former Peasant Village in the Republic of Guinea* and articles on rural class formation and drought in the Sahel.

Kathryn G. Dewey teaches community and international nutrition at the University of California, Davis. Her research has focused on human lactation and the relationship between agricultural development and nutrition in Mexico.

John M. Donahue received his doctorate from Columbia University and presently teaches at Trinity University in San Antonio, Texas. A medical anthropologist, he has done research in Colombia, Peru, and Nicaragua.

Kenneth W. Eckhardt is an associate professor of sociology at the University of Delaware and is currently working with Norman Schwartz on problems of rural development in Central American countries. His research interests are primarily methodological—he has coauthored a book with M. D. Ermann, *Social Research Methods*, on this subject— but he is also interested in cross-cultural studies of social change. Recently he completed a summary report on U.S. fertility for inclusion in a series for the International Statistical Institute World Fertility Survey project. He has published extensively in sociological journals.

Ray Funk is a rural development consultant in Prince Albert, Saskatchewan. He received his masters in adult education from Michigan State University. He was a candidate for the federal New Democratic party in 1972 and 1974 and he also operates a mixed farm with his wife, Bonnie, and their three children.

Polly F. Harrison received her doctorate in anthropology from the Catholic University of America and has carried out extensive fieldwork in Central America, Panama, and Peru. She is currently coordinator of Latin American Programs for Management Sciences for Health in Boston.

Peter M. Meehan was a graduate student at the University of Michigan at the time of his death. He had completed a masters degree in journalism and anthropology at Iowa State University. His research was done in Sri Lanka and Costa Rica.

E. Philip Morgan is associate professor and director of international programs in the School of Public and Environmental Affairs at Indiana University. His research and consulting work focus on relationships between public policy and organization/management in international development.

Christine Obbo is a Ugandan anthropologist currently teaching at Wheaton College, Massachusetts. She obtained her B.A. and M.A. degrees at Makerere University and a Ph.D. from the University of Wisconsin, Madison, where she also had training in regional and urban planning. She is the author of *African Women: Their Struggle for Economic Independence*.

Charles A. Reilly is research director of the Center for U.S.-Mexican Studies and teaches political science at the University of California, San Diego. He previously worked for the Inter-American Foundation.

Desiré Yande Sarr has completed graduate degrees at the University of Vincennes in France and Michigan State University. Upon completion of his study, he returned home to Senegal where he works with the Farming Systems Team of the Senegalese Institute for Agricultural Research.

Norman B. Schwartz is professor of anthropology at the University of Delaware. He has been doing basic research on Meso-American rural communities, particularly in northern (Peten) Guatemala since 1960, and has also worked as a development consultant in several Central American countries. Most recently he worked on an USAID-funded community managed fish pond project in western Panama. He has published extensively on Peten and has written several articles on community development for the *Annual Review of Anthropology* and *Human Organization*.

Robert Stock is an assistant professor of geography at Queen's University in Kingston, Ontario. He is a medical geographer and has done considerable research on health care systems, both Western and traditional, in northern Nigeria.

Michael B. Whiteford is professor of anthropology at Iowa State University. His research in Colombia, Costa Rica, and Mexico has focused on nutrition, migration, and social change. His publications include *The Forgotten Ones: Colombian Countrymen in an Urban Setting*.

Scott Whiteford is associate professor of anthropology at Michigan State University and has done extensive research in Mexico and South America on rural transformation. His most recent research examined the social impact of the development and salinization of the Colorado River on the Mexicali Valley, Mexico. Previous publications include *Workers from the North: Plantations, City, and Migration in Northwest Argentina*, and the jointly edited volumes *Forging Nations* and *Population Growth and Urbanization in Latin America*.

Ben Wisner is a geographer whose research has focused on agrarian issues in Africa. His extensive list of publications includes articles on political economy, migration, and agriculture. He teaches in the Department of Human Ecology at Rutgers University.

Index